The Right Tools for the Job

Also by the Authors

BUSINESS RELATIONSHIPS FOR COMPETITIVE ADVANTAGE

The Right Tools for the Job

On the Use and Performance of Management Tools and Techniques

by

Andrew Cox, Chris Lonsdale, Joe Sanderson and Glyn Watson

macmillan

First published 2005 by
PALGRAVE MACMILLAN
Houndmills, Basingstoke, Hampshire RG21 6XS and
175 Fifth Avenue, New York, N. Y. 10010
Companies and representatives throughout the world

PALGRAVE MACMILLAN is the global academic imprint of the Palgrave Macmillan division of St. Martin's Press, LLC and of Palgrave Macmillan Ltd. Macmillan® is a registered trademark in the United States, United Kingdom and other countries. Palgrave is a registered trademark in the European Union and other countries.

ISBN 1–4039–1881–3 hardback

This book is printed on paper suitable for recycling and made from fully managed and sustained forest sources.

A catalogue record for this book is available from the British Library.

Library of Congress Cataloging-in-Publication Data
The right tools for the job : on the use and performance of
    management tools and techniques / by Andrew Cox ... [et al.].
      p. cm.
    Includes bibliographical references and index.
    ISBN 1–4039–1881–3 (cloth)
      1. Industrial management. I. Cox, Andrew W.
HD31.R525 2004
658–dc22   2004048876

10   9   8   7   6   5   4   3   2   1
14   13   12   11   10   09   08   07   06   05

Printed and bound in Great Britain by
Antony Rowe Ltd, Chippenham and Eastbourne

Contents

Conclusions

List of Figures

List of Tables

Preface

This volume could not have been produced with out the support of a great number of people and organisations. The research was generously funded by the Engineering and Physical Sciences Research Council under Grants No: GR/L86395 and GR/N34161/01. The work could not have been completed without the generous assistance of the staff in the 237 companies participating in this study, that gave generously of their time to participate in the interview process to enable the survey reported here to be carried out.

The research was guided by the authors who alone are responsible for any sins of omission or commission that may appear in the text, but it could not have been produced without the assistance of a great many researchers who worked on the project over the past five years. The authors would like to thank, therefore, Rachel Anthony, Adam Cox, Aidan Coglan, Rachel Farmery, Lindsay Mangham and Andy Passey for the valuable research work they contributed to the project. In undertaking the administrative work supporting the project the sterling efforts of Michelle Donovan must also be acknowledged. Finally, and as always, Jackie Potter made the task of turning the raw data into a meaningful manuscript an easier task than it would have been without her.

Finally, we hope that those who manage to read this volume learn something about the current state of business management practice in the use of tools and techniques. Much is written about how tools and techniques are created and whether or not they are of any real value for managers. Despite the millions of words written about this topic it is surprising that there has been so little rigorous analysis of the actual use and performance of the tools and techniques that managers use in practice. If this volume goes some way to beginning a debate that is based on robust empirical evidence then it will have served its purpose. This study could only analyse some of the industries and some of the functions involved in business management. It will perhaps serve as a starting point for comparison for those who may wish to assess the merits of management tools and techniques in the future.

Andrew Cox, Chris Lonsdale, Joe Sanderson & Glyn Watson
Birmingham,
May 2004.

Introduction

1
The Case For and Against the Use of Management Tools and Techniques

'Imagine going to your doctor because you are not feeling well. Before you've had a chance to describe your symptoms, the doctor writes out a prescription and says, "Take two of these three times a week and call me next week"'.
"But – I haven't told you what's wrong", you say. "How do I know this will help me?"
"Why wouldn't it?" says the doctor. "It worked for the last two patients".
No competent doctors would ever practice medicine like this, nor would any sane patient accept it if they did. Yet professors and consultants routinely prescribe such generic advice, and managers routinely accept such therapy, in the naïve belief that if a particular course of action helped other companies to succeed, it ought to help their's, too'.

Christensen & Raynor (2003), p. 67.

The amusing quote above might lead one to conclude that business managers are the unwitting dupes of unscrupulous academics and consultants selling snake oil. Yet the major argument in this volume, which reports the findings from a survey of the use and performance of business management tools and techniques across 237 firms in 16 different industrial sectors, is that managers are not always as gullible as some may believe (Micklethwaite & Wooldridge, 1996). Indeed, the research reported here shows that there is a definite link between the willingness of managers to use management tools and techniques and the risks that have to be managed given the functions and the types of industry sectors that they operate in. This implies that there is evidence of practitioners being able to understand when specific tools and techniques are appropriate (*the right tools for the job*) and also when they are not (*the wrong tools for the job*).

That said there is also considerable evidence that managers in many firms do not use tools and techniques extensively, or at all. This implies that managers may be more guilty of *flying blind* (managing without any at all) than they are of using inappropriate tools and techniques. This also implies that practitioners may be much more sceptical about the use of tools and techniques in general than the authors quoted above suspect. This is not, of course, to deny that there is considerable evidence of inappropriate use of management tools and techniques within business. But this is to run ahead of the argument, which is briefly outlined in what follows.

This chapter focuses, first, on the cases for and against the use of management tools and techniques and shows that, while much is written about the gullibility of managers, rather less is known about the actual use and performance of tools and techniques in practice. In fact there has been little systematic empirical study of the actual use of tools and techniques in particular functions and specific industries to allow any one to make any clear statements about whether or not managers are regularly duped or whether when they use them they do so rationally. The second part of the chapter outlines the structure of the survey that was undertaken to analyse the use and performance of tools and techniques reported here. The basic structure of the subsequent analytic chapters is outlined and a brief overview of the overall findings is presented.

1.   The case for and against the use of management tools and techniques

Central to the human condition is the problem of uncertainty. It affects everybody, takes many forms and operates in all spheres of human existence. In everyday life, a parent must decide on the school to which they should send their child, aware that the wrong choice may adversely affect their life prospects. Later on, that same child, by this time a prospective student, must choose not only the institution at which to study but the degree programme to follow and the courses to take. Having graduated the student needs to decide on a career, whether to buy or rent a home and must also make choices about how his or her children are to be educated. All of these are critical choices for an individual that impact materially on his or her happiness. There is no certainty, however, that the choices made will prove to be the right ones. Hindsight is a wonderful thing.

This problem of choice with potentially sub-optimal outcomes bedevils both our private and our working lives. Wherever an individual ends up working they are confronted with choices that can significantly affect the performance of an organisation for better or for worse. Managers, therefore, hope that they are making the right choices but frequently they are working in the dark. The CEO of a large corporation may have to commit scarce resource to the development of new product lines, aware that as many of 90% of new products fail in their first year of life, and anxious that his or her choices will be amongst the lucky few. A marketing manager will brief an advertising agency in the hope that the campaign created will actually generate sufficient sales to warrant the time, effort and cost incurred in devising it. Operations managers must strike the balance between flexibility and efficiency in their production strategies; and procurement managers must choose one supplier from amongst many, in the hope that the one selected will deliver on the promises that it has made and the contract that it has signed. In short, all managers must take risks with their employer's resources and their own careers.

In doing so they frequently look outside of the company for inspiration and practical advice (Brindle & Stearns, 2001). External assistance comes in many forms: from benchmarking leading competitors; from consultants; and, from a range of business 'gurus' – including academics. In many instances the assistance can take the form of general philosophies or approaches to business problems. In other cases firms can import structured tools and techniques with specific and limited applications. The range and number of formalised techniques employed is itself extremely diverse and reaches into every area of business management. This includes high profile business functions like strategy and marketing and sales, as well as some of the less visible areas of operations and production and procurement and supply management. In recent years, concepts like outsourcing and lean thinking have, therefore, become almost as familiar as Business Process Reengineering (BPR), core competence thinking and economic value-added (EVA).

The advice game is now a multi-billion dollar industry. It spans the globe and few firms remain untouched by it. In theory at least the management tools and techniques, and the codified practices that are proffered by a growing army of external advisers, are supposed to help firms cope more effectively with the problem of risk and uncertainty. Enthusiasts for this burgeoning industry suggest that the ever-increasing amounts being spent on such services each year is clear evidence of its value. After all, business managers are worldly-wise, hard-headed individuals. If such tools and techniques were not of proven value surely they would not part with their money?

Other commentators, however, are not so sure. Indeed, the more critical students of business management argue that many of the tools and techniques foisted on the more unsuspecting and credulous business managers do not even meet the most basic standards of scientific enquiry. Rather, they are put together on the back of an envelope by avaricious consultants anxious to turn a quick buck. Sometimes such consultants, it is argued, go to the trouble of developing new tools but as often as not they fall back on the tried and tested technique of repackaging a pre-existing idea that has currently fallen out of fashion (Spell, 2001). Once the new wine (or rather the old wine in its new bottle) has been put together it will then be aggressively promoted through one of a small number of high profile, but largely uncritical business journals, in the hope that, with the backing of such an imprimatur, it will prove to be an easy sell. To assist in this promotional process the apparent effectiveness of the new tool will be demonstrated by pointing to a number of concrete examples in which it has apparently been used with great success.

Recently, this process was pithily described in the following terms: 'Get an article in the Harvard Business Review, pump it up into a book, pray for a best-seller, then market the idea for all its worth through a consulting company' (O'Shea & Madigan, 1997, p. 198).

If this is what happens – and there is no doubt that this process does occur in practice within business – can we assume that all managers are guilty of gullibility or is it only that some are more gullible than others? This is a crucial question that this study sets out to resolve. One of the most important questions asked in this study is, therefore, whether or not there are rational grounds for the patterns of tool and technique usage reported in the 237 companies surveyed, or is it all based on chance and managerial myopia? A second major question that this study seeks to answer is whether or not managers are broadly satisfied with the tools and techniques that they use, and whether managers in some functions and industries are more or less satisfied than others.

Before describing in more detail how the survey was constructed and the structure by which the findings from it are reported herein it is first necessary to discuss theoretically the case for and against the use of tools and techniques in business management. This takes the form of a discussion of the relative merits of approaches to business management based on principles of scientific rationality or the art of muddling through.

Best practice through scientific rationality

One of the fundamental problems for managers is that they are often at the mercy of what appear to them to be corporately unique demands and pressures. In responding to such challenges managers may (serendipitously) stumble across solutions to their problems. Necessity is after all the mother of invention. Yet there is no guarantee of success. While no one is more intimately acquainted with a problem than the person experiencing it many solutions require the problem-solver to have a sense of perspective that only comes with distance. Furthermore, why risk the uncertainty of untried techniques when there might already exist a model of proven pedigree. It is for just these sorts of reasons, plus the need to deal with problems quickly, that in undertaking their day-to-day activities many managers look externally for assistance and advice. It is perhaps fortunate for them, therefore, that there is no shortage of people who are prepared to offer it.

The codification of business life has been ongoing for sometime and it is arguable that here has been a standard process based on the empiricist tradition through which this occurs. Confronted with a clearly identifiable business management problem academics or consultants normally develop an approach to tackle it (Abrahamson, 1996; Abrahamson & Fairchild 1999). On the back of a successful trial, the model is aggressively marketed and, thereafter, widespread adoption follows until the technique hits the buffers and fails in implementation somewhere. This might be because of inappropriate application or it may be because of inadequate implementation. Regardless of the proximate cause, at this point the new approach is discredited and it quickly passes into folk law.

Despite a very high mortality rate over time the overall supply of such tools and techniques remains undiminished. The question is why? The answer is undoubtedly complex. Part of it lies in the fact that ideas perform such a critical function for managers. Such is the complexity of the manager's existence that anything that offers even a degree of clarity (or certainty) is welcomed. The supply remains undiminished because the demand remains undiminished. However, this seems to be only part of the answer. A deeper explanation may have its origins in the general approach to business management that stresses the importance of rationality.

The emphasis on rationality has a long tradition in Western thought generally. Its ascendance often dates back to the Enlightenment. Prior to this period the social world was often held to be a world of mysteries. The world was made by God: but his purpose was hidden and even though the Bible might shed some light on the human condition it did not allow it to be changed. The writings of scientists like Isaac Newton began to change this. In exploring the physical world Newton showed that not only could it be understood and explained but, as a result, it could be altered. If this were true, so it followed, so could the social world. If something was not working it needed to be studied until the reason for the failure had been understood. Thereafter, the problem could be resolved.

Richard Whittington has noted that this tradition is the dominant one in business management thought. For example, he has commented that while there are forty books or more using the title *Strategic Management* all of them say much the same thing. What also characterises this output is an overweening confidence on the part of its authors in the malleability of the commercial environment. There is in the literature "*little variety, little self-doubt*", so that the message takes on the aspect of generally accepted truth (Whittington, 2000, p. 1). It can be argued that this consistency and certainty does scant justice to the subject. Furthermore, outside the textbook mainstream the discipline sometimes resembles more of a jungle than a safe and well-trodden track.

However, as far as the mainstream is concerned – and business managers rarely read anything other than the mainstream – the business environment, while undoubtedly complex, is amenable to investigation, and malleable when it comes to operational practice. For those in this tradition effective business management requires: 'the determination of the basic, long-term goals and objectives of an enterprise, and the adoption of courses of action and the allocation of resources necessary for those goals' (Chandler, 1962, p. 13).

Best practice by muddling through

The idea that business management is, or indeed could ever be treated as, a branch of science has of course been challenged. Some sceptics even question the whole concept of scientific business management. Such a view holds that the future emerges rather than is rationally planned. This perspective is fundamentally pessimistic in orientation, likening the process of business management and corporate survival to that which occurs in the natural world: 'businesses are like the species of biological evolution: competitive processes ruthlessly select out the fittest for survival; the others are powerless to ward off extinction' (Whittington, 2000, p. 3).

According to this perspective, therefore, it is the market and not the firm that makes all of the important decisions. Business strategies specifically, and functional/departmental strategies more generally, emerge through a process of natural selection as the market passes judgement on them. By such a reckoning planning is simply an irrelevance. By the time managers have devised their programmes of action the world has moved on and they have become an irrelevance. Managers who believe that by buying in advice that they can ride the vicissitudes of the market are simply deluded. This is because, if management tools or techniques work at all, it will be at greatly reduced levels of functionality or by chance. In such an environment 'muddling through' – operating on a short-term reactive basis to constantly changing external circumstances – could actually be seen as a more rational approach than scientific planning.

However, while scientific planning is not necessarily capable of delivering all the promises made for it, in a rapidly changing market environment a management tool of limited use may be better than none at all. The analogy here is the evolution of the human eye. Critics of theories of evolution and the evolutionary process often point to the human eye to support their arguments. The human eye, so the argument goes, is a complex organ that only works properly if all of the parts are functioning fully. If the lens is the wrong shape, for example, it will not focus the light properly – leaving the individual either short or long-sighted. The gap between the eyes possessed by modern vertebrates and more primitive forms of organism is so large as to make it hard to explain how it could have been bridged by simple natural selection. Any shift from the primitive version to its more modern variant would fall far short in terms of performance. Not until all of the elements of the modern eye were present and assembled in their current form, would the eye work properly. And the point about evolution is that it punishes the sub-optimal. To evolutionary theorists, however, this rather misses the point. It is not necessary for the eye to be fully functioning in order for it to be of value. All that is necessary is that it be an improvement on what went before. Even a 1% improvement in the battle for survival can improve the odds. In the kingdom of the blind the one-eyed man is king. So it is with business management. As long as the gain derived from the experiment exceeds the resource expended in developing it, it has been of value – assuming of course that one has factored in the opportunity costs of alternative actions when calculating the expense.

The problem of theory and evidence in business management thinking

Perhaps more pertinently, however, while it is clearly true that some markets are so complex and dynamic as to make systematic planning difficult, it is not true that all markets are like this. Some industries and firms experience prolonged periods of stability. Even in industries where change occurs more quickly, not all business functions are necessarily affected by such change in the same way or to the same degree. Furthermore, it is clearly true that some firms have derived significant benefit from introducing rationally structured management tools and techniques.

The Japanese automotive industry is a case in point. Not only did practices like Total Quality Management and Just-in-Time transform the fortunes of the companies that used them domestically, it has also changed production practices internationally. For the firms that have gained from using such tools and techniques it is inconceivable that they should turn back the clock to the time before they were used. Consequently, it seems that management tools and techniques are not inappropriate *per se*, but can cause problems if the tool is inappropriate for the problem at hand, or appropriate but misapplied. And, it is at this point that one has to understand the problem that is created by the method by which most tools and techniques are created and then sold into firms.

If firms are to attempt to guide their activities according to scientifically rational principles then it is important that these principles should themselves have been scientifically derived. This is a question of epistemology: sometimes defined as the study of the process by which people acquire knowledge. In order for something to meet the standard of being *known* three things must hold. First, and critically, people must believe something to be true. A procurement manager must believe that if collaborative relationships are created with suppliers then this will add value to the association. A strategy manager must believe that if the competitive environment is better understood then there is a better likelihood of knowing whether or not there is a profit to be earned from it. However, belief, while being necessary to obtain knowledge and understanding, is not sufficient to allow us to be certain that knowledge has in fact been acquired. For many years people believed (wrongly) that the earth was flat. It is necessary, therefore, that in order for beliefs to be valid that what is believed to be true is actually true. For example, if partnerships with suppliers are adopted then they should deliver the gains that were expected. Again, however, belief and truth are not sufficient in themselves to give certainty. People believe in God. God may in fact exist. But we do not know for certain that such is the case. What exists here is not knowledge but faith. What is missing for truth and certainty is a third element – evidence. And this is where theory comes in.

The development of good and bad theory follows certain obvious patterns. Bad theory is essentially empiricist in that it lets the facts simply speak for themselves (Willer & Willer, 1973; Cox, 1997). Typically, it will make broad claims without necessarily spelling out the relationship between cause and effect. Businesses are successful when senior managers exercise strong leadership. Markets are enough to keep executives honest. Both statements may or may not be true but in neither statement is the basis for the belief that event Y should follow from action X, spelt out. Furthermore, bad theory is often overconfident in the strength of its message. A bad theory will frequently draw strong conclusions that simply are not warranted by the evidence available. Simply because a particular practice worked well for company A that used it at time T1, this does not mean that it will work equally well for company B using it at time T2. Finally, in its most acute form bad management theory is guilty of hubris. Not only will it promise on the basis of limited explanation and evidence to transform all organisations in many different contexts, it will also promise to tear up the business management rule book.

One recent writer offers a particularly amusing account of this particular brand of grandiose management theory (Collins, 2000). In doing so the author critically examines the work of a number of the most eminent business thinkers and comments on the inconsistencies contained in their work. Tom Peters is particularly criticised for apparently giving powerful support to senior managers prepared to grasp the nettle and downsize their organisations, yet only four years later he appears to turn his original position on its head. As Collins puts it: 'In a typically grand and dismissive gesture, Peters tells us that all bets are off! His work is inconsistent, he tells us, because the world is! Only a cynic would ask for anything more. Only a "sinner" would have the temerity to venture that inconsistency is the product of flabby modelling, populist thinking and ready-made science' (Collins, 2000, p. 167).

In contrast to this notion of bad theory based on simplistic empiricism three stages are suggested as necessary for the development of good theory (Christensen & Raynor, 2003). First, when induction rather than deduction is used the analyst must begin by describing the phenomena that they are observing in all of its breadth and detail. Rather than looking for the few occasions when the practice worked well they should also be keeping an eye out for the examples of failure. Thus, if partnerships are formed with suppliers, where did they work well, where were the results mixed and where were they outright failures? Second, and following on from this, the different cases must be arranged into categories that are capable of highlighting the most important differences. From this it is possible to move to stage three: the formulation of a hypothesis. This is a statement of cause and effect. It allows us to suggest that if actor A adopts practice P1 under conditions C1, then this will (with a certain specified degree of probability) lead to outcome Q1. It also allows us to say that if actor B adopts practice P1 under conditions C2, then this will (with a certain specified degree of probability) lead to outcome Q2.

However, even this is but the first step. Notice that predictions must be qualified with the caveat 'with a certain specified degree of probability'. Good theory never proves anything. It simply suggests that the evidence is, to a high degree of probability, consistent with the prediction. A good theorist is always prepared to modify or even reject a deeply held belief as new evidence presents itself. The contrast between good and bad knowledge development could not be starker and it perhaps explains better than anything else why so many business models fail in implementation. The reason is that they simply have not been thought through properly and then tested in the real world before being offered as ready-made solutions to the immediate business problems of managers.

Or does it? If the critics of scientific management are correct in their assertions one should expect that most management tools and techniques would prove to be of little value to those who use them, irrespective of the tool, the industry or the context in which it is applied. When managers continue to use such tools and techniques regardless of the results this simply emphasises their fundamental irrationality. When, however, they do not use them this suggests a manager's capacity to understand the tragedy of the human condition. And this is that uncertainty simply completes the triumvirate of certainties (including death and taxes) that people just have to learn to live with.

However, if advocates of rational scientific management are correct then the experience of tool and technique usage by managers should be broadly positive, but at the same time rather mixed. If satisfaction levels are positive this suggest that firms derive some value from using them, even when tools do not achieve everything that is promised. At the same time, one might expect satisfaction levels to be mixed. As the critics observe, some business contexts are simply more fertile than others for implementation and respond better to the introduction of particular management tools and techniques.

The overall findings from the survey of management tools and techniques

The survey results reported in this volume generally support this latter interpretation. The findings show that there is evidence that managers use management tools and techniques more in some industries than in others. They also show that the nature of risks that have to be managed within specific business functions and industries is also significant. Furthermore, the findings show that managers are broadly positive about the use of tools and techniques. All of this indicates that managers using tools and techniques appear to understand when it is appropriate to do so. There is also evidence that when they do so they also broadly understand for which functional business activities they should be utilised most often.

That said there is, indirectly, also evidence in the survey that also supports the anti-rational muddling through view of business management. While the survey findings demonstrate that, when managers use tools and techniques they do so for rational reasons, the major finding from this study is that managers do not use them very much at all. Rather than managers consistently understanding what are the *right tools for the job* the overwhelming evidence from the survey is that managers and their companies are *flying blind*. What this means is that, while the proponents of rational scientific management approaches can point to the evidence from this survey to support the view that some managers do appear to understand when it is appropriate to use tools and techniques in particular functions and in specific industries, most do not. This means that most companies and most managers are in fact muddling through.

The study therefore provides evidence for both of the viewpoints briefly outlined above. But it is worth stressing at the outset that even though this somewhat unsatisfactory outcome may have occurred at least one misconception can be laid to rest. The evidence in this study demonstrates overwhelmingly that when managers use tools and techniques they rarely do so as the gullible dupes of unscrupulous snake oil salesmen. In fact the evidence shows that most managers are inherently conservative and do not use very many tools and techniques at all. This does not mean that there are no circumstances when managers are duped by the unscrupulous. Clearly there will be some circumstances when suppliers of management ideas take advantage of gullible managers. Despite this the evidence here shows that tool and technique usage appears to be based on fairly rational principles and that most managers are subjectively at least, relatively satisfied with performance.

2.   The research project and the structure of the book

Methodological background to the survey of management tools and techniques

This volume is one of the products of a six-year study between 1998 and 2004 funded by the Engineering and Physical Research Council in the UK into the development, use and performance of management tools and techniques (the other major outputs from this study can be found in: Cox,

Sanderson and Watson, 2000; Cox et al., 2001, 2002, 2003, 2004a and 2004b). As part of the study the authors identified the most commonly cited tools and techniques in the business management literature with the intention of undertaking a survey of which tools are actually being used, by which firms and to what effect. The meaning of the term tool or technique, and what should be covered by this concept, caused some internal debate amongst the research team. Eventually it was decided that the concept should cover all (software and non-software) processes and systems based on structured ways of thinking and acting created to provide support for management decisions and operational practices. To provide rigour, the survey assessed these management practices in four different business functions: *strategy, marketing and sales, operations and production and procurement and supply*.

Furthermore, these management practices were surveyed in a wide and representative range of companies and industries. In total 237 companies (listed in Table 1.1) from 16 *manufacturing, combined manufacturing and services* and *services* industries were analysed using a structured questionnaire in face-to-face interviews over a four-year period. The number of companies surveyed within each industry sector ranged from a minimum of 11 to a maximum of 20, although it was not always possible to analyse all four functions in each of the firms surveyed. This explains why in some of the analysis that follows the number of company cases by function is less than 11. In total 123 individual tools and techniques (for the full list see Appendix A) were reported to be in use, although 1,830 management tool and technique usages were recorded.

Most of the firms surveyed were large nationally – based companies, although a considerable number were multinationals, but an attempt was made to achieve comprehensive coverage of as many different types of industries as possible, with a variety of operational systems and processes to be managed. To achieve this, as Figure 1.1 demonstrates, companies were selected not only on the basis of the types of industry (*manufacturing, combined manufacturing and services* and *services*) but were also segmented by the frequency and standardised nature of the business systems and processes to be managed. Thus a basic distinction was made between two broad types of business management system and process. Companies and industries were either categorised as *process-based* (i.e. producing a product and/or service of a fairly standardised type using fairly routinised systems and processes on a regular basis) or *project-based* (i.e. producing a product and/or service of a fairly non-standard type using fairly non-routinised systems and processes).

As Figure 1.1 demonstrates this approach ensured coverage of six very different types of industry and the companies within them. The rational for this approach was to ascertain to what extent there might be variance in the use and performance of tools and techniques in general and across the

Table 1.1 The Total Sample of 237 Companies Surveyed by Industry Sectors

Aerospace (15)	Construction (11)	Media & Entertainment (20)	Retail & Distribution (13)
Aeropia	Alfred-McAlpine	Anglia Television	Allied Carpets
BAE Systems	Amec	BBC	Amtrak
Britax International	Anglo-Holt	BBC Resources	Autologic
CJ Fox & Sons	Balfour Beatty	BRMB	Britannia Music
Computing Devices	Bovis Homes	BRMB Radio	C Butt Ltd
Dowty Aerospace	Carillion	Carlton Central	Courts
Dunlop Aviation	Crosby Homes	Carlton Television	Next plc
GKN Westland	Drake & Scull	Channel 4	Somerfield
Linread Northridge	Faithfull & Gould	Channel 5	Statesman
Martin-Baker	How Group	Galaxy FM	Tesco
McKechnie	Tilbury Douglas	Heart FM	Tibbet & Britten
PMES		Phoenix Television	Tradeteam
Rolls-Royce		Rank Group	WHSmith
TRW		Scottish Media Group	
Umeco		Sky	
		Sony Music (S2)	
		Telewest Communications	
		UCI	
		Warner B ros Home Cinemas	
		Wildtrack Television	

Basic Chemicals (15)	Financial Services (13)	Oil & Gas (15)	Telecommunications (13)
Air Products	Alliance & Leicester	Agip UK	Advent Communications
ACKROS	Barclays	Amerada Hess	BCH
BASF	Barclays Mercantile	BG	Canon
BOC	Bradford & Bingley	BP	Comdev
BP Chemicals	Britannia	Centrica	Crown Castle
CIBA Chemicals	Cheltenham & Gloucester	Edecco	European Antennas

Basic Chemicals (15)	Financial Services (13)	Oil & Gas (15)	Telecommunications (13)
Crosfield Chemicals	Churchill Insurance	Enterprise Oil	Hughes
Eka Chemicals	Endsleigh Insurance	Global Marine	Infonet
Houghton	Hill House Hammond	Intrepid	Motorola
ICI Chlor Chemicals	Nationwide	Lasmo	Motorola GSM
Nalco-Exxon Energy	Norwich Union	Ranger	Motorola GTSS
Rhodia	Virgin Direct	Rigblast	Orange
Rohm and Haas	Woolwich	Salamis	Voice
Solvay Interox		Shell	
Unichem Limited		Weir Pumps	

Computer Hardware (16)	Healthcare (17)	Power & Water Utilities (17)	Tourism & Leisure (20)
Apple	Acambis	British Energy	Airtours
Compaq	Advanced Medical Solutions	British Gas	Blue Harbour
Dell	AstraZeneca	Calor Gas	Britannic Travel
Fujitsu-Siemens	Biocompatibles	Corby Power Station	Compass Group
Hewlett Packard	Biofocus	Dynegy	First Choice Travel
IBM	Deltex Medical	GPU Power	Going Places Leisure
Integrated Dev Tech	Evotec OAI	Innogy	Hilton Group
Lexmark	GlaxoSmithkline	International Power	Holiday Autos Int.
Mitac	Goldshield	London Electricity	JAC Travel
Psion	Hypoguard	Magnox Electric	Keyline Continental
Sharp Electronics	Intercare	Northern Electric and Gas	Lancaster Landmark
Sun Microsystems	Martindale	npower	Queens Moat Houses
Synnex Info Tech	Nycomed Amersham	Severn Trent Water	Regent Inns
Tatung	Profile Therapeutics	United Utilities	Scottish Courage
Tulip	Quadrant Healthcare	Vivendi Water Partnership	Shearings Holidays
Xyratex	Smith and Nephew	Yorkshire Electricity & Gas	St. Giles Hotel
	SR Pharma	Yorkshire Water	STA Travel
			Sunsail
			Travel By Appointment
			Travelbag

Table 1.1 The Total Sample of 237 Companies Surveyed by Industry Sectors – *continued*

Confectionary (15)	IT Solutions (13)	Publishing (13)	Transport Equipment (11)
Allied Domecq	Action	Birmingham Post & Mail	Adtranz
Bernard Matthews	Bull Info Systems	Butterworth Heinneman	Dennis Eagle
Britvic	Cisco	Cambridge UP	LDV
Cadburys	CSC	Heinneman Secondary	Mayflower
Coca-Cola	Docent	IPC Media	Pendennis Shipyard
Fox's Biscuits	EDS	John Wiley & Sons	Reynard Motorsport
Geest	Electron Economy	Oxford UP	Schmidtz Cargobull
Golden Wonder	ICL	Pearson	Unipart
Lindt Chocolates	Kalamazoo Computer	Pearson Education	West Coast Traincare
Nestle	Logica	REPP	Whale Tankers
Paynes	Peoplesoft	Sage Publications	Wrightbus
Red Bull	Perot Systems	Taylor & Francis	
Sela Sweets	Unisys	Yorkshire Post	
Thorntons			
Trebor-Basset			

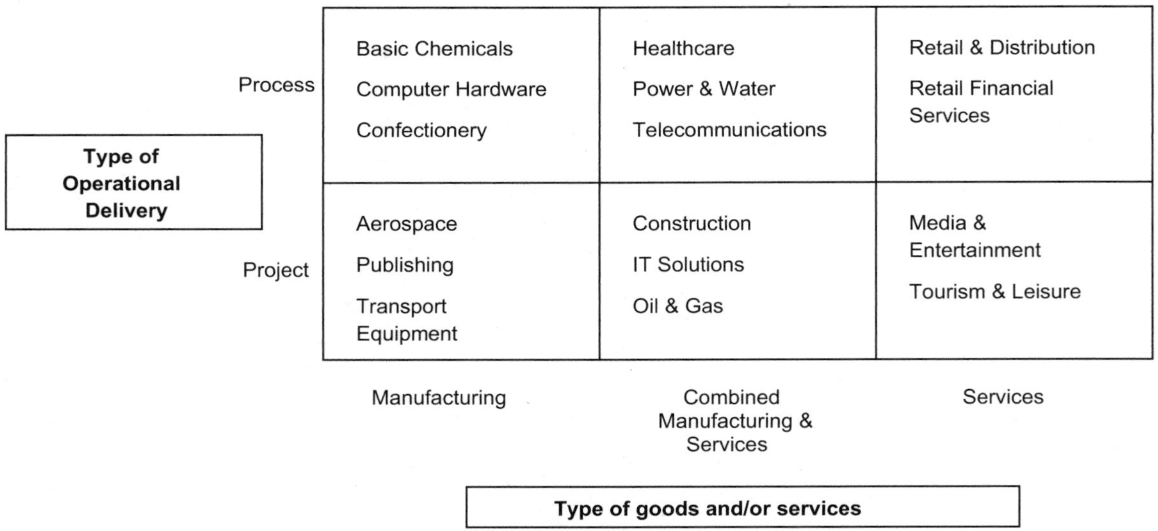

Figure 1.1 The Survey Segmentation of Industry Sectors

four different specialist functions, within very different types of industrial sector circumstance.

In undertaking the survey research, before analysing the tools that were being used and with what effect, the initial aim was to ascertain the universe of potential management tools and techniques theoretically available for use by managers in each of the four functional areas. This required the research team to undertake extensive desk based research of the business management literature to identify as comprehensive a list as possible of the tools and techniques that have been developed by academics, consultants and practitioners. The authors do not, however, claim that this list is in anyway a definitive guide to the tools and techniques that are available. The reason for this is that the research team was not able to read all of the literature in business management and not every academic, consultant and practitioner is prepared to publicise freely the tools and techniques that they use to analyse and resolve problems. Some individuals understand that retaining particularly useful tools and techniques exclusively for their own (or their client's) use may be more valuable than sharing them indiscriminately with others.

The literature survey discovered 253 functional-specific tools and techniques in total, with 56 in the strategy, 59 in the marketing and sales, 73 in the operations and production and 65 in the procurement and supply functional areas (although some of these were duplicated across functions as we shall see). A summary guide to these tools and techniques is provided by function in this volume as a reference source. The book is divided into four parts (A, B, C and D), and the first chapter in each part (chapters 2, 4, 6 and 8 respectively) provides a reference guide to the tools and techniques in the literature that have been developed for use in that functional area of business. This is followed, in each part, by an analytical chapter (chapters 3, 5, 7 and 9) that describes what the survey discovered about the actual pattern of tool and technique used in general and by industry sector, with a summary of which were not being used at all. The analytical chapters also focus on the performance of particular tools and techniques within specific industrial sectors and the barriers to their successful implementation.

In general terms there appears to be a disjuncture between the total number of tools and techniques that have been developed (or that were discovered in the literature survey) and those that are actually being used. This is indicated by the statistics in Table 1.2.

As the summary data above indicates overall only 184 tools and techniques were actually being used within the 237 companies surveyed and this means that at the functional level 69 potential tools and techniques were not being utilised. This demonstrates that some tools and techniques are used more frequently and by many companies than others. The analytic findings in chapters 3, 5, 7 and 9 outline which tools and techniques

Table 1.2 A Comparison of the Number of Tools and Techniques Available and the Number of Tools in Actual Use

	Strategy	Marketing & Sales	Operations & Production	Procurement & Supply	Total
The Number of Tools and Techniques Discovered in the Literature Survey	56	59	73	65	253
The Number of Tools and Techniques in Actual Use in the 237 Companies Surveyed	44	48	50	42	184
The Number of Tools Found Not to be in Use in the 237 Companies Surveyed	12	11	23	23	69
The average Tool use by Company	3.65	4.01	3.78	3.74	3.80

were most heavily used within each function. Notwithstanding the popularity of certain tools and techniques it is clear that there is considerable evidence of non-use. This in itself is interesting because it indicates either that the tools and techniques are of limited utility or that managers may not be aware of them at all. The research demonstrates that both causes of non-use operate in practice, but that lack of knowledge is clearly a major issue for most managers, as is a lack of the time and/or resources to implement those tools and techniques that are known about. These findings are described in more detail for each of the four functions in the first part of each of the analytical chapters that follow. Each chapter explains in general and by industry sector, which tools were actually used and which were not.

Having seen in general terms that there is a disjuncture between the number of tools in use and the number that have been developed, the research then focused on which business management activities within each function are most likely to have tools and techniques in use. In undertaking this each of the four functions was treated in exactly the same way. Since the task of analysing the number of tools and techniques was complex, to make the task of analysis across functions and industry sectors manageable it was decided to analyse performance by grouping the tools and techniques into the key management tasks undertaken within each function. This required the research team to identify those tasks and activities in each function that posed acute problems for the management of risk and uncertainty.

In the case of **strategy**, the function was broken down into the following 7 risk and uncertainty management categories:

market and environmental analysis;
product and competence development;
the make-buy decision;
resource allocation;
performance measurement;
financial management; and,
the use of IT and Internet solutions.

In the case of **marketing** some of the activities were the same. This is perhaps not surprising given the overlap in agendas between the two functions. This function was analysed using 6 categories:

market and environmental analysis;
product and competence development;
promotion and relationship management;
pricing;
performance measurement; and,
the use of IT and Internet solutions.

When it came to **operations and production** 5 principal categories were analysed:

planning, design and work organisation;
product and competence development;
process and systems improvement;
performance measurement, and,
the use of IT and Internet solutions.

Finally, for **procurement and supply** there were a total of 7 main categories:

the make-buy decision;
segmentation of spend;
supplier selection and negotiation;
supplier development;
process enhancement;
performance measurement; and,
the use of IT and Internet solutions.

This being done it was now possible to ascertain in general which broad types of business activity within each function was most amenable to the use of tools and techniques. Following this general analysis the research focused on whether there was any significant difference in usage across different industry sectors in each function. This analysis focused on the overall use of tools and techniques as well as on the objectives for implementation as well as the impact of tools and techniques on performance.

The overall structure of the book

The results of the research into the 16 different industry sectors are presented in the four parts I to IV that follow. Each part focuses on the experiences of the four major functions. Part I deals with *strategy*, Part II with *marketing and sales*, Part III with *operations and production* and Part IV with *procurement and supply*. Each of these parts is then divided into two chapters. In the first chapter in each part (chapters 2, 4, 6 and 8) a comprehensive list of the management tools and techniques commonly used in that function is provided. Following this there is an analytical chapter (chapters 3, 5, 7 and 9) that focuses on the use and performance of the tools and techniques used in each function. Each of these analytical chapters is arranged with the same structure to facilitate the process of comparison.

Each chapter begins with a short introduction that says something about the tradition of scientific management within that function. The issue of tool and technique usage in general is then considered. The discussion here focuses on which tools were being used and how often (Table 1 in each part), and which were not (Table 2). This is followed by a discussion of the use of tools and techniques by the major functional business activities for managing risk and uncertainty. Table 3 in each part assesses which of the different business activities that were identified as part of the initial research design accounts for the highest proportion of tools used within that function. Secondly, the table lists which of the tools and techniques featured most prominently in the performance of each particular activity.

Having analysed the use of tools and techniques in general each analytic chapter then focuses directly on their use and performance by individual and grouped industrial sectors. Table 4 records three sets of data for each functional area: the number of tool and technique usages; the number of companies interviewed; and, each individual industry sector's average propensity to use tools. Figure 1 provides a breakdown of the overall pattern of tool and technique usage across the individual and grouped industry sectors.

The remainder of each analytic chapter focuses on the objectives and performance of the tools and techniques used. Table 5 analyses what managers hoped to achieve by introducing tools and techniques for the organisation as a whole (*the firm level*). They were asked whether it was expected to contribute to increasing the competitive advantage of the organisation as a whole, or simply to help it function more operationally effectively. Three distinct measures of strategic competitive advantage were used in the survey questionnaire. The first two equate with Michael Porter's models of strategic fit – product differentiation and cost leadership (Porter, 1980). The third measure equates with strategic stretch or competitive repositioning (Hamel & Prahalad, 1993). The analysis compares respondents by individual and grouped industry sectors.

Table 6 deals with the range of benefits that managers anticipated they might obtain for their functional area from the use of particular tools and techniques (*the function level*). A number of potential functional benefits were identified. These included direct benefits: such as the ability to improve the functionality of a service being offered. Other categories dealt with more indirect benefits. These included the ability to improve: communication levels and/or information flows; the flexibility of the function; skill levels; and, employee numbers. The data is provided for individual and grouped industry sectors.

The final part of each analytic chapter analyses the general perception of the performance of tools and techniques by industrial sector. Table 7 records the subjective perception of respondents to the overall performance of tools and techniques in general. Respondents were asked to rate the performance of the tools and techniques they had implemented according to a scale that ran from highly positive to highly negative. A score of high positive is recorded as +1, while a score of highly negative is recorded as –1. Consequently, +1 and –1 describe the boundaries for the range of possible scores. A score of zero indicates a neutral impact. That is to say, the introduction of the tools and techniques were perceived neither to have benefited nor harmed the organisation or the administrative function. Finally, information was also recorded when the respondent had no clear idea of the impact of a particular management tool. This provided a mechanism by which to check whether managers were investing considerable effort into an activity without having any idea of whether the investment was actually paying-off. Once again the data is provided by individual and grouped industrial sectors.

Table 8 provides a comparison of both the rank order for usage rates and for satisfaction with performance across the 16 industry sectors. The findings show that there is only rarely a strong correlation between usage and performance satisfaction. Table 9 examines the barriers to implementation. It draws distinctions between those occasions when the source of the difficulties was the tool or technique itself, those occasions where the difficulties could be attributed to the internal environment into which the tool or technique was being introduced, and those occasions when respondents had no data. The Table also breaks down the internal barriers category into seven sub-categories: culture (resistance due to the existing standard operating procedures and political structures internally); the wrong performance measures; insufficient resources to implement effectively; senior management opposition; disruptive internal reorganisation; unrealistic expectations; and, other (a catch all category).

Finally in Table 10 an attempt is made to provide an overall explanation for the pattern of tool and technique usage and performance within each function. The original working assumptions that informed this survey were based on the idea that process-based industries would probably have a much greater propensity to use tools and techniques than project-based industries. The reason for this working assumption was that it was felt that firms operating in process-based industries were more likely to see value in routinised and standardised tools and techniques than those operating in project environments. Similarly, a second assumption was that firms operating in manufacturing industries, with high levels of operational and technical complexity to be managed on a regular basis, would also be more likely to see value from the use of management tools and techniques than services-based industries that rely on innovative ideas and non-product supply offerings. The combined manufacturing and services based industries were expected to be somewhere between these two extremes of use and non-use.

Given this the working assumption originally was that *Process/Manufacturing* industries would be the most likely to use tools and techniques, closely followed by the *Process/Combined* industry sectors, with the *Project/Services* and *Project/Combined* sectors expected to use tools and techniques least of all, and with the *Process/Services* and *Project/Manufacturing* industries somewhere in between. The findings reported here does offer some support for the two extreme assumptions that informed the starting point of the research survey – that is that *Process/Manufacturing* tend to have the heaviest usage with *Project/Services* having the lowest usage. Unfortunately the evidence is not quite as clear cut across all of the other sectors and it is for this reason that the data was finally analysed using an approach that attempted to analyse the types of risks and uncertainties that each of the four functions has to manage, and to what extent the 16 industry sectors can be categorised as high, medium or low risk for the particular function being analysed.

Table 10, therefore, shows what the use and performance scores are for each of the 16 industry sectors when they are categorised into high, medium and low risk. The evidence clearly shows that there is a clear correlation between the level of risk and uncertainty to be managed and the use, but not the performance, of tools and techniques. This means that the findings support the argument that there are rational reasons behind the use of tools and techniques, but only partial evidence that regular and heavy tool and technique use always leads to high levels of performance satisfaction. This conclusion is consistent across all of the four functions analysed.

These general findings support the view that managers do appear to be behaving relatively rationally when they use tools and techniques, and that they also understand which are the *right tools for the job* when it comes to the business activities to be managed within particular functions. The findings also support the view that managers, when using tools and techniques, may be far less gullible than some writers think. But this is to run ahead of the argument presented in what follows.

References

Abrahamson, E. (1996) 'Management Fashion' *Academy of Management Review*, 21(1).

Abrahamson, E. & Fairchild, G. (1999) 'Management Fashion: Lifecycles, Triggers, and Collective Learning Processes' *Administrative Science Quarterly*, 44.

Brindle, M. & Stearns, P. (2001) *Facing Up to Management Faddism: A New Look At an Old Face*, West Point, US and London, UK.

Cox, A. (1997) *Business Success* (Helpston, UK: Earlsgate Press).

Cox, A. et al. (2001) 'The Power Perspective in Procurement and Supply Management', *The Journal of Supply Chain Management*, Vol. 37, No. 2, Spring.

Cox, A. et al. (2002) *Supply Chains, Markets and Power: Mapping Buyer and Supplier Power Regimes*, London: Routledge.

Cox, A. et al. (2003) *Supply Chain Management: A Guide to Best Practice*, London: Financial Times/Prentice Hall.

Cox, A. et al. (2004a) *Business Relationships for Competitive Advantage*, Basingstoke & New York: Palgrave Macmillan.

Cox A. et al. (2004b) 'Power Regimes and Supply Chain Management', *Supply Chain Management: An International Journal*, October.

Cox, A., Sanderson, J. & Watson, G. (2000), *Power Regimes: Mapping the DNA of Business and Supply Chain Relationships* (Helpston, UK: Earlsgate Press).

Chandler, A. D. (1962) *Strategy and Structure*, Cambridge, MA: MIT Press.

Christensen, C. & Raynor, M. (2003) 'Why Hard-Nosed Executives Should Care About Management Theory' *Harvard Business Review*, September.

Collins, D. (2000) *Management Fads and Buzzwords: Critical-Practical Perspectives*, London: Routledge.

Hamel, G. & Prahalad, C. K. (1993) 'Strategy as Stretch and Leverage', *Harvard Business Review*, March/April.

Micklethwaite, J. & Wooldridge, A. (1996) *The Witch Doctors*, London: Heinemann.

O'Shea, J. & Madigan, C. (1997) *Dangerous Company: Management Consultants and the Businesses They Save and Ruin*, New York: Time Books.

Porter, M. E. (1980) *Competitive Advantage: Creating and Sustaining Superior Performance*, New York: Free Press.

Spell, C. (2001) 'Management Fashions: Where Do They Come from, and Are They Old Wine in New Bottles?' *Journal of Management Enquiry*, 10(4).

Whittington, R. (2000) *What is Strategy and Does it Matter?* London: Thomson Learning.

Willer, D. & Willer, J. (1973) *Systematic Empiricism: A Critique of a Pseudo-Science*, New York: Prentice Hall.

Part I

Strategic Management

2
Tools and Techniques for Strategic Management

The 56 tools and techniques listed below are not definitive but they do provide a comprehensive listing of some of the major tools and techniques regularly used by managers in the strategy function, as well as some of the most recently developed by academics and consultants. When appropriate a reference source is provided for further reading. These tools and techniques provide a basis for comparison with the actual tools and techniques found to be in use by strategy managers in the research survey. These findings are reported in chapter 3.

1. Activity-Based Costing

Providing a company with 'management information' rather than traditional 'accounting information', an activity-based cost management system enables managers to slice into their business in many different ways – by product or group of similar products, by individual customer or client group, and by distribution channel. Offering a close-up view of the particular slice under consideration, ABC analysis also illuminates the exact activities associated with each part of the business, and how those activities are linked to the generation of revenues and consumption of resources. Managers are thus given a framework for understanding precisely where to take the actions necessary to drive profits. Whilst assigning material cost to products in the same manner as conventional accounting, ABC does not assume that direct labour and direct material automatically generate overhead. Instead, products are recognised as incurring indirect cost by requiring resource-consuming activities, and these costs are specifically assigned rather than being estimated as a function of direct cost. Additionally, ABC assigns below-the-line costs, such as those attributable to sales, marketing, R&D, and administration. The system also separates product- and customer-driven costs. *Pareto analysis* can subsequently be used to focus on key costs concurrently in each dimension, the aim being to eliminate serious loss-making customer and product combinations. Key manufacturing and business process costs are assigned to activity centres, and thereafter, to products.

Recognising that many costs are not directly proportional to volume, but rather, to the number of batches produced, the main differentiating feature of ABC is its sophisticated treatment of second-stage drivers. It understands that whilst some costs should be assigned to batches, others, such as direct engineering, are related to entire products. Unlike traditional costing, there is also an awareness of formal systems within which costs can be stimulated at a variety of hierarchical levels. Individual units may trigger some costs, but others occur at the level of the batch, and even at that of the market segment. By separating out these costs, ABC facilitates an effective process of management decision-making. Hierarchical costs can be segmented both by product and customer:

> Product-driven activities: unit level, batch level, product level
> Customer-driven activities: order level, customer level, market level, enterprise level

Though predominately applied in the manufacturing industry, ABC principles are becoming increasingly relevant to the business sector, a deregulated and more competitive environment increasing the strategic importance of cost analysis. Central to design of a successful system is the choice of cost drivers, which should occur on the basis of system use, company complexity, and available resources.

- ❖ Cooper, R., 'The Rise of Activity-Based Costing – Part One: What is an Activity-Based Costing System?', *Journal of Cost Management* (1988).
- ❖ Cooper, R., 'Implementing an activity-based costing system', *Journal of Cost Management* (1990).
- ❖ Cooper, R., & Kaplan, R. S., 'Profit Priorities From Activity-Based Costing', *Harvard Business Review* (1991).
- ❖ O'Guin, M. C., *The Complete Guide to Activity-Based Cost* (1991).
- ❖ Rotch, W., 'Activity-Based Cost in Service Industries' *Journal of Cost Management* (1990).
- ❖ Turney, P. B. B., 'Activity-Based Costing: a Tool for Manufacturing Excellence' *Target* (1989).

2.   *Balanced Scorecard*

A management control system, the balanced scorecard utilises financial performance measures but sees these as a blunt instrument for performance measurement on their own, and argues for the use of measures of intangibles like skills, knowledge and communications etc. The balanced scorecard measures internal, customer, innovation/learning as well as financial indicators.

- ❖ Kaplan, R. S. & Norton, D. P. *The Balanced Scorecard* (1996).

3.   Benchmarking
Benchmarking is widely employed as a methodology to learn about best practice techniques from one's competitors. There are usually around ten generic categories for designing benchmarking architecture:

1) customer service performance
2) product/service performance
3) core business process performance
4) support processes and services performance
5) employee performance
6) supplier performance
7) technology performance
8) new product/service development and innovation performance
9) cost performance
10) financial performance

The first condition for design of a benchmarking architecture is that it must enable management to achieve the organisation's strategic objectives. This necessitates creation of a common language for performance measurement, a language consistent with the corporate culture. Plans must then be developed for the collection, processing, and analysis of this data. However, careful planning must be augmented by other critical factors to guarantee a successful benchmarking process:

- top management support
- benchmarking training for the project team
- suitable management information systems
- appropriate information technology
- appropriate corporate culture internally
- adequate resources

Precise benchmarking processes vary from company to company according to internal culture and needs. Successful implementation usually demands simplicity. The system recommended by the Council on Benchmarking at the Strategic Planning Institute involves a five-step process.

- ❖ Anonymous, 'Leadership through quality: implementing competitive behaviour', *Xerox Corporation Booklet* (1987).
- ❖ Anonymous, 'Benchmarking: Focus on World Class Practices', *AT&T* (1992).
- ❖ Anonymous, 'Benchmarking: PIMS Letter on Business Strategy', *PIMS Europe Ltd* (1993).
- ❖ Bogan, C. E. & English, M. J., *Benchmarking for Best Practices: Winning through Innovative Adaptation* (1994).

❖ Garvin, D., 'Building a learning organisation', *Harvard Business Review* (1993).
❖ McNair, C. J. & Liebfried, K. H. J., *Benchmarking* (1992).
❖ Walleck, S. A., O'Halloran, D. & Leader, C. A., 'Benchmarking and World Class Performance', *The McKinsey Quarterly* (1991).

4.   *Best Practice Club Initiative*

Introduced by the Department of Trade and Industry, the Best Practice Club Initiative aims to improve the competitive performance of UK companies through a programme called 'Inside UK Enterprise'. Implementation of best practice is encouraged through a series of one-day visits to these businesses. Over 170 'host' companies from a range of industry sectors, both manufacturing and service-oriented, openly share their experiences, and engage in a business-to-business exchange of information. Managers have the opportunity to visit other firms, to observe new techniques and innovations "hands-on" and hence, to judge compatibility with their own business.

5.   *Brainstorming*

This simple technique involves creative group discussion. For best results, criticism is withheld, and freewheeling is welcomed. The greater the number of ideas generated, the greater the likelihood of identifying an idea worth pursuing, and hence, quantity is encouraged. Combination and improvement of ideas is another key theme.

6.   *Break-Even Analysis*

This analysis demonstrates the relationship between fixed costs, variable costs, and revenue. For each product, there is a variable cost, and when deducted from the sales value, this generates a contribution. The volume level of sales at which the sum of unit product contribution equals the fixed and variable costs constitutes the break-even point. Construction of the appropriate chart (Figure 2.1) enables management to identify which expenses are controllable, which cost items contribute most to total expenditure, and how much these might possibly be reduced. Care must be taken in the allocation of fixed costs. Some that were previously considered fixed could be made variable by adopting techniques such as re-engineering and activity-based costing.

Break-even analysis has, however, been criticised by Dyson on the following grounds:

• Cost can't easily be divided into fixed and variable categories
• Variable costs don't always vary in direct proportion to activity – the cost of direct materials may change as a result of shortages of supply, or owing to bulk buying, while direct labour costs may be fixed in the

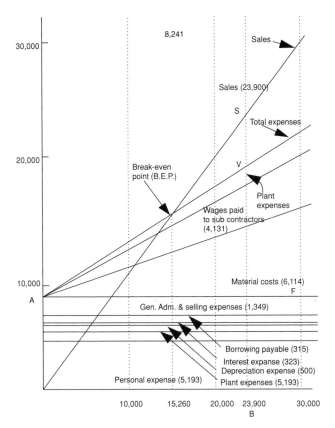

Figure 2.1   The Break-Even Point Chart
Source: Nagashima, S., *100 Management Charts* (1987), Tokyo: Asian Productivity Organisation.

short-term, since the company may need to give a minimum period of
notice to employees before they can be dismissed
- Fixed costs will change to some extent as activity increases or decreases
- It is difficult to determine the period of time over which costs remain
  fixed – in the long-term, all costs become variable, since the company
  can avoid them altogether (by going into liquidation, for example)
- A specific decision affecting one product may affect others too, especially if they are complementary (when a garage sells both oil and petrol,
  for example)
- Fixed costs can't be ignored entirely, since survival of a company
  demands that it recover all its costs
- The break-even and profit/volume charts are too simplistic – they don't pay
  attention to individual products, and they assume that any change in one
  product will have an identically proportionate effect on the others

- Non-cost factors, such as the security of suppliers, and availability of finance, can't be ignored in arriving at a specific decision

❖ Dyson, J. R., 'Accounting for Non-Accounting Students', *Financial Times* (1997).

❖ Nagashima, S., *100 Management Charts* (1992), Tokyo: Asian Productivity Organisation.

7.   Business Process Re-Engineering

BPR is normally seen as the radical reshaping of existing business processes linked with the application of IT technology to map and remodel internal processes and systems so that they are less complex and easier to operate. BPR is essentially an attack on silo or functional management structures within organisations and is focused on waste removal and the focus on value adding activities.

❖ Hammer, M. & Champy, J., *Re-engineering the Corporation* (1993).

8.   Business Stream Analysis

Rather than a standardised technique, this is a process of strategic planning. A large British aerospace company, for example, had a timetable, a nine-month cycle during which it examined the basics – Which sectors are we operating in? Who are the competitors? What choices do we have? Where will business growth come from? What sectors are we missing? What new competitors are coming in?

9.   Capital Asset Pricing Model

Providing a framework to analyse the trade-off between risk and return, this model calculates the rate of return that investors will require in order to compensate for the risk involved with investing in a particular firm (as opposed to investing in risk-free government bonds). This measure is known as a firm's 'cost of capital'. Firms tend to utilise the model themselves when considering prospective stocks for investment. A finance department may also wish to determine the return required by shareholders in their own firm, ensuring that they only pursue projects meeting this expectation.

❖ Clinton, D. & Chen, S., 'Do new performance measures measure up?', *Management Accounting* (1998).

10.   Cause-and-Effect Analysis

The cause-and-effect, or fishbone diagram, attempts to identify the various factors of cause and effect in the *cost structure* of a business (Figure 2.2).

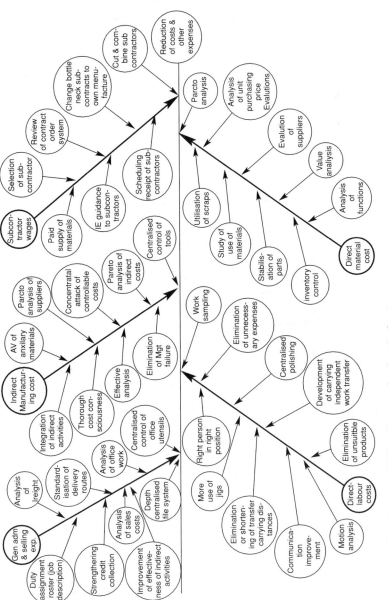

Figure 2.2 The Causes and Effect Diagram for Cost Reduction
Source: Nagashima, S., *100 Management Charts* (1992), Tokyo: Asian Productivity Organisation.

Careful analysis of all the factors included in such a diagram enables the firm to plan a feasible cost reduction programme, which can thereafter be integrated into its overall cost structure to re-establish competitive advantage. Identification of the inter-relationship between factors provides a mechanism to establish contingency plans and reduce political pressures within an organisation.

❖ Nagashima, S., *100 Management Charts* (1992), Tokyo: Asian Productivity Organisation.

11.   Change Management
A rather generic term, change management encompasses a number of tools and techniques. Most are models that demand adherence to a particular series of steps. For example, the academic, Charles Baden-Fuller, outlines a change model in his book, *Rejuvenating the Mature Business*, a model with four distinct stages – simplifying, galvanising, leveraging, and building. Another concept is 'Transition From-To Analysis', used to monitor and understand the changing direction of actions. Though useful, it perhaps concentrates too heavily on logical, rather than emotional, issues of change. The DVF>R formula is another diagnostic tool, where R is resistance, D is dissatisfaction with the present, V is the vision, and F is the first step. However, there is a feeling that these sorts of processes are best developed internally.

12.   Cognitive Mapping
Aiming to identify important elements in causation, cognitive mapping involves a diagram in which the causation between concepts is linked by arrows (Figure 2.3). This provides an effective technique for problem analysis and the brainstorming of possible scenarios.

13.   Competency Models
These skill matrices address questions of skill-set requirement across different functional areas of the business – competence in financial management, international management, etc. They are sometimes employed as a

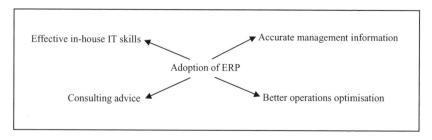

Figure 2.3   Cognitive Mapping Diagram

performance measure on a bi-annual, perhaps even on a monthly basis. There are also measures such as 'added value' per employee.

14. *Competitive Position-Market Attractiveness Matrix*

In conjunction with McKinsey, GE developed a nine cell portfolio model to measure the relative attractiveness of a company's multiple business for investment purposes based on market attractiveness (high/medium/low) and competitive position (strong/medium/weak). Alternate investment strategies are advised for the portion of business contained within each cell of the matrix.

Positioning in the two composite dimensions is conditioned by a quantitative scoring system. *Market attractiveness* is assessed using data on the market/industry characteristics of a business. Important variables are size (on a segment-by-segment basis), historic growth rate, projected growth rate, number of competitors, competitor concentration, market profitability, barriers to entry, barriers to exit, supplier power, buyer power, degree of product differentiation, and market fit. According to its relative position, a value between 1 (very unattractive) and 5 (highly attractive) is assigned to the business. If the variables are weighted, this weight is also applied, and the scores summed to arrive at an overall total. This figure is then divided by the maximum possible score to generate a *market attractiveness* co-ordinate. A calculation of *competitive position* is operationalised by scoring the company on a series of appropriate dimensions selected by the management on the basis of their detailed knowledge of the business, and weighted according to their assessment of the relative importance of each dimension. Measures include absolute market share, relative share, trend in market share, relative profitability, relative product quality, relative price, customer concentration, rate of product innovation, and relative capital intensity. Each of these factors can be scored from 1 (very weak competitive position) to 5 (very strong competitive position). The co-ordinate for *competitive position* is determined by following the same procedure as for *market attractiveness*. Business units can then be plotted on the matrix, relative size indicated by the area of each circle. This means of analysis is not without its flaws, however. Not only does it require accurate identification of a multiplicity of variables in positioning the business correctly, but the weighting and numerical scoring system can also deceive with its pseudo-scientific approach. Data is often not available to provide an accurate assessment of position, and as a consequence, there is a tendency to drift towards the moderate score. Furthermore, it is difficult to ensure consistency of analysis across business units, and when markets change, very misleading positioning can occur in terms of *market attractiveness*.

❖ Channon, D. F., *Australian Pacific Bank Case* (1993) London: Imperial College.

❖ Hax, A. C., & Majlus, N. S., *Strategic Management: An Integrative Perspective* (1984).
❖ Hofer, C. W., & Schendel, D., *Strategy Formulation: Analytical Concepts* (1978).

15.   Competitor Analysis
More of a systematic process than a specific technique, the main objective of this activity is to assess the likely response of competitors to a specific course of action. This is sometimes very formal, as with firms like Rolls Royce, who operate complex cost models of their competitors to determine strategy for winning particular business. However, in other cases, it may be quite informal, simply a question of company visits and networking at trade shows. It can be carried out internally, or via an independent market researcher.

16.   Consumer Profiling
This approach is normally associated with understanding the psychology of customers so as to understand their attitudes and motives in relation to the strategy for particular products and services. The approach often focuses on the four major profiles of consumers – complexity, variety-seeking, dissonance – reducing and habitual behaviour.

❖ Assael, H., Consumer Behaviour and Marketing Action (1987).

17.   Core Competence Thinking
Core competencies have been defined as 'a set of differentiated skills, complementary assets, and routines that provide the basis for a firm's competitive capacities and sustainable advantage in a particular business'. Quinn and Hilmer's understanding is that, rather than products or functions, they constitute amalgamations of skill and knowledge. Competencies thus involve activities such as product design, technology creation, customer service, and logistics, tending to be grounded in knowledge rather than ownership of assets or intellectual property. In this light, knowledge-based activities are seen to account for most of the value in a supply chain. Furthermore, the core competence is envisaged as a unique source of leverage in the value chain, and hence, must exist in an area where the firm can dominate. Unlike the traditional approach to strategy, emphasising products and markets, and focusing competitive analysis on product portfolios, core competency thinking analyses the firm as a bundle of resources that can be configured to provide firm-specific advantages. A resource-based model addresses issues beyond the remit of mainstream strategic analysis, issues of diversification and changing competitive environment. It recognises that globalisation, deregulation, technological change, and questions of quality, are eroding the traditional sources of competitive advantage.

According to Hamel and Prahalad, core competencies have three identifying elements:

1) They provide potential access to a wide variety of markets
2) They make a significant contribution to the customer's perceived benefits of the end product
3) They are difficult for competitors to imitate

Development of competencies is clearly a challenge. Acquisition, alliance, and licensing can all prove critical. The time necessitated for development demands a long-term and committed approach to a firm's strategic direction. A corporate-wide architecture must be the aim of senior management, establishing objectives for competence building. 'Ownership' within the firm tends to be the crucial factor in maintaining core competencies and ensuring their longevity. Firms need to review their competency portfolio on an ongoing basis, retaining only those which continue to provide advantage.

❖ Hamel, G. & Prahalad, C. K., *Competing for the Future* (1994).
❖ Klavans, R., 'The Measurement of a Competitor's Core Competence', in Hamel, G. & Heene, A., (eds), *Competence-Based Competition* (1994).
❖ Leonard-Barton, D., 'Core Capabilities and Core Rigidities: A Paradox in Managing New Product Development', *Strategic Management Journal* (1992).
❖ Mahoney, J. T. & Pandian, J. R., 'The resource-based view within the conversation of strategic management', *Strategic Management Journal* (1992).
❖ Prahalad, C. K. & Hamel, G., 'The Core Competence of the Corporation', *Harvard Business Review* (1990).
❖ Quinn, J. B. and Hilmer, F., 'Strategic Outsourcing', *Sloan Management Review* (1994).
❖ Rumelt, R. P., *Strategy, Structure and Economic Performance* (1974).
❖ Stalk, G., Evans, P. & Shulman, L., 'Competing on Capabilities: the new rules of corporate strategy', *HBR* (1992).

18.   Cost-Benefit/Trade-Off Analysis
The primary aim of such analysis is to weigh benefit against risk:

• low benefit, high risk – forget it
• low benefit, low risk – forget it
• high benefit, low risk – absolutely do it
• high benefit, high risk – be careful

Most firms go through this process intuitively. The main issues are formality and frequency of use, together with the relevance of the information input. A methodology need not always address risk, but may contrast resource requirements against cost instead.

19.   Customer Profitability Matrix

Companies can define themselves by the type of customer they seek to service. For this purpose, the customer profitability matrix provides four categories. It requires detailed cost analysis and allocation of indirect costs for all customer segments. This encompasses pre-sale costs (location, need for customisation, etc), production costs, distribution costs, and after-sale service costs. The actual prices charged to different customer segments are subsequently assessed, together with the volume consumed over time and its value. The matrix (Figure 2.4) has net price on the vertical axis, and cost on the horizontal, and is divided into four quadrants:

1) carriage trade – high cost, high price
2) bargain basement – low cost, low price
3) passive – low cost, high price
4) aggressive – high cost, low price

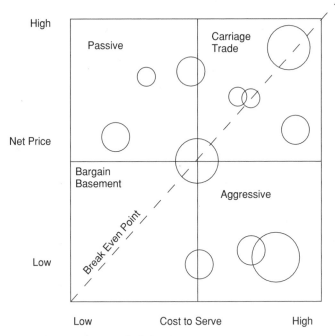

Figure 2.4   The Customer Profitability Matrix
Source: Reprinted by permission of *Harvard Business Review* from 'Manage Customers for Profits (Not Just Sales)' by Shapiro, Ragan, Moriarty, and Ross (Volume 65 Issue 1; Sept/Oct 1987), p. 103, 104.

The size of each circle represents the value of that customer segment. Very large customers may be identified individually. The cross-lines represent average price and cost, while the diagonal line shows the break-even point at which price equals cost. Interrogation of the matrix enables development of strategies that maximise profitability.

❖ Shapiro, B. P. et al., 'Manage Customers for Profits (Not Just Sales)' *Harvard Business Review* (1987).

20. Decision Gates
This technique provides a framework for organising and structuring the process of new product development. The aim is to reach a given target in order to pass through a stage/decision gate. Often implemented as a formalised procedure, it tends to demand a cross-functional team. By setting target dates every two to three months, the progress of a project can be monitored and reviewed. The process assists with time, cost, and resource allocation, and also ensures appropriate staff involvement. Rather than concentrating on technical aspects, decision gates encourage firms to be market driven. There are four sequential stages:

1) Project-idea stage, and assessment of technical issues. Is it feasible? Are the raw materials available? Does the firm have the necessary equipment?
2) Planning, research & development. Focus groups gather information. Samples are developed, and assessment is undertaken to determine whether products can be produced within the customer price range.
3) Trial stage. Customer review questionnaires gather feedback on the product, and information is fed back to enable improvement. Technical standards approval must also be obtained.
4) Production and marketing of the product.

21. Directional Policy Matrix
This three-by-three matrix was developed by Royal Dutch Shell Group as a portfolio-planning tool. It integrates business sector prospects with a company's competitive capabilities (Figure 2.5). Positioning is determined in a similar manner to the competitive position-market attractiveness matrix. Though developed by Shell with specific reference to the petrochemical industry, the model is generally applicable in relation to all diversified enterprises. Shell uses four criteria to assess business sector prospects:

1) Market growth rate
2) Market quality
3) Industry feedstock situation
4) Environmental aspects

Company's Competitive Capabilities	Business Sector Prospects: Unattractive	Average	Attractive
Weak	Disinvest	Phased Withdrawal	Double or Quit
Average	Phased Withdrawal	Custodial	Avis or Try Harder
Strong	Cash Generation	Growth	Leader

Figure 2.5 The Shell Directional Policy Matrix
Source: Reprinted from *Long Range Planning,* Robinson, S. J. Q., Hichens, R. E., and Wade, D. P., 'Planning a Chemical Company's Profits: Royal Dutch Shell Group of Companies – the Directional Policy Matrix, a Tool for Strategic Planning' © 1978, with permission from Elsevier.

The company's competitive capabilities are assessed by three further criteria:

1) Market position
2) Production capability (process economies, hardware, feedstock)
3) Product research and development

Shell has also developed a second-order DPM, enabling managers to combine two parameters for investment decisions, to relate product strategy criteria to the company's priorities in other areas, most notably as regards location and feedstock security. It identifies a range of strategic positions (Figure 2.6):

- Robinson, S. J. Q., Hichens, R. E. & Wade, D. P., 'Planning a Chemical Company's Profits: Royal Dutch Shell Group of Companies – the Directional Policy Matrix, a Tool for Strategic Planning', *Long Range Planning* (1978).
- Royal Dutch Shell Company, *The Directional Policy Matrix: a New Guide to Corporate Planning* (1975).

22. Discounted Cash Flow Analysis

This method of investment appraisal recognises the 'time value' of money (91p today will be worth £1 in a year's time if the rate of interest is 10%). Clearly, over the duration of a five-year project, the cost of capital, and

Criteria	• Matrix position
	• Profit record
	• Other product-related criteria
	• Judgement
Category I	Hardcore of good quality business. Consistently generating good profits. (engineering thermoplastics)
Category II	Strong company position. Reasonable/good sector prospects. Variable profit record. (chlorinated solvents)
Category III	Promising product sector. (new chemical business)
Category IV	Reasonable/modest sector prospects. Company role is minor. Variable profit record. (chemical solvents)
Category V	Unfavourable prospects. Company has significant stake. (detergent alkalyte)

Figure 2.6   Shell Classification for Investment Decisions
Source: Reprinted from *Long Range Planning*, Robinson, S. J. Q., Hichens, R. E., and Wade, D. P., 'Planning a Chemical Company's Profits: Royal Dutch Shell Group of Companies – the Directional Policy Matrix, a Tool for Strategic Planning' © 1978, with permission from Elsevier.

when the revenue is earned, are crucial variables in appraising that investment. The two main DCF techniques are Net Present Value (NPV) and Internal Rate of Return (IRR). NPV ascertains the total change in wealth that would result from undertaking a particular project. IRR is the discount rate that would make NPV equal zero. If IRR is higher than the firm's cost of capital, then a project is regarded as being worthwhile.

23/24/25.   *E-Business Applications*

Since the emergence of the Internet there have been a wide number of software applications developed to enable businesses to manage their strategic and operational direction more effectively, especially in relation to the management of internal and external processes and relationships. Perhaps the major factor here has been the ability to use and manipulate information faster, further and with greater speed than ever before. This has provided opportunities for seller-side software to find and manage customers more effectively (like efficient customer response (ECR) and customer relationship management (CRM) technologies) as well as to provide channels to market (through portals, exchanges and hubs) that allow for easier access to customers.

Relatedly there has been a growth in internal software applications to improve information and system and process optimisation (such as Peoplesoft, Oracle, SAP and other enterprise planning systems). On the buyer-side there has also been a growth in supplier relationship management (SRM) and leverage tools and techniques, such as reverse auctions, hubs and exchanges and supply chain management and optimisation software.

❖ Evans, P. & Wurster, T. S., Blown to Bits (2000).
❖ Liebowitz, S., Rethinking the Network Economy (2002).
❖ Narasimhan, R., Evaluating E-Procurement Solutions (2003).

26.   *Economic Profit*
This measure attempts to determine the profitability of brands and customers after allowing for costs. Described as the antidote to marginal costing, firms like Cadburys and Trebor Bassett believe the technique offers a comprehensive insight into profit and loss, checking whether products are actually profitable. Economic profit also enables firms to identify where future investment should be targeted, highlighting the opportunity provided for Cadburys by the differentiated brand of Turkish Delight. Responding positively to advertising, it has achieved comparatively high economic profit. Basically, economic profit simply provides another means of overhead accounting. By enabling firms to question the drivers of economic profit and identify where value is located, it facilitates achievement of value for money from the resources committed to their brands and customers. Its impact is similar to that of EVA.

27.   *Economic Value Added (EVA)*
This is a method of measuring financial performance and aligning management goals more closely with those of their shareholders. It involves a charge for the 'cost of capital' being subtracted from net operating profit, and can be performed either at the level of the firm or for investment in particular assets. The added dimension provided by 'cost of capital' should ensure that projects likely to diminish 'shareholder value' are not pursued. 'Old economy' businesses with large tangible assets are best suited to EVA, its calculations proving less practical and relevant for the software and media companies of the 'new economy'. Furthermore, it needs to be complemented by other measures to prove effective. Stern Stewart, the pioneering consultants, regard EVA as a revolutionary valuation tool, but in truth, its input is greater from a behavioural viewpoint.

28.   *Five 'S' Strategy*
Derived from the first letters of five Japanese terms, '5S' encompasses organisation (Seiri), neatness (Seiton), cleaning (Seiso), standardisation (Seiketu), and discipline (Shitsuke). Dramatic improvements in quality and productivity have been seen to result from adoption of these simple principles:

Seiri (Organisation)
Organisation of the workplace involves continuous efforts to implement systems that eliminate the unnecessary. The Pareto diagram, and a Japanese variant, the KJ method, are both heavily utilised.

Seiton (Neatness)
Neatness aims to eliminate the time losses involved in searching. Studies are undertaken on a regular basis to improve space utilisation on the basis of the '5Ws and 1H' (what, when, where, why, who, and how), questions that are posed with regard to every item.

Seiso (Cleaning)
Cleaning seeks to achieve zero dirt, and to eliminate minor defects and faults at key inspection points. This is an historic and traditional concept for the Japanese, operating in the spirit that 'to clean is to inspect'.

Seiketu (Standardisation)
Standardisation means continuous and repeated maintenance of organisation, neatness and cleanliness. The emphasis is on visual management. Ironically, this method of inspection is both simple and cheap in comparison to the more sophisticated, computer-based systems often attempted by Western corporations.

Shitsuke (Discipline)
Discipline means instilling in everyone how things ought to be done, thus eliminating bad habits and reinforcing those deemed to be good.

❖ Channon, D. F., *Canon B Case* (1993).
❖ Takashi, O., The 5Ss (1991).

29. Gap Analysis
During the course of business, gaps develop between the corporate objectives of a firm and its expected business outcomes. Gap analysis involves the development of measures to reduce or eliminate these gaps. It might demand a change of objectives, or even alteration of strategy across the business. A revision of corporate objectives is certainly the first possibility – if expected outcomes exceed aspiration, the objectives could be revised upwards, but if aspirations substantially exceed possible performance, it might be necessary for a downwards revision. If a significant gap still remains after such adjustment, new strategies need to be developed. To forecast the sales increases likely to result from introduction of these alternative growth strategies, managers can estimate the following measures of market structure:

• Industry market potential (IMP)
• Relevant industry sales (RIS)
• Real market share (RMS)

IMP represents the maximum possible unit sales for a particular product, RIS encompasses the firm's current sales and competitive gap, and RMS is current sales divided by the RIS (Figure 2.7).

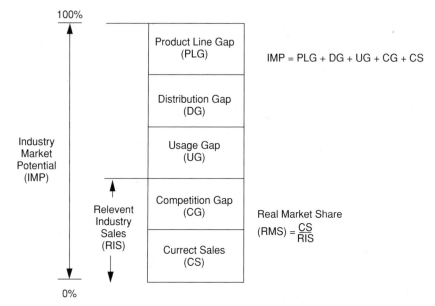

Figure 2.7   Gap Analysis
Source: Rowe, A., Mason, R., Dickel, K. and Snyder, N., *Strategic Management: A Methodological Approach* (1989). Reading, MA: Addison-Wesley, p. 115.

If the expected gap can't be closed by decreasing market potential or gaining additional market share, it is possibly time to assess the firm's business portfolio. This is open to potential modification, either by diversification into higher-growth activities, or by the divesting of low-growth businesses.

❖ Ansoff, I., *Corporate Strategy* (1987).
❖ Drucker, P., *The New Realities* (1989).
❖ Rowe, A. J., Mason, R. O., Dickel, K. E., Mann R. B. & Mockler, R. J., *Strategic Management* (1994).
❖ Weber, J. A., 'Market Structure Profile and Strategic Growth Opportunities', *California Management Review* (1977).

30.   *Growth Share Matrix*

This technique is also referred to as the Product Portfolio Matrix and assesses the relative value of particular products or services against two variables – the market growth rate growth of the product or service set against its relative market share. This provides an easy way of understanding the strategic position of products and/or services under four strategic outcomes – stars, question marks, cash cows and dogs.

This portfolio model (Figure 2.8), developed by BCG during the 1960s, is widely used within diversified companies to influence investment and cash management policy.

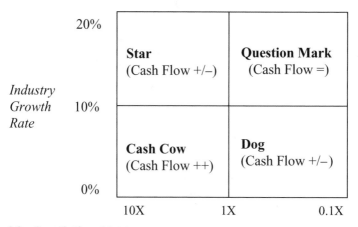

Figure 2.8   Growth Share Matrix
Source: Adapted from: Hax, A. C., and Majlus, N. S., *Strategic Management: An Integrative Perspective* (1984), New Jersey: Englewood Cliffs.

The horizontal axis is drawn on a logarithmic scale, and identifies the relative market share of each of the businesses within a company's portfolio. Relative market share is defined in relation to that of the company's largest single competitor. By definition, only one company within a defined market can have a relative share greater than one. The vertical axis depicts industry growth rate in real terms, the impact of inflation having been discounted. Businesses are mapped on the matrix, their size reflected in circle area. Relative position of each business within the four quadrants indicates its expected generation of cash-flow, suggesting an appropriate investment strategy. The primary advantage of the growth share matrix is that it permits a company to map its businesses, enabling rapid management visualisation of its portfolio positioning. Respective sequences for development (Figure 2.9) and disaster (Figure 2.10) are outlined here:

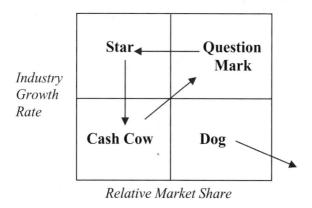

Figure 2.9   The GSM Sequence for Success
Source: Hax, Arnoldo C., Majluf, Nicholas S., *Strategic Management: An Integrative Perspective*, 1st Edition © 1984. Reprinted by permission of Pearson Education Inc., Upper Saddle River, NJ.

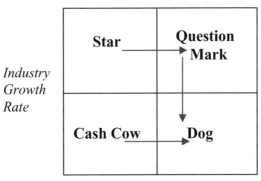

Relative Market Share

Figure 2.10   The GSM Sequence for Disaster
Source: Hax, Arnoldo C., Majluf, Nicholas S., *Strategic Management: An Integrative Perspective*,
1st Edition © 1984. Reprinted by permission of Pearson Education Inc., Upper Saddle River, NJ.

The matrix, it has been argued, represents no more than a static snapshot of the business portfolio. However, development of the share momentum graph (Figure 2.11) has subsequently addressed such criticism:

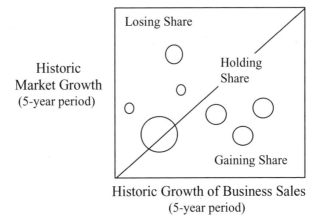

Historic Growth of Business Sales
(5-year period)

Figure 2.11   Share Momentum Graph
Source: Hax, Arnoldo C., Majluf, Nicholas S., *Strategic Management: An Integrative Perspective*,
1st Edition © 1984. Reprinted by permission of Pearson Education Inc., Upper Saddle River, NJ.

By plotting the position of each business unit against the dimensions of total market growth and growth in business sales, it is easy to observe where the company has been gaining or losing share over a relevant time period. This can perform a useful corrective function. In general terms, growth share analysis can also prove effective in evaluating competitive

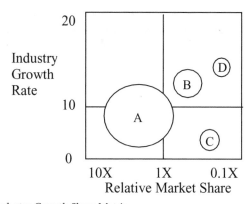

Figure 2.12   Industry Growth Share Matrix
Source: Hax, Arnoldo C., Majluf, Nicholas S., *Strategic Management: An Integrative Perspective*,
1st Edition © 1984. Reprinted by permission of Pearson Education Inc., Upper Saddle River, NJ.

dynamics. Illustrating the relative market position of major competitors (Figure 2.12), the matrix can indicate how different companies classify their business.

With the largest market share, Competitor A is clearly operating as a cash cow, but by growing at less than the market rate, it is also trading this market share for cash, allowing competitors B and D to see their businesses as question marks, and therefore, investment opportunities. Competitor C alone is forced to recognise its business as a dog. Examining the same industry over time (Figure 2.13), it is clear that competitors B and D have been growing faster than A, faster than the market as a whole. Additional to analysis at industry-level, further refinement allows assessment of the

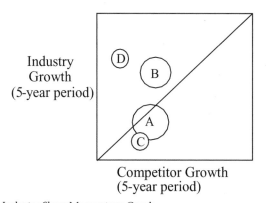

Competitor Growth
(5-year period)

Figure 2.13   Industry Share Momentum Graph
Source: Hax, Arnoldo C., Majluf, Nicholas S., *Strategic Management: An Integrative Perspective*,
1st Edition © 1984. Reprinted by permission of Pearson Education Inc., Upper Saddle River, NJ.

business by product and technology. The growth share matrix has thus provided a useful management tool for both diagnosing the position of the multi-business and multi-product firm, and for understanding industrial and competitive dynamics. It has, however, been subject to criticism for the following reasons:

- GSM positioning implies that relative market share can be used as a surrogate for cost.
- Detailed analysis is rarely undertaken due to cost and lack of appropriate data.
- The model assumes that only the two variables of relative market share and industry growth rate are necessary to establish the strategic position of a business.
- In calculating relative market share, it is assumed that the 'market' has been accurately defined, which is not always the case, particularly when market boundaries are in a state of flux as a result of geographic, product, or customer segment changes.

❖ Bogue, M. C., & E. S., Buffa, *Corporate Strategic Analysis* (1986).
❖ Hax, A. C. & N. S., Majluf, *Strategic Management: an Integrative Perspective* (1984).
❖ Henderson, B. D., 'The Experience Curve Reviewed: The Growth Share Matrix of the Product Portfolio', *Perspectives* (1973).
❖ Lewis, W. W., *Planning by Exception* (1977).
❖ Henderson, B. D., *The Logic of Business Strategy* (1984).

31.   Key Performance Indicators (KPIs)
KPIs provide a commonly accepted means of assessing firm performance. Chosen indicators vary by firm. They may be internally generated, or alternatively, bought-in from an external source in benchmarking against other companies within the marketplace. Regularity of assessment will depend upon the particular measure.

32.   Knowledge Management
In order to manage a business effectively, it is often necessary to have a system by which to store and organise internal knowledge in order that it be easily accessed and utilised. Computer-based software usually provides the means to this end.

33.   Management Information System (MIS)
MIS provides for the bespoke or customised presentation, reporting, and manipulation of data appropriate to the running of an organisation, enabling a firm's management to turn data into useful management information for planning and control activities. The software will usually collate figures and generate reports on a regular basis, and there is also the

facility to pull out information on a more informal basis. These unique (firm specific) tools are distinct from generic E-Business internal software applications and/or ERP or MRP systems, which are dealt with separately.

34. Manpower Planning

This process, also referred to as 'resource profiling', facilitates allocation of people, perhaps for a programme at bid stage. It might operate as an off-the-shelf software package (AMS Real Time), or might simply be a communicative activity, an element of the budgeting process. At a more formal level, resource codes are sometimes used to ascertain how many people are required for a task, and activities such as 'what if?' analysis undertaken. Manpower planning is often a critical task in project-related companies, assigned to a dedicated co-ordinator. It tends to work better in an operational arena rather than indirect areas of spend.

35. Market Research

This is such an obvious indicator of competence in business that it often goes unremarked. It is clearly essential for companies to have a structured process, by which they undertake market analysis as part of their business strategy thinking, in order to understand what actual and potential customers want and need. There are structured survey based approaches to undertaking market research that provide insights into the socio-psychological attitudes of customers to understand their rank order preferences for particular products and services and the value propositions that link best with particular segments of marginal utility.

❖ Malhorta, N. K., *Marketing Research: An Applied Orientation* (1993).

36. Market Value Added (MVA)

This measure, an extension of the EVA concept, is the difference between a firm's current value, inclusive of equity and debt, and the cumulative money invested in and retained by the company. It underscores wealth creation since the firm's foundation.

37. Outsourcing Analysis Procedures

Increasingly the traditional highly vertically integrated business model developed in the last century has been challenged by the growth of outsourcing. Two phenomena are particularly relevant here. First, the focus on core and non-core activities and, second, the emergence of developing countries as competitors for many standard product and service supply offerings at much lower costs than western companies. In this environment it has become essential for well-managed companies to have a strategic make-buy methodology to allow them to assess the risks and opportunities of outsourcing.

❖ Lonsdale, C. & Cox, A., Outsourcing (1998).

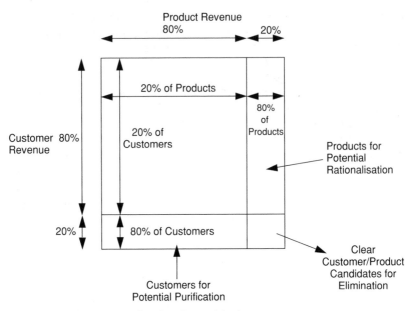

Figure 2.14   The Customer/Product Pareto Matrix
Source: Channon, D. F., *Bank Strategic Management and Marketing* © 1986. John Wiley & Sons Limited. Reproduced with permission.

38. *Pareto Analysis*

Developed by economist, Vilfredo Pareto, in the nineteenth century, this provides a means to evaluate the desirability of alternate economic and social states, and of change from one to another. It recognises that in order for a maximum welfare position to be reached then the benefits of some should not increase to the detriment of others. In these terms, Pareto efficiency can only be achieved when it is no longer possible to make anyone better off without an adverse impact on someone else. From a practical perspective, this is a very strict criterion, and hence, has limited use. Even if it were possible for the beneficiary of a transaction to fully compensate those who were losing out, such compensation would never be paid. Analysis of the customer-product relationship can be organised through a Pareto matrix (Figure 2.14). From this observation, it follows that 20% of products will account for 80% of sales.

The Pareto effect can also be applied along other dimensions – sales force, critical machinery, etc. By combination of significant variables (Figure 2.15), it is possible to produce a useful guide to strategy. Unfortunately, a strong tendency in business is to add new products and customers without eliminating the obsolete and unprofitable. It is thus important that Pareto analysis along a firm's major strategic dimensions be undertaken periodically to guard against inefficiencies.

❖ Baumol, W. J., *Economic Theory and Operational Analysis* (1977).

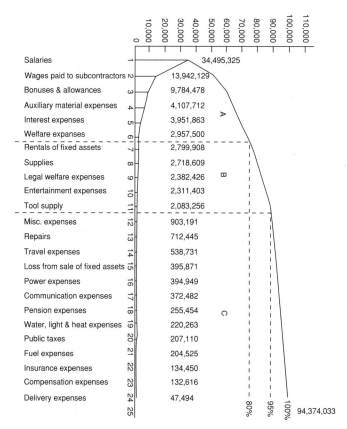

Figure 2.15   Pareto Analysis of Production Cost and Manufacturing Expenditure
Source: Nagashima, S., *100 Management Charts* (1987), Tokyo: Asian Productivity Organisation.

❖ Channon, D. F., *Bank Strategic Management and Marketing* (1986).
❖ Nagashima, S., *100 Management Charts* (1992).

39.   Payback Analysis
Easy to understand and communicate, payback analysis is a method of investment appraisal that calculates the time taken to repay the original capital outlay. Slightly nonsensical, it ignores returns after this point in time, and fails to account for the 'time value' of money. It can, nevertheless, prove useful in fast-moving industries (computers), as it is often vital to recoup investment in a short space of time.

40.   PEST Analysis
Used to define and measure the effect of variables outside the control of an organisation, PEST is an acronym of the four categories of change – political, economic, social, and technological. A broad-brush instrument, it constitutes an environmental checklist of the external elements that augment

or constrain industry profitability, attempting to reduce strategic risk by *scenario planning*. Not a precise technique in quantification, PEST is applied specifically to individual products and markets. Whilst following the same general outline, each analysis will specify different item variables, subsequently allocated different weightings. Having determined the probability ranking of each item variable, the next step is to evaluate the quantitative and qualitative effect of these occurrences on the achievement of corporate objectives. Multiplying probability by effect, a crude ranking index of corporate vulnerability/opportunity can then be established. This index can be further refined by removal of limited-impact items, enabling more detailed analysis of the significant variables.

- ❖ Fahey, L. & King, W., 'Environmental Scanning for Corporate Planning', *Business Horizons* (1977).
- ❖ Hofer, C. W. & Schendel, D., *Strategy Formulation: Analytical Concepts* (1978).
- ❖ Rowe, A. J., Mason, R. O., Dickel, K. E., Mann, R. B. & Mockler, R. J., *Strategic Management* (1994).
- ❖ Utterback, J., 'Environmental Analysis and Forecasting in Strategic Management', in Hofer, C., and Schendel, D., (eds), *A New View of Business Policy and Planning* (1979).
- ❖ William, R. E., *Putting it All Together: A Guide to Strategic Thinking* (1976).

41.   PIMS

This acronym stands for the Profit Impact of Market Strategy. The PIMS programme operates through a business-unit, research database that captures the real-life experiences of over 3,000 businesses. Each business is a division, product line, or profit centre within its parent company, selling a distinct set of products or services to an identifiable group of customers, and competing with a well-defined set of competitors. Meaningful analysis must be possible in terms of revenue, operating costs, investment, and strategic plans. PIMS research has seemed to indicate that profit performance varies enormously both across and within businesses. However, care must be cautioned in interpreting the database, as it is extremely misleading to use general findings without evaluating the appropriateness of each strategic move. PIMS provides an insight, provides guidelines for business judgement, but these are far from being hard dogma. It extends across several areas of analysis:

Marketplace Standing
There are several measures of marketplace standing – market share, market share rank, and relative market share. However, whichever measure is adopted, there is a strong positive correlation between marketplace strength and profitability. PIMS has highlighted the danger of low market share in an environment that is either marketing- or R&D-intensive, both

of which exhibit fixed cost characteristics. When companies are trapped in the low-profit cell, the strategic options are to reduce the role of marketing and R&D, to strengthen share, either organically or by merger/alliance, or to re-segment and dominate a niche in the market. When none of these appear feasible, the small-share competitor is inevitably undermined by his larger competitor's 'virtuous circle'

Differentiation from Competitors

PIMS assesses the value-for-money position of a business by judging its relative competitive standing in terms of quality and price. Quality is defined from the perspective of the external marketplace. Customers evaluate the total benefit bundle of products and services, providing a ranking relative to leading competitors. A 'relative perceived quality' measure is then computed by subtracting the percentage of product and service attributes judged as superior to competitors from that judged as inferior. The relationship between quality/market share and return is one of the key determinants of performance in the database.

Capital and Production Structure

It is with regards to investment intensity that PIMS perhaps exhibits its most powerful findings. This is measured in two ways – the conventional ratio of investment to sales revenue, and a ratio of investment to actual value add generated by the business (net sales revenue, less all input from external suppliers). As the investment intensity of a business increases, its ROI falls dramatically. This is the most powerful negative relationship in the database – ROI averages only 8% for investment intensive businesses compared to 38% for low investment intensity businesses. The behavioural element of the investment intensity effect is vividly illustrated by analysis of the return on sales (ROS) achieved at different levels of investment. If a business is to hold ROI as investment intensity increases, ROS should increase smoothly. In practice, however, ROS is at best flat, and actually begins to tail off at higher levels of intensity. It is perhaps the case that management focuses too heavily on the profit margin on sales, ignoring the more important criterion of return on investment. A more substantive explanation, however, relates to the destructive nature of competition (price war) that typically accompanies high levels of investment intensity. The fact that fixed capital intensity usually represents a major barrier to exit only serves to compound this problem.

- ❖ Buzzell, R. D. & Gale, B. T., *The PIMS Principles* (1987).
- ❖ Buzzell, R. D., Gale B. T. & Sultan, R. G., 'Market Share – a Key to Profitability', *Harvard Business Review* (1975).
- ❖ Schoeffler, S., Buzzell, R. D., & Heaney, D. F., 'Impact of Strategic Planning on Profit Performance', *Harvard Business Review* (1974).

❖ Woo, C., 'Market Share Leadership: Not Always so Good', *Harvard Business Review* (1984).

42.   Porter's Five Forces

Originating in the work of Michael Porter, this model specifies five main sources of competition – the bargaining power of suppliers, the bargaining power of buyers, the threat of potential entry from outside the industry, the threat posed by industries producing substitute goods or services, and competition from companies in the same sector. Development of a viable strategy involves identification and evaluation of all five forces (Figure 2.16), the nature and importance of which vary by industry and company, with the ultimate aim of protecting the firm from associated dangers.

❖ Cowley, P., 'Margins and Buyer/Seller Power in Capital Intensive Businesses', *PIMS Asso. Ltr* (1986).
❖ Porter, M. E., 'How Competitive Forces Shape Strategy', *Harvard Business Review* (1979).
❖ Porter, M. E., *Competitive Strategy: Techniques for Analysing Industries and Competitors* (1980).
❖ Thompson, A., 'Competition as a Strategic Process', *Anti-Trust Bulletin* (1980).
❖ Thompson, A. & Strickland, A. J., *Strategic Management* (1993), New York: Irwin.
❖ Yip, G., 'Entry of New Competitors: How Safe is Your Industry?', *PIMS Asso. Ltr* (1979).

43.   Product Market Diversification Matrix

Originally developed by Ansoff, this matrix divides a company's product market activities into four areas, each assigned a particular strategy (Figure 2.17).

The concept has been further refined to include the added complexity of geography (Figure 2.18). In its three-dimensional format, the matrix can be used to define the strategic thrust and ultimate scope of business. The firm can opt for different variations of market need, product/service technologies, and geographic scope to define its market.

Ansoff believes that there are two means of achieving strategic flexibility. Externally, it is possible to diversify the firm's geographic scope, the needs it serves, and the technologies it utilises, so that sudden changes in strategic business need not result in serious repercussions. Resources and capabilities can also be made easily transferable amongst the firm's businesses. Ironically, optimising one of the four components of the portfolio strategy growth vector is likely to depress the firm's performance with regard to the other components. In particular, maximising synergy is likely to reduce strategic flexibility.

❖ Ansoff, I., *Corporate Strategy* (1987).

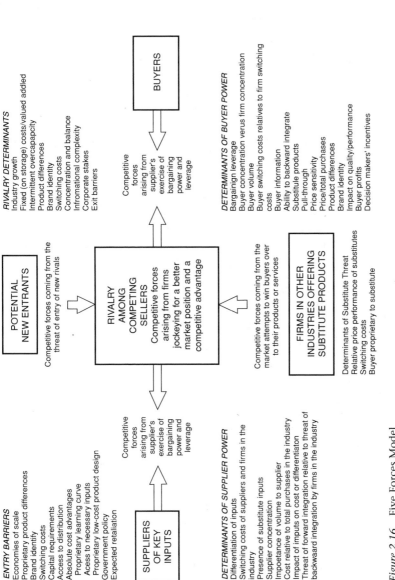

ENTRY BARRIERS
Economies of scale
Proprietary product differences
Brand identity
Switching costs
Capital requirements
Access to distribution
Absolute cost advantages
Proprietary learning curve
Acess to necessary inputs
Proprietary low-cost product design
Government policy
Expected retaliation

Competitive
forces
arising from
supplier's
exercise of
bargaining
power and
leverage

**POTENTIAL
NEW ENTRANTS**

Competitive forces coming from the
threat of entry of new rivals

**RIVALRY
AMONG
COMPETING
SELLERS**
Competitive forces
arising from firms
jockeying for a
better market
position and a
competitive advantage

RIVALRY DETERMINANTS
Industry growth
Fixed (on storage) costs/valued added
Intermittent overcapapcity
Product differences
Brand identity
Switching costs
Concentration and balance
Infromational complexity
Corporate stakes
Exit barriers

Competitive
forces
arising from
supplier's
exercise of
bargaining
power and
leverage

BUYERS

DETERMINANTS OF SUPPLIER POWER
Differentiation of inputs
Switching costs of suppliers and firms in the
industry
Presence of substitute inputs
Supplier concentration
Impoetance of volume to supplier
Cost relative to total purchases in the industry
Impact of imputs on cost or differentiaton
Threat of forward integration relative to threat of
backwaard integration by firms in the industry

Competitive forces coming from the
market attempts to win buyers over
to their products or services

**SUPPLIERS
OF KEY
INPUTS**

**FIRMS IN OTHER
INDUSTRIES OFFERING
SUBSTITUTE PRODUCTS**

Determinants of Substitute Threat
Relative price performance of substitutes
Switching costs
Buyer proprietary to substitute

DETERMINANTS OF BUYER POWER
Bargainign leverage
Buyer concentration verus firm concentration
Buyer volume
Buyer switching costs relatives to firm switching
costs
Buyer information
Ability to backward integrate
Substitute products
Pull-through
Price sensitivity
Price/total purchases
Product differences
Brand identity
Impact on quality/performance
Buyer profits
Decision makers' incentives

Figure 2.16 Five Forces Model
Source: Reprinted with the permission of The Free Press, a Division of Simon & Schuster Adult Publishing Group, from *Competitive Advantage: Creating and Sustaining Superior Performance* by Michael E. Porter. Copyright © 1985, 1998 by Michael E. Porter. All rights reserved.

Current Products	New Products
Market Penetration Strategy	Product Development Strategy
Market Development Strategy	Diversification Strategy

Figure 2.17 The Product/Market Diversification Matrix
Source: From Ansoff, I. (1988) *The New Corporate Strategy*, New York; John Wiley, pp. 82–84.

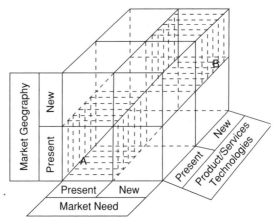

Figure 2.18 Dimensions of the Geographic Growth Vector
Source: From Ansoff, I. (1988) *The New Corporate Strategy*, New York; John Wiley, pp. 82–84.

44. Project Management

This is an established set of controls associated with contract life cycle management, operating from inception to closure. The tool has standardised metrics for performance, reported on a regular basis. It is predominately focused on *risk management*, particularly within long-term, project-based businesses.

45. Resource Agreement Model

This is a framework for resource allocation, and often provides a basis for the strategic plan that shapes a firm's future. The model is regularly utilised in the context of annual budgeting and forecasting. Demanding a continuous review process to define a clear strategy, to identify a firm's position and priorities in relation to market dynamics, this approach clearly supports the alignment of functions.

46. Risk Analysis Tools

Since all companies have to make decisions in situations of both risk and uncertainty and because the pace of modern technological change is much faster than ever before it is always essential for strategy managers to have risk management tools and techniques in place.

❖ Ritchie, B. & Marshall, D., *Business Risk Management* (1993).

47. Scenario Planning

Enabling the visualisation of alternative futures, scenario planning facilitates the design of flexible strategies to cope with these visions of the future. The key characteristic of this process is its implicit incorporation of the subjective assessment of individuals/groups, and its recognition that decision-makers have the potential to condition future development. Scenarios tend to be constructed on the basis of indisputable facts and assumptions that have proved accurate in the past. These are then extrapolated through the process of scenario development to create a series of alternate futures, which, in themselves, are mutually consistent. A series of scenarios, usually no more than three, are subsequently developed as the basis for alternate predictions. Gross-impact analysis can then be undertaken to examine the effect of contrary variables on alternate futures. At the end of this process, established scenarios are issued to individual business units, providing a background against which to develop their strategic plans.

❖ Anonymous, 'Shell's multiple scenario planning: a realistic alternative to the crystal ball', *World Business Weekly* (1980).
❖ Schwartz, P., *The Art of the Long View* (1991), New York.
❖ Wack, P., 'Scenarios: uncharted waters ahead', *Harvard Business Review* (1985).

48. Succession Planning

Increasingly gaining competitive advantage from the knowledge of their people, companies are beginning to recognise the criticality of certain key individuals. Succession planning is a means of identifying these people, together with key areas of technology, critical success factors, and points of vulnerability. Replacements are identified for important members of staff. Occasionally, this is also relevant at 'lower' levels of the organisational hierarchy.

49.   SWOT Analysis
An acronym of Strengths, Weaknesses, Opportunities, and Threats, SWOT analysis provides a simple, but powerful, tool for evaluating the strategic position of the firm In formulating strategy, the firm attempts to build on its strengths and eliminate its weaknesses. When it does not possess the skills required to take advantage of opportunities or avoid threats, the necessary resources to rectify this situation must be identified, and appropriate steps taken to procure strengths and reduce weaknesses.

❖ Channon, D. F., *Bank Strategic Management and Marketing* (1986).
❖ Channon, D. F., *Strategic Management Workbook* (1994).
❖ Thompson, A. J. & Strickland A. J., *Strategic Management* (1993).

50.   Target-Based Costing
Market research is undertaken to establish what consumers might be prepared to pay for the functions offered by a new product. Once this is established, it is possible to determine the retail price (before discounts). Allowing for the required level of profitability, this establishes the cost at which the company must produce in order to achieve a satisfactory return on its investment. Having established target price and corresponding costs, designers, engineers, and procurement officers set out to achieve the desired cost level. Conducted in extreme detail, this process will consider component re-engineering, changes in assembly method, function elimination, and the application of pressure to suppliers. If the target cost is not attainable, the product may need to be aborted.

❖ Channon, D. F., *Canon B Case* (1993), London: Imperial College.
❖ Kotler, P., *Marketing Management* (1994), Englewood Cliffs, NJ: Prentice-Hall.

51.   Technology Watch
This is a simple technique to identify future technological development, to pinpoint key trends and the potential niche positioning these might facilitate. By highlighting a company's limitations in terms of systems, processes, and skills, it is possible to determine areas of the business that require attention.

52.   Value-Based Management
This is basically a generic phrase covering several shareholder value techniques. Stern Stewart contributed EVA, L.E.K. are responsible for Value-Based Management, and Holt Consultancy brought us CFROI. Active management of future value has increasingly been deemed critical to business. Consultants are seen to add value to this process through their access to databases.

Figure 2.19   Value Chain Analysis
Source: Channon, D. F., *Blackwell's Encyclopaedic Dictionary of Strategic Management* (1999)
Blackwell Publishing.

53.   Value Chain Analysis

The activities performed by a firm are part of the value add process that a raw material undergoes as its progresses through to its ultimate consumption. Hence, the value chain for a firm (Figure 2.19) must be understood in the context of the entire supply chain. The benefit of the value chain concept is that it allows a firm to be disaggregated into a variety of strategically relevant activities. In particular, it allows identification of those with different economic characteristics, those with a high potential for creating differentiation, and those most important for developing cost structure. From this analysis, different courses of action should be identifiable in order to develop differentiation and less price sensitive strategies. Competitive action subsequently aims to perform strategic activities better or cheaper than competitors.

Michael Porter produced the generic value chain in 1985, classifying activities into primary and support functions. There are five primary activities – inbound logistics, operations, outbound logistics, marketing & sales, and service (though the extent to which they feature will depend upon the nature of the industry). The four support activities are firm infrastructure, human resources, technology development, and procurement. In order to diagnose competitive advantage, it is necessary to define a firm's value chain within a particular industry and draw comparison with those of its key competitors, enabling identification of the potential areas for reconfiguration.

❖ Channon, D. F., *Blackwell's Encyclopaedic Dictionary of Strategic Management* (1999).

54.   Variance Analysis

This is the comparison of actual and budgeted figures (on a component basis). As a performance measure, it supports the notion of 'responsibility accounting'. However, flexible budgeting should respond to changes in volume. For example, if a production manager was budgeted to spend £100,000 on materials, but spent £110,000, he shouldn't be deemed to have overspent by £10,000 if volume was 10% higher than budgeted.

55.   Virtual University

The growing trend within large companies is to develop knowledge and learning in-house. The aim is to become more structured with regard to the firm's development, to develop core material that is consistent with the company's vision and values.

56.   *Vulnerability Analysis*

This is a means to assess the potential damage that might result if a firm's key strategic underpinnings were removed. These bastions have been identified as:

- Customer needs and wants served by the firm's products or services
- Resources and assets – people, capital, facilities, raw materials, and technology
- Relative cost position compared with its competitors
- Consumer base – size, demographics, and trends
- Technologies required
- Special skills – systems, procedures, and structures
- Corporate identity – image, culture, and products
- Institutional barriers to competition – regulations, patents, and licensing
- Social values – lifestyles, common norms, and ideals
- Sanctions, supports, and incentives to do business
- Customer goodwill, product quality, safety and corporate reputation
- Complementary products or services in the stakeholder system

Conducting vulnerability analysis involves the following steps:

1) Identify the key underpinnings
2) Identify the threat caused by their removal
3) State the most conservative consequence of each threat
4) Rank the impacts of the worst consequence of each threat
5) Estimate the probability of each threat occurring
6) Rank the firm's capability to deal with each threat
7) Determine whether the company's vulnerability to each threat is extreme or negligible

Having conducted this assessment, it is necessary to rank the impact on a scale of 0 (no impact) to 10 (catastrophe), and similarly, to rank ability to respond to each threat from 0 (defenceless) to 10 (absorb the threat). The company's overall vulnerability to each threat can then be plotted on a vulnerability assessment matrix.

❖ Hurd, D. A., 'Vulnerability Analysis in Business Planning', *SRI International Research Report* (1977).
❖ Rowe, A. J., Mason R. O., Dickel K. E., Mann R. B. & Mockler R. J., *Strategic Management* (1994).

3
The Use of Strategic Management Tools and Techniques

Business strategy thinking has been responsible for producing more than its fair share of business gurus and management fads (Moore, 1992; Micklethwait & Wooldridge, 1996). When assessing the scope and value of strategic tools and techniques three things stand out. First, the breadth of the advice being offered and, second, the diversity of approaches and ideas being recommended. Third, and perhaps most significantly, is the contradictory nature of much of the advice proffered. This state-of-affairs is curious when one bears in mind that the discipline has a reputation for having a strong 'scientific' orientation. Although there are writers of business strategy who treat the development and implementation of corporate plans as a fundamentally sociological activity, the majority of writers err towards treating it as a technocratic exercise. For such technocrats, the secret to developing an effective strategy lies in identifying goals, developing a programme of action (plan) capable of meeting the objectives, and executing it. Indeed, when writing about business strategy, many authors have a predilection for talking in military metaphors.

However, in the case of business strategy it can be argued that the claims for scientific rigour are merely pretensions. This is because the literature on business strategy is contradictory and diverse and because nobody really knows what leads to business success – except in the most generalised sense. When analysing what makes firms successful one sees very different causal factors. The success of Toyota rests on a combination of good design and highly effective production and contracting techniques. By contrast, Bill Gates and Microsoft rely on a set of proprietary technologies that quite inadvertently happened to have become the industry standard. For Stella Artois beer is the brand that is critical to success. For each firm the ability to differentiate is critical but what individuals or firms should do to differentiate in particular markets and supply chains is not always clear or easy to replicate.

For the senior leadership of firms this creates something of a problem. On the one hand they need guidance. After all, nothing is more important than that they should have a clear idea about what it is they need to do in order to be successful. Unfortunately, it would appear that firms succeed at different times for different reasons. Every business guru or consulting practice, therefore, justifies their strategic approach by citing examples when the recommended strategy worked for some or other business. The dilemma for senior managers, therefore, is which advisers should they listen to and which tools and techniques should they operationalise.

This chapter seeks to address this problem for senior managers by, first, analysing just how 'scientific', as a function, business strategy actually is. The chapter seeks to answer this question by first asking how frequently business managers use management tools, in which industries and for which activities? Second, the objectives behind the use of tools and techniques and their performance are analysed. Finally, we address the question of whether or not the current strategy tools and techniques appear to be used appropriately or not.

1.   The general use of tools in the strategy function

The discussion that follows provides a description of the general use of strategy tools and techniques in total, and across the 7 business activities outlined earlier in chapter 1. The analysis then focuses on the use of tools and techniques across the 16 industry sectors and the 6 industry sector groupings also outlined in chapter 1.

The use of tools and techniques in general

Despite the millions of words written on the subject of business strategy and the millions of dollars spent on strategic advice within companies, what is perhaps the most surprising finding from the survey research reported here is the relative low level of use of strategy tools and techniques. As Table 3.1 indicates, although 131 firms (see Appendix B) in 16 different industrial sectors were surveyed for the strategy part of the study, only 44 individual tools and techniques were found to be in use. At one level this is not surprising because the literature survey uncovered only 56 strategy tools and techniques in total, which indicates that at least one firm or another appears to being using most of the tools and techniques available, with only 12 in the literature survey (as outlined in Table 3.2) not found to be in use in at least one of the companies surveyed.

Despite this the survey shows that strategy tool and technique usage is heavily weighted in favour of just a few major tools and techniques. As Table 3.1 indicates undertaking a structured approach to market research recorded the highest usage rate (with 10.04% of total strategy tool uses across the 131 respondent companies). Benchmarking was the next most used tool and technique (7.53% of total usages), followed closely by core competence thinking (6.90% of total usages), SWOT analysis (6.70%),

Table 3.1 The Total Use of Strategy Tools and Techniques (*44 Tools with 478 Tool Usages in Total Recorded*)

Tool	Incidence	%	Tool	Incidence	%
Market Research	48	10.04	E-Business-Internal Applications	7	1.46
Benchmarking	36	7.53	Economic Value Add (EVA)	7	1.46
Core Competence Thinking	33	6.90	Decision Gates	6	1.26
SWOT Analysis	32	6.70	Value Chain Analysis	6	1.26
Discounted Cash Flow Analysis	26	5.44	Growth Share Matrix	5	1.06
Scenario Planning	22	4.60	Technology Watch	5	1.06
Balanced Scorecard	21	4.39	E-Business-Buy Side Software	4	0.84
Competitor Analysis	19	3.98	Brainstorming	3	0.62
Key Performance Indicators	18	3.77	Competency Model	3	0.62
E-Business-Seller Side Software	17	3.56	Manpower Planning	3	0.62
Activity Based Costing	16	3.35	Outsourcing Analysis	3	0.62
Porter's Five Forces	14	2.93	Pareto Analysis	3	0.62
Gap Analysis	13	2.72	Business Stream Analysis	2	0.42
Business Process Reengineering	12	2.51	Cost Benefit Analysis	2	0.42
Consumer Profiling	12	2.51	Competitive/ Market Attractive	2	0.42
Management Information System	12	2.51	Economic Profit Measures	2	0.42
Project Management Tools	12	2.51	Resource Agreement Model	2	0.42
Value Based Management	11	2.30	Succession Planning	2	0.42
Risk Analysis Tools	9	1.88	Virtual University	2	0.42
Knowledge Management	8	1.67	Best Practice Club Initiative	1	0.21
PEST Analysis	8	1.67	Payback Analysis	1	0.21
Change Management	7	1.46	Variance Analysis	1	0.21

Table 3.2   **The 12 Strategy Tools and Techniques Not Found in Use**

Break-Even Analysis
Capital Asset Pricing Model
Cause-and-Effect Analysis
Cognitive Mapping
Customer Profitability Matrix
Directional Policy Matrix
Five "S" Strategy
Market Value Added (MVA)
Product Market Diversification Matrix
PIMS
Target-Based Costing
Vulnerability Analysis

---

discounted cash flow analysis (5.44%), scenario planning (4.60%), the balanced scorecard (4.39%), competitor analysis (19%), KPIs (18%), E-Business seller-side software (3.56%) and activity based costing (3.35%).

Beyond these 11 major tools and techniques, that each scored over 3% of total usages, there are 33 other tools and techniques reported to be in use, some of which are extremely well known approaches in the academic and consulting literature. Key tools and techniques that stand out in this regard are Porter's Five Forces (2.93% of total usages), BPR (2.51%), PEST Analysis (1.67%), EVA (1.46%), Boston Portfolio or Growth Share Matrix (1.06%) and Outsourcing Analysis (0.62%). That these tools and techniques appear is not surprising what is however is the fact that companies appear not to be using tools and techniques extensively in the companies analysed. This may be a surprise to some – especially to those who argue that corporate leaders are often the gullible dupes of self-interested academics and consultants peddling shoddy goods (Christensen & Raynor, 2003).

Given the critical importance of the strategy process for all firms the findings reported here demonstrate that rather than being duped many companies are not using structured tools and techniques to think about strategy issues at all. Thus, if we consider the most frequently cited strategy tool and technique in use – market research – only 37% of companies in the survey (48 users from a universe of 131 respondents) were using this approach. Similarly, low-level usage figures were recorded for most of the major tools and techniques actually in use. Thus, only 28% of respondents were using benchmarking, only 25% were using core competence thinking and SWOT analysis, while only 17% were using scenario planning and the balanced scorecard. For some of the other famous strategy tools and techniques the usage rates were even worse. Porter Five Forces was only being used by 11% of respondents, BPR by 9%, EVA by 5% and the Boston or Growth Share Matrix by about 4%.

What all of this clearly indicates is that tools and techniques are not used as extensively as some may claim in the companies surveyed. This does not mean that consultants are not being used extensively – clearly they are. What this means is that, while consulting firms and academics may employ many of the structured tools and techniques when they provide strategic business advice, there is less evidence that managers develop the capability to operationalise and use these tools and techniques on their own in the business when consultants are not involved. This implies that there is a significant competence gap within companies about the availability of tools and techniques for strategizing, as well as a general lack of focus on the continuous analysis of key strategic business problems within the strategy functions of the firms surveyed.

The use of tools and techniques by business activity

It is interesting to consider the uses to which particular strategy tools and techniques are put when companies do decide to use them. The evidence seems to indicate that, while companies may not use these tools as extensively as they should, when they do decide to use them they tend to focus broadly on key strategic rather than operational issues. This is borne out by the findings reported in Table 3.3.

The table has been constructed by first disaggregating the key business activities that the strategy function normally has to discharge within any company, as described in chapter 1, and then linking these seven business activities with the particular types of tools and techniques found to be in use. These key business activities were defined as *market and environmental analysis, product and competence development, resource allocation, performance measurement, financial management, the make/buy decision* and the *use of IT and Internet solutions.*

As the table demonstrates, unsurprisingly, the bulk of the tools and techniques that were being used were focused disproportionately on the key concerns of *market and environmental analysis* (assessing customer wants and needs, understanding socio-political, economic and technological change and competitor and value chain positioning) and *product and competence development* (analysing customer value propositions, benchmarking competitors and non-competitors, assessing core and non-core activities, developing new products, understanding product and service markets and developing internal capabilities). These two activity sets accounted for 46.06% and 40.62% of all tools usage respectively.

These can be regarded as the two most important strategic activities and this is borne out by the somewhat lesser usage rates for tools and techniques to assist with operational delivery after the strategic positioning decisions have been made. *Resource allocation* activities accounted for 24.05% of tools and techniques total usages, with *performance management* activities scoring 18.63%, *financial management* activities 16.74% and *IT and Internet solutions* a

Table 3.3   The Use of Strategy Tools and Techniques by Business Activity

(The total figures do not sum to 100% because some tools and techniques can be used for more than one business activity).

Rank Order of Tools and Techniques by Business Activities	Tools and Techniques	% of Total Usage Recorded	Total Business Activity Usage Score
1 Market & Environmental Analysis	Market Research	10.04	46.06%
	Benchmarking	7.53	
	Swot Analysis	6.70	
	Scenario Planning	4.60	
	Competitor Analysis	3.98	
	Porters Five Force	2.93	
	Consumer Profiling	2.51	
	Risk Analysis Tools	1.88	
	Pest Analysis	1.67	
	Value Chain Analysis	1.26	
	Technology Watch	1.06	
	Business Stream Analysis	0.42	
	Competitive/Market Attractiveness	0.42	
2 Product And Competence Development	Market Research	10.04	40.62%
	Benchmarking	7.53	
	Core Competence Thinking	6.90	
	Competitor Analysis	3.98	
	Gap Analysis	2.72	
	Consumer Profiling	2.51	
	Knowledge Management	1.67	
	Decision Gates	1.26	
	Growth Share Matrix	1.06	
	Technology Watch	1.06	
	Brainstorming	0.42	
	Competitive/Market Attractiveness	0.42	
	Succession Planning	0.42	
	Virtual University	0.42	
	Best Practice Club Initiative	0.21	
3 Resource Allocation	Scenario Planning	4.60	24.05%
	Balanced Scorecard	4.39	
	Key Performance Indicators	3.77	
	Activity Based Costing	3.35	
	Management Information Systems	2.51	
	Project Management	2.51	
	Value Chain Analysis	1.26	
	Manpower Planning	0.62	
	Pareto Analysis	0.62	
	Resource Agreement Model	0.42	

Table 3.3   The Use of Strategy Tools and Techniques by Business Activity –
continued

(The total figures do not sum to 100% because some tools and techniques can be used for more than one business activity).

Rank Order of Tools and Techniques by Business Activities	Tools and Techniques	% of Total Usage Recorded	Total Business Activity Usage Score
4 Performance Management	Balanced Scorecard	4.39	18.63%
	Key Performance Indicators	3.77	
	Activity Based Costing	3.35	
	Business Process Re-Engineering	2.51	
	Management Information Systems	2.51	
	Value Chain Analysis	1.26	
	Succession Planning	0.42	
	Virtual University	0.42	
5 Financial Management	Discounted Cash Flow Analysis	5.44	16.74%
	Activity Based Costing	3.35	
	Management Information Systems	2.51	
	Value Based Management	2.30	
	Risk Analysis Tools	1.88	
	Cost Benefit Analysis	0.42	
	Economic Profit Analysis	0.42	
	Payback Analysis	0.21	
	Variance Analysis	0.21	
6 Make/Buy Decision	Core Competence Thinking	6.90	7.52%
	Outsourcing Procedures	0.62	
7 It And Internet Solutions	E-Business Seller-Side Software	3.56	5.86%
	E-Business Internal Applications	1.46	
	E-Business Buyer-Side Software	0.84	

mere 5.86%. Perhaps the one business activity set that stands out as somewhat anomalous is *the make/buy decision*, which reported a relatively low activity score of 7.52% total usages. This is surprising given that there has recently been a growth in outsourcing activity in many western companies. It may well be, however, that the research only captured the beginning of this trend and that, in the future, we might expect to see the number of companies using make/buy tools and techniques increasing strategically.

The use of tools and techniques by industry sector and by industry sector groupings

When considering which industry sectors use strategy tools and techniques more than others it is clear that in general terms some use them much more than others. Manufacturing industries (Basic Chemicals with an average usage rate of 7.50, Aerospace 7.10, Transport Equipment 6.38 and Confectionery 4.36) in highly competitive and heavily capital-intensive industries account for four of the top six places in the rank order of average tool usage outlined in Table 3.4. Furthermore, large scale and heavily capital-intensive industries in the manufacturing and services combined category (Power & Water with 6.14 average uses and Oil & Gas with 5.56) account for the other two top ranking places.

It seems clear therefore that there is some correlation between the type of industry measured by whether it is manufacturing-based, service-based or combined (manufacturing and service). This is borne out by the data presented in Table 3.4 and also in Figure 3.1. As Figure 3.1 indicates manufacturing-based industries tend to use strategy tools and techniques far more than any other industries. The average usage figure for manufacturing is 5.04, while that for combined manufacturing and services is 3.30 and for services only 2.19. There would appear also to be a slightly greater use of strategy tools and techniques in the process-based industries (that have standardised and routinised systems and processes to be managed) compared with the project-based industries (that have discrete and often one-off supply offerings, with relatively non-standard and non-routinised operating systems and processes). The average usage figure for process-based industries is 3.92, while it is only 3.51 for project-based industries.

Table 3.4   The Rank Order Use of Strategy Tools and Techniques by Industry Sector

Industry	Total Tools	No. of Firms	Average
Basic Chemicals	45	6	7.50
Aerospace	71	10	7.10
Transport Equipment	51	8	6.38
Power & Water	43	7	6.14
Oil & Gas	50	9	5.56
Confectionery	35	8	4.36
Healthcare	28	8	3.50
Retail Financial Services	34	10	3.40
Computer Hardware	29	9	3.22
Retail & Distribution	21	8	2.63
Construction	10	6	1.67
Publishing	13	8	1.63
Telecommunications	12	8	1.50
IT Solutions	13	9	1.44
Tourism & Leisure	11	8	1.38
Media & Entertainment	12	9	1.33
Overall Average	**478**	**131**	**3.65**

	Process/ Manufacturing	Process/ Manufacturing & Services	Process/ Services	Total Process Average Usage: 3.92
	Group Average Usage 5.03	Group Average Usage 3.71	Group Average Usage 3.02	
PROCESS	Basic Chemicals (7.50)	Healthcare (3.50)	Retail & Distribution (2.63)	
	Computer Hardware (3.22)	Power & Water (6.14)	Retail Financial Services (3.40)	
	Confectionery (4.36)	Telecommunications (1.50)		
	PROJECT/ MANUFACTURING	PROJECT/ MANUFACTURING & SERVICES	PROJECT/ SERVICES	Total Project Average Usage: 3.51
	Group Average Usage 5.04	Group Average Usage 2.89	Group Average Usage 1.36	
PROJECT	Aerospace (7.10)	Construction (1.67)	Media & Entertainment (1.33)	
	Publishing (1.63)	IT Solutions (1.44)	Tourism & Leisure (1.38)	
	Transport Equipment (6.38)	Oil & Gas (5.56)		
	Total Manufacturing Average Usage 5.04	Total Combined Average Usage 3.30	Total Service Average Usage 2.19	
	MANUFACTURING	COMBINED MANUFACTURING & SERVICES	SERVICES	

TYPE OF OPERATIONAL DELIVERY

TYPE OF GOODS AND/OR SERVICES

Figure 3.1 The Use of Strategy Tools and Techniques by Industry Groups

The reason for these differences may not, however, be primarily to do with the operational processes that have to be managed but it may rather be a function of four factors. First, the level of capital investment that firms have to sustain in the management of particular processes and systems to make a profit may force them to consider the environmental and product and competence requirements of their businesses more than those that do not have these same pressures. Relatedly, and the second factor here, is the overall level of competition and/or regulation that firms face. In a highly contested and regulated environment firms have to consider their strategic options far more carefully than those in less competitive or regulated environments.

The third variable, is combination of all of the previous factors and relates to the overall level of operational and financial risk that is involved in managing a business strategically. Clearly, firms operating with heavily capital-intensive processes and systems, in highly contested and regulated industries, will experience severe financial and operational penalties if they make the wrong strategic decisions about market and value chain positioning for particular products and services. The fourth factor relates to the frequency and scale with which firms have to make these decisions. Clearly firms that have to constantly 'bet the business' (in the sense of making decisions that could have overall catastrophic consequences for corporate survival), and on a frequent basis are, arguably, more likely to require a comprehensive approach to strategy formulation, with the use of many standard tools and techniques on a regular basis, than those who do not.

If one takes these four variables together it is clear that most of the heavy users of strategy tools and techniques appear to operate in heavily contested or regulated markets, with high levels of capital investment required, with high levels of operational and financial risk that must be managed on a regular basis. This is certainly true of the top six users of strategy tools and techniques. This group of high risk users includes Basic Chemicals (7.50 uses) and Confectionery (4.36 uses) in the *Process/Manufacturing* industry grouping; and also Aerospace (7.10 uses) and Transport Equipment (6.36 uses) in the *Project/Manufacturing* industry grouping; Power & Water (3.71 uses) in the *Process/Combined* industry grouping; and, Oil & Gas (5.56 uses) in the *Project/Combined* industry grouping. The only anomalies in the data for these industry groupings are the Telecommunications (1.50 total average uses), the Construction (1.67) the IT Solutions (1.44) and the Publishing (1.63) sectors.

The Telecommunications results are difficult to explain because firms in this sector suffer from many of the same problems as those experienced by other firms operating in the *Process/Combined* industry sector grouping. The cause may be simply a function of the practices of the companies interviewed and their particular approaches to strategy, which may not be representative of the sector as a whole. The low usage scores recorded for the

Construction and IT Solutions sectors may be less difficult to explain. When compared with the relatively heavy usage industry sectors above, while both of these industries face severe competition, they do not experience the same levels of regulation or requirements for capital intensive investment prior to bidding for work. Furthermore, since they operate within a project environment, in which they bid for work often without having to make extensive investments prior to starting the work, it can be argued that the levels of financial and operational risks they face are, relatively speaking, much lower than for those who have to sustain costly operating processes without certainty of market share or growth. Relatedly, while firms in these sectors will regularly seek sales opportunities, they do not 'bet the business' on a regular basis (although they sometimes may do so in major Construction projects) when they bid for work. In such circumstances it is likely that the perceived need to develop a comprehensive approach to strategy formulation will be lower than for the Oil & Gas industry sector in the *Project/Combined* industry grouping, where the process is regular and continuous with very heavy capital intensive investment that can last for twenty years or more with very high operational and financial risk. As a result these two sectors can be categorised as medium rather than high-risk industry strategy sectors.

A similar explanation can also be used to explain the lowest usage industry sectors of Media & Entertainment (1.33 average usages) and Tourism and Leisure (1.38 usages). Clearly in these *Project/Services* industries similar factors will be at work. While there is clearly extensive competition in both industry sector, the nature of the initial financial investments that have to be made are not as high as those required to be made by the firms operating in the heavier usage sectors. It can also be argued that the level of operational and financial risks being managed in these two industry sectors, while obviously significant for the individuals involved, are not relatively of the same order of magnitude, nor do they have to be made on as regular a basis. Once again this implies that the need for a comprehensive and continuous approach to strategy formulation is unlikely.

This argument can also be extended to the Publishing sector in the *Project/Manufacturing* industry sector grouping, whose average usage score of 1.63 stand in stark contrast to the Aerospace score of 7.10 uses and Transport Equipment with 6.38. The explanation for this marked difference of usage rates is clearly similar to that presented above. In the publishing business the nature of the investments made in particular product offerings are relatively low compared with Aerospace and Transport Equipment. Firms in this industry rarely, if ever, 'bet the business' on one book or magazine. This means that the need for a continuous and comprehensive strategy formulation process is unlikely in this sector. This tendency is reinforced, it can be argued, by the historic 'gentleman's club' approach in the industry, in which entrepreneurial individuals or book editors search for new talent and back their market hunches. In this type of industry, with low financial and operational risks, even though there is fierce competition, the need for a heavy use of strategy tools and techniques is not apparent.

Finally, there is what can be called medium-level risk industry sectors that have some need for strategy formulation tools and techniques (because they have some but not all of the four factors outlined above) but not on as frequent or comprehensive a basis as the heavy users (who normally experience all of these factors at once). The firms in this middling user category are those to be found in the *Process/Services* industry sector grouping (Retail & Distribution (2.63 average uses) and Retail Financial Services (3.40 uses) and Healthcare (3.50) from the *Process/Combined* grouping and, finally, Computer Hardware (3.22 uses) from the *Process/Manufacturing* grouping. Clearly, while each of these industry sectors has broad similarities with the other heavy user process-based industry sectors none of them experience exactly the same level of financial and operational risks or competitive pressures as the heavy user groups.

In Retail & Distribution, for example, while there is extensive competition firms rarely 'bet the business' on particular contracts, and the operational failure of what is provided as a service is often focused on relatively small operational transactions that can be easily rectified without fundamentally challenging the strategic positioning of the company. The same is true in the Retail Financial Services industry, where there is often restricted competition, and services are provided to small consumers who rarely have the power and leverage to affect the corporate strategy of the selling company on an individual basis. Customers are also notoriously risk-averse in the financial services industry and extremely reluctant to switch accounts. In Healthcare, there is also restricted competition and an ageing population, which provides relative stability for market conditions and new product offerings, making the need for constant strategy reformulation unlikely. Computer Hardware, although fiercely competitive amongst the few players in the market, also suffers from restricted competition and this may also reduce the financial and operational risks in new product development – although the pace of technological innovation is certainty a factor that needs to be considered actively. For all of these reasons it seems likely that, while firms in this medium risk category are likely to use tools and techniques to some extent the pressure to do so will be somewhat less than for those firms regularly operating in sectors with very high levels of financial and operational risk.

2.   The performance of the tools and techniques used in strategy

Having analysed the use of strategy tools and techniques in some detail, and seen that they are not used as extensively as they might be, but that there are potentially rational reasons for the variability in use across industry sectors and groupings, it is now possible to focus on the performance of the tools and techniques that were adopted. This section focuses on the objectives behind the use of strategy tools and techniques and the impact of these on both the firm and the function. This is followed by an analysis of their impact by industry sector and by industry sector grouping. Finally, there is a discussion of the major barriers to effective implementation.

The corporate and functional objectives for implementing tools and techniques

Table 3.5 provides a general overview of the major objectives behind the implementation and use of strategy tools and techniques. As the table demonstrates strategy managers appear to be using tools and techniques equally for strategic as for operational objectives. This is interesting because the findings are broadly similar for the marketing function (see Table 5.5, chapter 5) the other functions, as one might expect, tend to use tools and techniques more for operational effectiveness considerations rather than for broad strategy objectives.

In compiling Table 3.5 managers in the 131 companies surveyed were asked to explain for what purpose they were using a particular tool or technique. The choices were either for strategic or operational effectiveness purposes. In the strategy context managers were provided with a further three choices. The tools and techniques could be used to assist with the search for differentiation, through the development of unique products or through cost leadership advantages, or they could be used to find repositioning opportunities within markets and value chains. The findings show that, as one mighty expect, managers in the strategy area were using tools and techniques 56% of the time to assist with strategic objectives. Of these strategic objectives, the search for differentiation through the development of unique products and services was the most popular (27%), closely followed by market and value chain repositioning (20%). The search for cost leadership was much less popular at 9% of responses recorded.

When one disaggregates by industry sector and grouping it is clear that the industry sectors in project-based industries are much more focused on strategic objectives than those in the process-based industries. Thus, the *Project/Services* industries had a 83%/17% split between strategic and operational objectives, while both the *Project/Manufacturing* and *Project/Combined* groupings had a strategy/operational split of 64%/36%. Conversely, the *Process/Services* grouping had a split of 52%/48% in favour of strategic objectives and the *Process/Combined* grouping had a 55%/45% split. The *Process/Manufacturing* grouping stands out with a strategic/operational split of 22%/78% in favour of operational objectives.

What these figures appear to demonstrate is that companies operating in *Process/Manufacturing* sectors by and large find it difficult to develop

Table 3.5 Overall Objectives for Introducing Strategy Tools and Techniques

Group	Industry	Strategic Objectives			
		Unique Products %	Cost Advantage %	Repositioning %	Operational Effectiveness %
Process/ Manufacturing Group	Basic Chemicals	16	12	3	69
	Computer Hardware	3	0	11	86
	Confectionery	18	0	3	79
	Group Average	*12*	*4*	*6*	*78*
Process/Combined Group	Healthcare	45	8	19	28
	Power and Water	13	0	8	79
	Telecommunications	33	18	21	28
	Group Average	*30*	*9*	*16*	*45*
Process/Services Group	Retail and Distribution	22	3	22	53
	Retail Financial Services	24	5	29	42
	Group Average	*23*	*4*	*25*	*48*
Project/ Manufacturing Group	Aerospace	23	10	34	33
	Publishing	42	0	14	44
	Transport Equipment	38	10	21	30
	Group Average	*34*	*7*	*23*	*36*
Project/Combined Group	Construction	27	14	36	23
	IT Solutions	10	0	31	59
	Oil & Gas	20	26	28	26
	Group Average	*19*	*13*	*32*	*36*
Project/Services Group	Media and Entertainment	82	12	0	6
	Tourism & Leisure	10	24	38	28
	Group Average	*46*	*18*	*19*	*17*
Overall Average (%)		27	9	20	44

uniquely differentiated products, cost leadership or market and value chain repositioning opportunities. This is largely a function of the relatively maturity of these industries in technological terms and the consolidation of the market that has taken place, with fierce, low margin competition taking place between the remaining industry incumbents in the Basic Chemicals, Computer Hardware and Confectionery sectors. Clearly, in the other process-based industries (which includes: Healthcare, Power & Water, Telecommunications, Retail & Distribution and Retail Financial Services), although there is fierce competition, incumbents appear to believe that there may be opportunities to improve product and service offerings, or to reposition within relatively dynamic and growing markets. The fact that all of these sectors have high levels of services rather than products as part of their market offering may well provide more opportunities for differentiation and repositioning than in the more product dominated process industries.

Interestingly, it is in the project environment that one notices the greatest incidence of strategic differentiation, cost leadership and repositioning objectives. Again this is not surprising because in a project environment there are constant opportunities to return to market with new product and service offerings that may achieve differentiation. Given this, one would expect that these areas would have the highest incidence of strategic, as opposed to operational, objectives behind tool and technique usage. It is also not surprising that the *Project/Services* grouping (including Media & Entertainment and Travel & Leisure) was the grouping that experienced the greatest incidence of differentiation objectives. In these industries the opportunity to provide new events, new programmes and new venues and artists on a regular basis is at a premium, and explains the higher focus on these strategic differentiation issues.

Overall, what is a little surprising is the relatively high incidence of operational effectiveness as a major objective in all sectors except the *Project/Services* industries. It is obvious that the *Process/Manufacturing* grouping might need to focus its strategies on internal operational effectiveness because of its lack of strategic opportunities externally. What is less clear, however, is why operational effectiveness – primarily through the use of *resource allocation, financial management, performance management* and *IT and Internet solution* tools and techniques – should be at such a premium in the other industry groupings. Nevertheless these industries do focus heavily on operational effectiveness in the strategy area as the figures for these sectors clearly demonstrate. Thus, operational effectiveness objectives range from a total of 38% in the *Project/Manufacturing* and *Project/Combined* industry sector groupings, to 45% for *Process/Combined* and 42% for *Process/Services* industries.

To some extent the reason for this may be because of the regular and/or complex processes and systems that have to be managed operationally within these businesses to deliver any strategic goal; a task that strategy managers recognise needs to be undertaken effectively and efficiently to assist bottom-line performance. In that sense the focus on operational delivery is clearly a sensible objective for companies, and one that firms in the mature *Process/Manufacturing* industries clearly appear to appreciate, given their score of 78% in favour of operational effectiveness objectives. The fact that companies do appear to understand the need to do both strategic visioning and operational delivery effectively is a measure of their competence and further indication that they are not the simple dupes of wily academics and/or consultants selling the latest business strategy fashions.

Having assessed the corporate level objectives behind the use of strategy tools and techniques it is also interesting to consider what are the functional (within the strategy department) objectives behind implementation. The survey findings about this topic are presented in Table 3.6, which was constructed from a series of questions asked of interviewees about the functional rather than corporate or firm level goals or objectives behind tool and technique selection. Interviewees were asked to choose from a range of options that might be seen to assist the work of the function or department when they selected particular tools and techniques to use. The choices available included: increasing the functionality (or service level delivery offered by the function to the rest of the business); reducing the costs of functional operations, encouraging greater communication of issues within the business: obtaining better information about issues affecting the business in general; encouraging flexibility within the business; improving functional skill sets through competence development; and, increasing the number of staff within the function. We also asked to what extent there might be other alternative options, as well as whether or not there was no data available about why tools and techniques were being used. This was a test of whether or not managers within firms understood why they were using any particular tool or technique.

Table 3.6 demonstrates that there are three primary functional objectives behind the implementation of strategy tools and techniques. The first is the need to collect better information about the environmental circumstances that the company is operating within. The overall score for this particular item was 36% of all responses. This response was perceived to be extremely important in all sectors and groupings, and was only the second most important objective in the *Process/Combined* grouping (27% of responses compared with 32% for functionality improvement) and the *Process/Services* grouping (with 24% of responses compared with 41% for improved functionality). The second most important functional objective, scoring 24% of all responses overall, was improving the functionality of service level delivery by the strategy function to the rest of the business. For the two groupings above this objective was clearly perceived to be the most

Table 3.6 The Functional Objectives for Introducing Strategy Tools and Techniques (%)

Industry	Functionality	Cost	Communication	Information	Flexibility	Skill Sets	Number Employed	Other	No Data
Process/Manufacturing									
Basic Chemicals	5	16	11	37	2	5	0	23	1
Computer Hardware	7	11	13	42	4	11	1	11	0
Confectionery	10	16	28	35	0	3	2	0	6
Group Average	*8*	*15*	*17*	*38*	*2*	*6*	*1*	*11*	*2*
Process/Combined									
Healthcare	13	14	23	41	1	6	0	1	1
Power & Water	47	18	4	18	2	0	0	5	6
Telecommunications	35	9	15	22	7	9	1	1	1
Group Average	*32*	*14*	*14*	*27*	*3*	*5*	*0*	*2*	*3*
Process/Services									
Retail & Distribution	47	11	13	26	0	1	1	0	1
Retail Financial Services	34	17	17	21	6	1	4	0	0
Group Average	*41*	*14*	*15*	*24*	*3*	*1*	*2*	*0*	*0*
Project/Manufacturing									
Aerospace	9	5	15	46	5	16	2	0	2
Publishing	25	6	19	25	7	9	3	1	5
Transport Equipment	17	12	24	31	3	12	1	0	0
Group Average	*17*	*8*	*20*	*34*	*5*	*12*	*2*	*0*	*2*

Table 3.6 The Functional Objectives for Introducing Strategy Tools and Techniques (%) – *continued*

Industry	Functionality	Cost	Communication	Information	Flexibility	Skill Sets	Number Employed	Other	No Data
Project/Combined									
Construction	31	8	11	25	3	15	0	5	2
IT Solutions	0	2	30	37	0	4	2	25	0
Oil and Gas	28	15	13	26	5	11	1	1	0
Group Average	*20*	*9*	*18*	*29*	*3*	*10*	*1*	*10*	*0*
Project /Services									
Media & Entertainment	38	9	7	38	0	4	2	0	2
Tourism & Leisure	39	15	13	23	8	2	0	0	0
Group Average	*39*	*12*	*10*	*30*	*4*	*3*	*1*	*0*	*1*
Overall Average	24	11	16	31	3	7	1	5	2

important objective. Beyond these two primary objectives came improved communication of the environmental circumstances within the business. This objective scored the third highest response rate at 16%. Clearly, the majority of the companies surveyed appear to recognise that obtaining information is not enough and that they must also have tools and techniques as well to assist in the communication process internally about what needs to be done.

Somewhat surprising is the fact that improving the skill sets of managers within the strategy department or function itself did not figure prominently as an objective for most respondents (it was in fact rated lower than cost reduction which scored 11% of total responses). Only 7% of total respondents saw this as a major objective. This is a concern on two grounds. First, it was argued earlier that most companies do not appear to see the need to use many of the basic strategy tools and techniques that are available. Second, anecdotal evidence indicates that tools and techniques are often initially introduced to managers within companies by academics and/or consultants, but that their use declines once the initial external intervention takes place. The fact that most respondents do not see tools and techniques as a way of improving the competence and skill sets of their internal staff is, therefore, quite worrying. Furthermore, this lack of interest in developing the competence and skill sets of internal staff is a problem that is to be found in all of the four functions analysed in this volume.

The impact of tools and techniques by industry sector and industry sector grouping

Prior to undertaking the survey it was expected that the most pronounced impact on the firm would come from the use of strategy tools and techniques. After all, the whole point of strategy tools is that they are supposed to assist the firm in making the key decisions effectively. These are the tools and techniques that are supposed to help the firm decide whether it should compete in one market rather than another, or which competencies it should develop. To some extent the marketing function shares in these decisions, as we shall see in chapter 5. What the findings from the survey reveal, however, is that while most managers using strategy tools and techniques claim that they add value to their organisations – either by enhancing the performance of the firm as a whole, or by contributing to the effectiveness/efficiency of the function – there is no significant difference between the performance of tools and techniques to assist the firm or the function. Indeed, the overall performance scores reported in Table 3.7 for tools and techniques supporting the function (0.69) were slightly higher than for those supporting the firm (0.63).

Table 3.7 was constructed based on a series of interviews in the survey companies that asked respondents to score the relative performance of the

Table 3.7   The use and Impact of Strategy Tools and Techniques by Industry Sector and Groupings

Rank Order of Most Usages by Industry Sector	Performance Score			No Data %	
	Firm	Function	Average Combined Score	Firm	Function
Basic Chemicals (7.50)	0.73	0.87	0.80	20	16
Aerospace (7.10)	0.55	0.59	0.57	12	6
Transport Equipment (6.38)	0.51	0.61	0.56	15	12
Power & Water (6.14)	0.56	0.67	0.62	43	33
Oil & Gas (5.56)	0.66	0.65	0.68	27	3
Confectionery (4.36)	0.75	0.80	0.78	27	12
Healthcare (3.50)	0.63	0.74	0.69	19	17
Retail Financial Services (3.40)	0.57	0.69	0.63	54	19
Computer Hardware (3.22)	0.71	0.81	0.76	2	2
Retail & Distribution (2.63)	0.61	0.69	0.65	60	11
Construction (1.67)	0.65	0.76	0.71	4	4
Publishing (1.63)	0.68	0.17	0.43	62	31
Telecommunications (1.50)	0.58	0.67	0.63	8	0
It Solutions (1.50)	0.70	0.75	0.73	0	0
Tourism & Leisure (1.38)	0.62	0.64	0.63	0	0
Media & Entertainment (1.33)	0.50	1.00	0.75	85	89
Overall Average	**0.63**	**0.69**	**0.66**	**27**	**16**
Project/Manufacture (5.04)	0.58	0.46	0.52	30	16
Process/Manufacture (5.03)	0.73	0.83	0.78	16	10
Process/Combined (3.71)	0.59	0.69	0.65	23	17
Process/Services (3.02)	0.59	0.69	0.64	57	15
Project/Combined (2.89)	0.67	0.72	0.70	10	2
Project/Services (1.36)	0.56	0.82	0.69	43	45
Overall Average	**0.63**	**0.69**	**0.66**	**27**	**16**

particular tools and techniques used on a score ranging from +1 for high positive performance to –1 for low negative performance, with 0 as a heutral mid-point, indicating neither positive nor negative impact on performance. The interviewees were also asked whether they had robust and objective data or not to assess the performance of the tools and techniques being used. This was a test of whether managers were actually measuring the post implementation impact of tool and technique in use. Interviewees were asked to assess the performance of the tools and techniques against both firm and function implementation objectives. The data in Table 3.7 was collated on the basis of industry sectors and grouped industrial sectors.

The findings show that in general most managers had a positive view about the impact of strategic tools and techniques, both at the firm (0.63) and the function level (0.69). Indeed, unlike managers in some of the other functional areas analysed here, there were no negative scores in the strategy area at all. More interesting, perhaps, was the fact that 27% of respondents did not have robust and objective data to actually measure the impact of tools and techniques in functional use, and 16% did not have measures for those used to improve the performance of the firm. This is further evidence, which recurs throughout this volume, that managers often use tools and techniques without understanding the need to measure and manage performance.

That said some industries appear to value the use of strategy tools and techniques more than others. The top performance scores for both firm and function combined were recorded in the Basic Chemicals (0.80), the Confectionery (0.78), the Computer Hardware (0.76), the Media & Entertainment (0.75), IT Solutions (0.73), and Construction (0.71) industry sectors. The lowest combined performance scores were reported in the Publishing (0.43), Transport Equipment (0.56) and Aerospace (0.57) sectors. In the middle performance rank came Power & Water (0.62), Retail Financial Services, Telecommunications and Tourism & Leisure (all scoring 0.63), Retail & Distribution (0.65), Oil & Gas (0.66) and, finally, Healthcare (0.69).

The scores between the highest satisfaction rating (0.80) and the lowest (0.56) are not that significant and demonstrate that, while managers in companies may not use strategy tools and techniques as extensively as they might, when they are used most managers appear to find them beneficial. It is worth remarking on the fact, however, that some industry sector groupings appear to use tools and techniques in this area more than others but they do not always achieve the same performance scores as those recorded by those using tools and techniques less often. Thus, as Table 3.7 demonstrates, The *Project/Manufacturing* grouping uses tools on average more than other groupings (5.04) but also reports one of the lowest average performance scores (0.52). This is interesting because the *Project/Services* grouping reports the lowest average usage (1.36) but the second highest performance score (0.69). On the other hand the Process Manufacturing grouping records the second highest usage score of (5.03) and the highest performance score (0.78). On the face of it this can only be explained either by the fact that heavy tool and technique usage is no guarantee of satisfaction with performance, or that a more selective approach may sometimes pay dividends if the user fully understands which tools and techniques are most appropriate for the purposes required.

In this regard it is interesting to note that the high performance score recorded in the *Project/Services* grouping is primarily a function of the high scores recorded for the use of functional (0.82) rather than firm (0.56) level tools and techniques. A similar pattern emerges in the *Process/Manufacturing* grouping, with a high functional score (0.83) compared with firm (0.73) level score and in the *Process/Combined* and *Process/Services* groupings, who both record usage and performance scores of 0.59 compared with 0.69. The obvious explanation for this is that managers are happier with functional tools and techniques because they can be operationalised more easily in their businesses when compared with firm level tools that often require the firm to analyse and manage complex external environmental factors – many of which cannot be controlled effectively despite the expectations before implementation.

This problem of correlating usage levels with performance levels is further demonstrated in Table 3.8. The table provides a quick reference point for understanding which industry sectors appear to be most satisfied with performance relative to their use of tools and techniques. As the table demonstrates in only one case is there a perfect fit between the rank order achieved for usage rates and performance scores. Interestingly enough, the Basic Chemicals sector recorded the highest usage rate (7.50) and the highest performance score (0.80). Once again, however, the performance score was highest at the functional level (0.87) rather that at the firm level (0.73). Despite this obvious correlation between use and performance levels, the second, third and fourth heaviest users of strategy tools and techniques were 14th, 15th and 13th respectively in the rank order for performance scores.

Once again, however, each one of these three sectors reported a higher satisfaction rate for function rather than firm level performance. This indicates that there is no simple correlation between the level of tool and technique use and performance, but that in general the use of those tools and techniques that affect functional performance appear to be more likely to

Table 3.8   **Rank Order Comparisons for Usage and Impact**

Rank Order Usage Scores	Industry Sector	Rank Order Combined Impact Scores	
1 (7.50)	Basic Chemicals	1	(0.80)
2 (7.10)	Aerospace	14	(0.57)
3 (6.38)	Transport Equipment	15	(0.56)
4 (6.14)	Power & Water	13	(0.62)
5 (5.56)	Oil & Gas	8	(0.66)
6 (4.36)	Confectionery	2	(0.78)
7 (3.50)	Healthcare	7	(0.69)
8 (3.40)	Retail Financial Services	10=	(0.63)
9 (3.22)	Computer Hardware	3	(0.76)
10 (2.63)	Retail & Distribution	9	(0.65)
11 (1.67)	Construction	6	(0.71)
12 (1.63)	Publishing	16	(0.43)
13 (1.50)	Telecommunications	10=	(0.63)
14 (1.44)	It Solutions	5	(0.73)
15 (1.38)	Tourism & Leisure	10=	(0.63)
16 (1.33)	Media & Entertainment	4	(0.75)

be successful than those that affect performance at the firm level. The reasons for tool use and performance outcomes is discussed in more detail in the concluding section of this chapter, where an alternative segmentation (based on strategic risks levels) is provided to explain some of these issues in more detail.

The barriers to successful implementation

Notwithstanding the fact that users view the use of strategy tools and techniques positively their implementation can be problematic, as Table 3.9 demonstrates. The table was developed by asking managers using strategy tools and techniques to explain what the proximate causes for failure were when tools or techniques were used unsuccessfully. The basic choices available to respondents were either that there were problems with the tools or techniques themselves (they did not work as expected), or there was nothing wrong with them but there were internal barriers to implementation. The interviewees were also asked if they had evidence to support whether or not the tools or techniques used had failed. If they did not have any data about success or failure and had not measured the performance of the tools or techniques used this was recorded in the no data category. When respondents reported that there were internal barriers they were then provided with a number of choices of internal barriers to select from: the culture of the organisation was opposed; the wrong performance measures were being used; insufficient resource was provided for implementation; senior management was opposed; there was an internal reorganisation that disrupted implementation; the users had unrealistic expectations; and, any other factors.

As the table demonstrates the most significant obstacle to successful implementation was perceived to be the tool or technique itself. As many as 58% of respondents reported that when tools and techniques failed in implementation it was because of tool and technique inadequacy. This seems to indicate that there may be some support for the argument of those who contend that managers are sometimes duped by academics and consultants who develop tools and techniques that do not work in practice. This conclusion may also be supported by the fact that 10% of respondents also lacked any data about the performance of the tools and techniques they were using. This appears to indicate that managers may sometimes be implementing the latest fads without understanding why. On the other hand 32% of respondents overall claimed that failure of implementation occurred due to internal barriers that stopped perfectly acceptable tools and techniques from being implemented.

Of the internal barriers reported three stand out. Fully 30% of the respondents who had experience of failed implementation blamed insufficient resource for failure. This is unsurprising because often managers assume that they can simply introduce new tools and techniques into the

Table 3.9 The Barriers to Effective Implementation in the Strategy Function

Industry	Causes of Failure 100%				Types of Barriers 100%					
	No Data (%)	Tool (%)	Barriers (%)	Culture	Wrong Performance Measure	Insufficient Resource	Senior Management	Disruptive Internal Reorganisation	Unrealistic Expectations	Other
Process/ Manufacturing										
Basic Chemicals	10	72	18	70	0	0	0	20	10	0
Computer Hardware	0	62	38	17	11	17	6	22	0	27
Confectionery	39	14	47	57	9	22	0	0	4	8
Group Average	*17*	*49*	*34*	*48*	*6*	*13*	*2*	*14*	*5*	*12*
Process/ Combined										
Healthcare	19	53	28	25	8	8	0	0	58	1
Power and Water	30	50	20	9	27	36	0	0	9	19
Telecoms	0	85	15	50	0	50	0	0	0	0
Group Average	*16*	*63*	*21*	*28*	*12*	*31*	*0*	*0*	*22*	*7*
Process/Services										
Financial Services	0	27	73	17	2	33	17	6	11	14
Retail and Distribution	13	42	45	35	0	41	6	0	18	0
Group Average	*7*	*34*	*59*	*26*	*1*	*37*	*11*	*3*	*15*	*7*

Table 3.9 The Barriers to Effective Implementation in the Strategy Function – *continued*

Industry	Causes of Failure 100%			Types of Barriers 100%						
	No Data (%)	Tool (%)	Barriers (%)	Culture	Wrong Performance Measure	Insufficient Resource	Senior Management	Disruptive Internal Reorganisation	Unrealistic Expectations	Other
Project/ Manufacturing										
Aerospace	10	50	40	29	3	0	5	16	24	23
Publishing	0	90	10	0	0	67	0	0	33	0
Transport Equipment	9	43	48	30	5	11	11	5	35	3
Group Average	*6*	*61*	*33*	*20*	*3*	*26*	*5*	*7*	*30*	*9*
Project/ Combined										
Construction	12	71	17	0	50	50	0	0	0	0
IT Solutions	0	81	19	0	17	0	17	0	0	66
Oil and Gas	0	68	32	24	5	43	0	5	5	18
Group Average	*4*	*73*	*23*	*8*	*24*	*3*	*5*	*2*	*2*	*28*
Project/Services										
Media & Entertainment	0	61	39	0	0	82	0	9	0	9
Tourism & Leisure	0	63	37	20	10	20	10	0	20	20
Group Average	*0*	*62*	*38*	*10*	*5*	*51*	*5*	*4*	*10*	*15*
Overall Average	10	58	32	24	9	30	5	5	14	13

business without understanding the significant change management resource requirements that are necessary to fully implement new ways of thinking. Relatedly, 24% of respondents reported that failure could also be blamed on cultural opposition. It is clear that this barrier is closely linked to the previous one because, once a new way of thinking is introduced into a business, it is always likely to generate internal opposition as existing standard operating practices are challenged by new ways of thinking and operating. The third most significant barrier to implementation was unrealistic expectations, which was reported by 14% of respondents. This barrier is closely linked to the previous two because managers who wish to innovate often have very high expectations that are not realisable in the short-term given the power structures that currently exist within organisations.

When disaggregating the results by industry sectors and groupings it is clear that, while most of the respondents broadly follow the pattern outlined above, some sectors and groups have slightly different emphasis than others. Thus, the *Project/Services* sector had a much greater concern about tool and technique failure (73%) rather than internal barriers (23%) when compared with *Process/Services*, with only 34% of failure blamed on tool and technique inadequacy. Some sectors were also much more concerned about the inadequacy of tools than others. Thus, the Publishing (90%), the Telecommunications (85%) and IT Solutions (81%) sectors tended to blame tool or technique inadequacy most for failure. In general terms, however, industry sector and grouping differences were not significant.

3.   Conclusions: The appropriateness of the use of tools and techniques for strategic management

Overall it is clear, however, that managers in the strategy function, when they use tools and techniques at all, have a fairly positive view about them. The satisfaction or performance rating is positive both for tools and techniques that assist with function and with firm level improvement, but it is slightly more marked for functional improvement than it is for the firm level. There is also some evidence that when tools and techniques fail they may do so because they are not really *the right tools for the job*. This is indicated by the fact that 58% of respondents reported that failures of implementation occur through the inadequacy of the tool or technique being used. This may support the claims made by some writers that in the strategy area desperate managers are sometimes the unwilling dupes of opportunistic or misguided academics and consultants selling shoddy goods. The reason why this problem may be more apparent in the strategy area is probably because managers in this area are often under constant pressure to develop new ideas. In many other functions the requirement is only for operational effectiveness and efficiency to deliver operationally on the strategic goals of the firm. In the strategy (and also perhaps in marketing and new product development) function managers must innovate or die. In this environment the scope for sometimes 'off the wall' ideas to be tried and tested (and then found wanting) is perhaps most conducive.

That said, it is not the case that all strategy managers are constantly testing new and untried tools and techniques. On the contrary, the evidence presented here shows clearly that managers, if anything, do not use tools and techniques for strategizing as often as they might. Indeed during the interviews the research team often discovered a real antipathy on the part of business managers towards structured ways of thinking about problems. Managers were often highly sceptical of the value of many of the tools and techniques on offer and this probably explains why only 37% of the companies surveyed had a structured tool or technique in place for market research, why only 17% used scenario planning, why only 11% used Porter's Five Forces and why only a derisory 4% used the Growth Share Matrix. The findings demonstrate fairly clearly that, while there may be some gullible managers in the strategy areas, when it comes to tool or technique usage most managers are either agnostic or they believe strategizing is an art not a science. Whichever it is, it is clear that most firms do not go to market very often to buy strategy tools and techniques.

Despite this it is clear that when managers do use tools and techniques for strategizing they tend to use the same tools and techniques as everyone else, and also that most of the tools and techniques that are available in the literature were found to be in use within one or other of the companies surveyed. There was, however, a heavy reliance amongst our survey sample on just a few major tools and techniques amongst users. Thus, market research accounted for (10.04%) of all usages, benchmarking (7.53%), core competence thinking (6.905), SWOT analysis (6.70%), discounted cash flow analysis (5.44%), scenario planning (4.60%) and the balanced scorecard (4.39%).

It is also clear that, despite the view that strategy managers spend most of their time thinking about innovative ideas (sometimes known as 'stretching the envelope' or 'blue skies thinking'), in practice most managers appear to recognise that strategy is only part innovation and it is also just as much about operational delivery, The findings here reinforce that view because there is clear evidence that managers in the strategy area focus just as much, if not more, on tools and techniques for operational effectiveness and efficiency as they do on environmental analysis and competence and product development. This may of course be because operational delivery is easier to manage and implement than external environmental and/or internal competence development, but it does show that strategy managers do understand that certain tools and techniques are right for the job operationally as well as strategically.

This implies that strategy managers that do use tools do have an understanding of *the right tools for the job*, what is more difficult to explain is why some managers in some industry sectors appear to use tools and techniques more than others and with very different levels of success and failure in implementation. The research findings presented here clearly demonstrate that across industry sectors and industry sector groupings there is variable performance and variable usage. It is our view that this difference can be largely explained by consideration of the strategic risks and uncertainty that managers in different industry sectors normally experience. Thus, as we discussed earlier, it can be argued that there are three broad categories of strategic risk that face companies. Companies experiencing *High Strategic Risk* will normally be those that operate in highly competitive or regulated markets and value chains, that have to incur very high levels of capital intensive sunk costs in operational delivery processes and systems, that face severe operational and financial risks if their chosen strategy fails, which results in them having to 'bet the business' on any new product or service offerings. In this category are located the Aerospace, Basic Chemicals, Confectionery, Oil & Gas, Power & Water, Telecommunications and Transport Equipment industry sectors.

At the other extreme is the *Low Strategic Risk* category. In this category are located those industry sectors that are the diametric opposite of high-risk industries. These are industries that do not face fierce competition or regulation, do not have heavy sunk costs in capital intensive operational and financial operating processes and systems and do not face extreme operational and financial risks and uncertainty or have to 'bet the business' on any new product or service offerings. The companies that are located in this category are those from the Media & Entertainment, Publishing and Tourism & Leisure industry sectors. The *Medium Strategic Risk* category includes those firms that are within industries where some but not all of these risks and uncertainty factors are at play. In this study we include the Computer Hardware, Construction, Healthcare, IT Solutions, Retail & Distribution and Retail Financial Services industry sectors.

Given this categorisation of strategic risk types it is fairly clear (as demonstrated in Table 3.10) that firms in the industry sectors characterised as *High Strategic Risk* are much the most likely to use tools and techniques than those that are not. The data confirms that the high-risk industries report an average usage rate of 5.51 compared with 2.64 in the medium and 1.45 in the low risk categories. The performance scores are more interesting. At one level they show that the low risk industry sectors do not experience the same level of performance as the other two risk category industries – whether this is at the firm or the function level. The combined score for firm and function impact in the low risk industries was 0.69. This was much lower than the combined firm and function score recorded for both the high risk (0.66) and medium risk (0.70) category industries.

The data indicates that low risk industries use tools and techniques much less than other industries and rate the performance of the tools and

Table 3.10 The Use and Performance of Strategy Tools and Techniques in High, Medium and Low Risk Sectors

Type of Industry Sectors	Indicators of Use and Performance			
	Average Tool Usage	Performance Impact Scores		
		Firm	Function	Average Combined Score
High Strategic Risk				
Aerospace	7.10	0.55	0.59	0.57
Basic Chemicals	7.50	0.73	0.87	0.80
Confectionery	4.36	0.75	0.80	0.78
Oil & Gas	5.56	0.66	0.65	0.66
Power & Water	6.14	0.56	0.67	0.62
Telecommunications	1.50	0.58	0.67	0.63
Transport Equipment	6.38	0.51	0.61	0.56
Group Average	**5.51**	**0.62**	**0.69**	**0.66**
Medium Strategic Risk				
Computer Hardware	3.22	0.71	0.81	0.76
Construction	1.67	0.65	0.76	0.71
Healthcare	3.50	0.63	0.74	0.69
IT Solutions	1.44	0.70	0.75	0.73
Retail & Distribution	2.63	0.61	0.69	0.65
Retail Financial Services	3.40	0.57	0.69	0.63
Group Average	**2.64**	**0.65**	**0.74**	**0.70**
Low Strategic Risk				
Media & Entertainment	1.33	0.50	1.00	0.75
Publishing	1.63	0.68	0.17	0.43
Tourism & Leisure	1.38	0.62	0.64	0.63
Group Average	**1.45**	**0.60**	**0.60**	**0.60**

technique used positively but at a lower level than the other industry types. This may be an appropriate thing for these industries to do. This is because in the low risk category the risk of not monitoring the external environment strategically may be less problematic than in other industries. This is not to argue that it is sensible to have a low usage rate only that the consequences of not adopting a structured 'scientific' approach to strategic management problems may be lower than in other industries.

The higher level of performance scores for the medium risk category industries, when compared with the high-risk category industries, is not as surprising as might at first be thought. This is because, while high risk industries are compelled to monitor the external environment more than others, their higher level use of tools and techniques in an environment of great risk and uncertainty is likely to result in more frequent disappointment than is likely amongst those who do not have to monitor the external environment or use tools as frequently. Thus, it is probable that the higher performance scores for medium risk category industries are a function both of lower expectations and the emphasis on functional rather firm level operational delivery (where the performance scores were extremely high (0.74) in these industries.

It would appear from this discussion, therefore that, while managers may not always use tools and techniques in the strategy area as extensively as they should, when they do the pattern of use is explicable in terms of the relative risks that have to be managed strategically. This indicates that, while there is evidence of tool and technique failure due to the inadequacy of some of the tools and techniques themselves, when strategy managers use tools and techniques they do so on what appear to be fairly rational calculations associated with the degrees of risk and uncertainty that have to be managed. In this sense, while it may not be possible to say that managers always understand that they are using the right tool all of the time, they do not appear to use them as indiscriminately as some have claimed.

References

Christensen, C. & Raynor, M. (2003) 'Why Hard-Nosed Executives Should Care About Management Theory'. *Harvard Business Review*, March/April.
Micklethwait, J. & Wooldridge, A. (1996) *The Witch Doctors*, London: Heinemann.
Moore, J. I. (1992) *Writers on Strategy and Strategic Management*, Harmondsworth: Penguin.

Part II

Marketing and Sales Management

4
Tools and Techniques for Marketing and Sales Management

The 59 tools and techniques listed below are not definitive but they do provide a comprehensive listing of some of the major tools and techniques regularly used by managers in the marketing and sales function, as well as some of the most recently developed by academics and consultants. These tools and techniques provide a basis for comparison with the actual tools and techniques found to be in use by marketing and sales managers in the research survey. These findings are reported in chapter 5.

1. *(ABC) Activity Based Costing*
See the reference in strategy tools and techniques (chapter 2).

2. *AIO Framework*
This approach to marketing sees respondents presented with questionnaires designed to measure their activities, interests and opinions (AIO). The major dimensions used to measure the AIO elements, and those that segment respondent demographics, are presented below (Figure 4.1):

Activities	Interests	Opinions	Demographics
Work	Family	Themselves	Age
Hobbies	Home	Social Issues	Education
Social Events	Job	Politics	Income
Vacation	Community	Business	Occupation
Entertainment	Recreation	Economics	Family size
Clubs	Fashion	Education	Dwelling
Community	Food	Products	Geography
Shopping	Media	Future	City size
Sports	Achievements	Culture	Stage in cycle

Figure 4.1 Dimensions of AIO Framework
Source: Reprinted with permission from *Journal of Marketing*, published by the American Marketing Association, Kotler, P., January 1974, p. 34.

Once collected, the data can be analysed on a computer to determine distinctive lifestyle groups. When developing a marketing campaign, the strategists will target a particular group, and the advertising department will develop the means of appealing to their distinctive AIO characteristics.

❖ Kotler, P., *Marketing Management* (1997).

3.   Audience Share Research

With particular applicability to audio-visual broadcasting, this is the technique of analysing market share, using third-party figures to monitor performance and benchmark in relation to one's competitors

4.   Balanced Scorecard

See the reference in strategy tools and techniques (chapter 2).

5.   BCG Competitive Advantage Matrix

A company must identify specific ways to differentiate its products and thus obtain competitive advantage. However, the number of differentiation opportunities varies by industry type. The Boston Consulting Group has distinguished four types of industry based on the number of potential competitive advantages and their size (Figure 4.2).

Volume Industry – companies can gain only a few, but rather large, competitive advantages. In the construction-equipment industry, for example, companies can strive for the low-cost position, or the highly differentiated position, and win big on either basis. Profitability tends to be correlated with company size.

Stalemated Industry – there are very few potential competitive advantages, and those available are small. In the steel industry, for example, it is hard to differentiate the product or decrease the manufacturing cost. Companies can attempt to hire better marketing staff, and can entertain more lavishly, but these are small advantages. Profitability is usually unrelated to market share.

Fragmented Industry – companies enjoy many opportunities for differentiation, but each competitive advantage is small. A restaurant, for example, can differentiate in many ways, but still ultimately fail to increase its market share. Profitability is not related to restaurant size.

Specialised Industry – companies have many means to differentiate, each offering a high payoff. A company manufacturing specialised machinery for a selected market segment might be an example. Small companies are potentially as profitable as larger ones in such a market.

❖ Kotler, P., *Marketing Management* (1997).

6.   Benchmarking
See the reference in strategy tools and techniques (chapter 2).

7.   Brand Equity Analysis
This is the process of valuing the intangible elements associated with a product and/or service that add value over and above the cash flow that would be generated if there was no intangible brand value. Often understood in financial transactions as purchasing the 'goodwill' in the products or services. Companies increasingly try to evaluate the financial dimensions of their brands and the equity that may arise from its possession.

8.   Brand Management/Branding Decisions
Serving the purpose of both differentiation and identification, branding constitutes a major issue in product strategy. The challenge for any organisation is to develop brand depth, to develop a customer perception that encompasses six distinct product dimensions – attributes, benefits, associated values, cultural orientation, projected personality, and user type. Branding certainly presents a wide range of decision-making necessities (Figure 4.2):

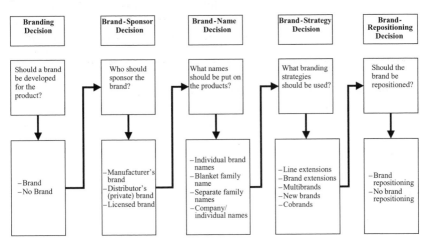

Figure 4.2   An Overview of Branding Decisions
Source: Kotler, Philip, Marketing Management: Analysis, Planning, Implementation and Control, 9th Edition, © 1997. Reprinted by permission of Pearson Education, Inc., Upper Saddle River, NJ.

❖ Kotler, P., *Marketing Management* (1997).

9.   Business Stream Analysis
See the reference in strategy tools and techniques (chapter 2).

10.   Buy-Grid Framework and Buy-Flow Maps
In order to buy necessary goods, business buyers move through a purchasing/procurement process. Organisational marketing has been analysed and

modelled as a cycle with various 'phases' or 'stages' in a *buy-grid framework*. There are three *buy-classes* – new task, modified re-buy, and straight re-buy. Robinson, Faris, and Wind (1967) have also identified eight stages of the industrial buying process, referred to as *buy-phases*:

1) Anticipation and/or recognition of need
2) Determination of features and quantity of required item
3) Specification of the purchase requirement – companies will often assign a product-value-analysis (PVA) engineering team, enabling cost reduction by careful study of components to determine if they can be redesigned, standardised, or produced by cheaper methods
4) Search for the most appropriate suppliers
5) Acquisition and analysis of proposals from potential suppliers – after evaluating the proposals, the buyer will eliminate some suppliers, perhaps inviting those remaining to make a formal presentation
6) Supplier selection – specification of desired supplier attributes, and indication of their relative importance, often through a supplier evaluation model (Figure 4.3).

   The choice and importance of different attributes varies in relation to the buying situation. Delivery reliability, price, and supplier reputation are important for *routine-order products*, but for *procedural-problem prod-*

	Rating Scale				
Attributes	Importance Weights	(1) Poor	(2) Fair	(3) Good	(4) Excellent
Price	0.3				X
Supplier reputation	0.2			X	
Product reliability	0.3				X
Service reliability	0.1		X		
Supplier flexibility	0.1			X	

Total score: 0.3(4) + 0.2(3) + 0.3(4) + 0.1(2) + 0.1(3) = 3.5

Figure 4.3   Supplier Evaluation Model
Source: Kotler, Philip, Marketing Management: Analysis, Planning, Implementation and Control, 9th Edition, © 1997. Reprinted by permission of Pearson Education, Inc., Upper Saddle River, NJ.

ucts, the three most important attributes are technical service, supplier flexibility, and product reliability.

7) Order-routine specification – the buyer negotiates the final order, listing the technical specifications, the quantity needed, the expected time of delivery, return policies, warranties, etc

8) Performance review by three common methods – the buyer may contact end users and ask for their evaluation, may rate the supplier on several criteria using a weighted score method, or may aggregate the cost of poor supplier performance to come up with adjusted costs of purchase

These are the buying stages in a new-task buying situation – in modified re-buy, and straight re-buy, some of the stages would be compressed or bypassed (Figure 4.4):

		Buy - Classes		
		New Task	Modified Re-buy	Straight Re-buy
BUY-PHASES	1. Problem recognition	Yes	Maybe	No
	2. General need description	Yes	Maybe	No
	3. Product specification	Yes	Yes	Yes
	4. Supplier search	Yes	Maybe	No
	5. Proposal solicitation	Yes	Maybe	No
	6. Supplier selection	Yes	Maybe	No
	7. Order-routine specification	Yes	Maybe	No
	8. Performance review	Yes	Yes	Yes

Figure 4.4   Applicability of Buy-Phases to each Buy-Class
Source: Adapted from Patrick J. Robinson, Charles W. Faris and Yoram Wind, *Industrial Buying and Creative Marketing*, 1967.

A *buy-flow map* provides a diagrammatic representation of the major steps in the business buying process. Though useful for descriptive purposes, the *buy-grid framework* should not, however, be taken literally as a managerial model, since it lacks predictive power, and is unable to offer a causative explanation of buying decisions.

❖ Kotler, P., *Marketing Management* (1997).
❖ Lewis, B. R. and Littler, D. (eds), *Blackwell's Encyclopaedic Dictionary of Marketing* (1999).

11. Capture Planning
An agreed approach on how to win a particular segment of business, this may involve a tender approval database. It tends to be quite prescriptive,

and provides a good means of centralising information. Operating as a standard approach across business units, sometimes through a template in paper format, a key challenge is its implementation from an IT perspective. Particularly useful in project-based businesses, capture planning is also utilised in large organisations constrained by the need to act in a co-ordinated way towards key customers.

12.   Competitive Advantage Mapping

An internally developed market assessment technique, competitive advantage mapping analyses the critical success factors for winning new business. It usually includes a variety of categories against which the firm positions itself in relation to competitors on a 1 to 10 scale.

13.   Competitor Analysis

See the reference in strategy tools and techniques (chapter 2).

14.   Consumer-Adoption Process/Innovation-Adoption Model

Marketing managers must understand the consumer adoption process to build an effective strategy for market penetration. It is important they recognise that any innovation – any good, service, or idea that is perceived as new – will take time to spread through the social system. Rogers defines the *innovation diffusion process* as 'the spread of a new idea from its source of invention or creation to its ultimate users or adopters'. Focusing on the mental process through which an individual passes from first hearing about an innovation to final adoption, he identifies five distinct stages – awareness, interest, evaluation, trial, and adoption. A number of factors should, however, be kept in mind:

- People differ markedly in their readiness to try new products. Rogers defines a person's innovativeness as 'the degree to which an individual is relatively earlier in adopting new ideas than other members of his social system'. Rogers categorises adopters on the basis of their relative time of adoption (Figure 4.5).

In line with such adopter classification, an innovating firm should research the demographic, psycho-graphic, and media characteristics of innovators and early adopters, directing communications accordingly.

- Personal influence plays a large role in the adoption of new products.
- Characteristics of the innovation affect its rate of adoption. Five of these are especially influential:

  1) Relative advantage – the degree to which it appears superior to existing products

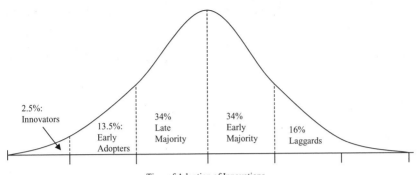

Figure 4.5 Innovation-Adoption Model
Source: Redrawn from Everett M. Rogers, *Diffusion of Innovations* (New York: Free Press, 1983).

2) Compatibility – the degree to which it matches the values and expectations of individuals in the community
3) Complexity – the relative difficulty of understanding and use
4) Divisibility – the extent to which it can be tested out on a limited basis
5) Communicability – the extent to which beneficial results can be
observed or described

- Like people, organisations vary in their readiness to adopt innovation.
Adoption is associated with variables in the organisation's environment
(community progressiveness, community income), the organisation
itself (size, profits, pressure to change), and the administrators (education level, age, sophistication). Once useful indicators are discerned,
they can be used to identify the best target organisations.

15. *Consumer Profiling*
Through market research, it is possible to segment the consumer base in
line with variables such as age, occupation, gender, and geographical location. Some companies extend this analysis to include behavioural and psychological factors. A selection of consumer profiles can be constructed to
enable stereotyping of the customer base. This can be useful for targeting a
strategy or promotional campaign.

Models that analyse consumer behaviour as they move from a state of
unawareness to the purchase of a product or service are summarised below:

AIDA Model
This model demonstrates how a targeted customer progresses from a state
of unawareness of a product or service to eventual purchase. AIDA is an
acronym for Attention ⇒ Interest ⇒ Desire ⇒ Action. Measures are taken
before and after communication, and subsequently used to set objectives

and analyse success. However, logic progression through the stages is not always possible.

❖ Lewis, B. R. and Littler, D. (eds), *Blackwell's Encyclopaedic Dictionary of Marketing* (1999).

Buy-Feel-Learn Model
Typically applies to impulse purchases, where attitudes, knowledge, and liking/preference are developed after purchase.

Feel-Buy-Learn Model
Rather than following the logical sequence of L-F-B, the customer has a feeling for a product or service prior to purchase, but only learns about its actual attributes subsequently.

Learn-Feel-Buy Model
Learning about a product or service through marketing communication, the customer recognises its benefits and develops positive feelings, moving from unawareness to awareness, interest, and liking. This eventually stimulates a sale, and may develop loyalty in the longer term.

❖ Lewis, B. R. and Littler, D. (eds), *Blackwell's Encyclopaedic Dictionary of Marketing* (1999).

Communications Model
An amalgamation from various sources, this is another model outlining stages in a consumer adoption/response hierarchy.

❖ Kotler, P., *Marketing Management* (1997).

DAGMAR Model
Defining Advertising Goals for Measured Advertising Results, this model was developed by Colley (1961) for the specific measurement of advertising effectiveness. It envisages the customer moving from a state of unawareness of the product or service, passing through comprehension and conviction on the route to eventual action.

❖ Lewis, B. R. and Littler, D. (eds), *Blackwell's Encyclopaedic Dictionary of Marketing* (1999).

Hierarchy of Effects Model
Developed by Lavidge & Steiner (1961), this model sees the consumer pass through a cognitive stage (awareness and knowledge) and an affective stage

(liking, preference, and conviction) in moving towards realisation of the conative stage (purchase).

❖ Lewis, B. R. and Littler, D. (eds), *Blackwell's Encyclopaedic Dictionary of Marketing* (1999).

Innovation-Adoption Model
Developed by Rogers (1962), this model postulates a number of stages through which a targeted customer passes from awareness, through interest, evaluation, and trial, to eventual purchase/adoption.

❖ Lewis, B. R. and Littler, D. (eds), *Blackwell's Encyclopaedic Dictionary of Marketing* (1999).

16. Contact Management System
Providing for better interaction with consumers, this tool is particularly useful for large organisations that need to 'speak to the customer with one voice'.

17. Core Competence Thinking
See the reference in strategy tools and techniques (chapter 2).

18. Decision Gates
See the reference in strategy tools and techniques (chapter 2).

19. Direct Marketing
This approach to marketing involves use of one or more communications media for the purpose of soliciting a direct and measurable consumer response. Socio-economic change, increasing use of credit, a customer convenience orientation, rising discretionary income, and developing computer technology and communications media have all stimulated increased use of direct marketing.

❖ Lewis, B. R. and Littler, D. (eds), *Blackwell's Encyclopaedic Dictionary of Marketing* (1999).

20/21/22. E-Business Applications
See the reference to the three applications (Seller/Internal/Buyer) in strategy tools and techniques (chapter 2).

23. Focus Groups
A form of qualitative market research, focus groups are mainly used as an alternative to structured interviews with questionnaires. They tend to come into play in complex situations where direct questioning might not provide satisfactory information.

24.   Four 'Ps' Analysis/Marketing Mix

It was Professor Neil Borden of Harvard Business School who first coined the term 'marketing mix' to describe the most important ingredients in marketing programmes. The best-known 'marketing mix' is McCarthy's 4Ps – product, price, promotion and place. For service industries, the mix is often extended to include people and processes.

❖ Lewis, B. R. and Littler, D. (eds), *Blackwell's Encyclopaedic Dictionary of Marketing* (1999).

25.   Gap Analysis

See the reference in strategy tools and techniques (chapter 2).

26.   Importance-Performance Analysis

An element within the overall analysis of service performance, this involves the rating of services in terms of both customer importance and company performance. By rating elements of the service bundle, such analysis can identify where action is required. Ratings can be displayed in a matrix emphasising those service attributes requiring attention.

27.   Key Account Management

This refers to the approach adopted in relation to those clients most important to a firm's success. In order to serve key customers as successfully as possible, a specific team is often assigned to this brief. The seniority of those involved and the flexibility allowed in negotiations tends to reflect the sensitivity of the account.

❖ Lewis, B. R. and Littler, D. (eds), Blackwell's Encyclopaedic Dictionary of Marketing (1999).

28.   Key Performance Indicators

See the reference in strategy tools and techniques (chapter 2).

29.   Knowledge Management

See the reference in strategy tools and techniques (chapter 2).

30.   Marketing Information Systems

♦ Marketing Decision Support Systems

This is an information system that allows marketing decision-makers to interact directly with databases and models. Examples include Brandaid, Callplan, Detailer, Geoline, Mediac, Promoter, ADCAD, and Coverstory.

❖ Lewis, B. R. and Littler, D. (eds), *Blackwell's Encyclopaedic Dictionary of Marketing* (1999).
❖ Kotler, P., *Marketing Management* (1997).

◆ Marketing Information Systems

These are designed to generate, analyse, store, and distribute information to appropriate marketing decision-makers on a regular basis. They have, however, largely been superseded by marketing decision support systems.

❖ Lewis, B. R. and Littler, D. (eds), *Blackwell's Encyclopaedic Dictionary of Marketing* (1999).

❖ Kotler, P., *Marketing Management* (1997).

◆ Marketing Intelligence Systems

This is a set of procedures used by managers to obtain their everyday information regarding developments pertinent to the marketing environment. Intelligence is gathered by reading books, newspapers, and trade publications; by talking to customers, suppliers, distributors, and other outsiders; and by liasing with other managers and personnel within the company. Successful companies will follow four steps to improve the quality and quantity of their marketing intelligence:

1) Training and motivation of the sales force to spot and report new developments
2) Encouragement of distributors, retailers, and other intermediaries to hand over important intelligence
3) Purchase of information from outside suppliers such as A. C. Nielsen Company and Information Resources Inc.
4) Establishment of an internal marketing information centre to collect and circulate marketing intelligence

❖ Kotler, P., *Marketing Management* (1997), London: Prentice-Hall.

31. *Market Research*

◆ Experimental Research

This is the most scientifically valid research. With extraneous variables kept under control, matched groups are subjected to different treatments, and observed response differences are checked for statistical significance. The aim is to capture cause-and-effect relationships by eliminating competing explanations of the observed findings.

❖ Kotler, P., *Marketing Management* (1997).

◆ In-depth Interviews

This is a qualitative market research technique that sees a highly-skilled individual conducting an unstructured personal interview with a single respondent to probe underlying feelings, motives, opinions, beliefs, and attitudes.

♦ Observation
This is a method of collecting data on a topic of interest by watching and recording behaviour, actions, and facts. Informal, unstructured observation is an everyday means of collecting market information, though better results are likely to be obtained from a planned study. Observers are occasionally disguised, can be human, electronic, or mechanical, and can operate within either a natural or contrived setting.

♦ Questionnaires
These provide a means of questioning respondents. They are the most commonly used instrument for collecting primary data. Questionnaires must be carefully developed, tested, and de-bugged before they are administered on a large-scale.

❖ Kotler, P., *Marketing Management* (1997).

♦ Survey Research
A major source of primary data, surveys can provide information on past and intended behaviour, attitudes, beliefs, opinions, and personal characteristics. The data provided by surveys is basically descriptive, but appropriate analysis can offer evidence of the association between variables.

❖ Lewis, B. R. and Littler, D. (eds), *Blackwell's Encyclopaedic Dictionary of Marketing* (1999).
❖ Kotler, P., *Marketing Management* (1997).

32.   *New Product Development Process*
This process involves eight stages – idea generation, idea screening, concept development and testing, marketing strategy development, business analysis, product development, market testing, and commercialisation (Figure 4.6).

❖ Kotler, P., *Marketing Management* (1997).

33.   *PEST Analysis*
See reference in strategy tools and techniques (chapter 2).

34.   *Plan-o-grams*
This is a technique used for display and merchandising of consumer goods. It enables manufacturers to advise retailers on better methods for the allocation of brands and packs within their available space. Cadburys and Coca-Cola have been pioneers in the use of computerised programmes that recommend both how to utilise retail space more effectively, and take advantage of consumer shopping patterns and perceptions. Such techniques have become common within a fast-moving consumer goods trade,

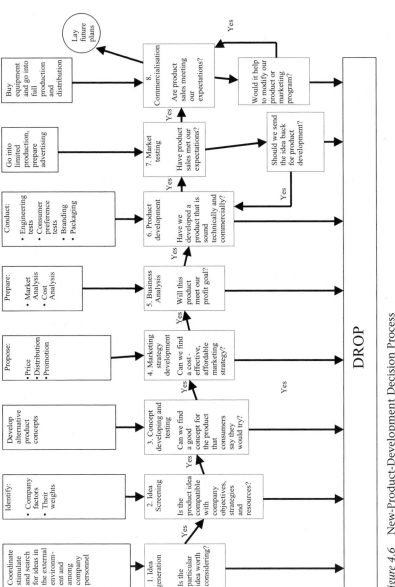

Figure 4.6 New-Product-Development Decision Process
Source: Kotler, Philip, Marketing Management: Analysis, Planning, Implementation and Control, 9th Edition, © 1997. Reprinted by permission of Pearson Education, Inc., Upper Saddle River, NJ.

since firms are increasingly battling for shelf-space with retailers' own brands.

35.   *Porter's Five Forces*
See reference in strategy tools and techniques (chapter 2).

36.   *Portfolio Analysis*
This form of analysis is employed both at a business and product level. At a business level, the aim is to assess the current mix in terms of balance (growing against maturing business, for example). Such techniques generally prescribe the actions to be taken with regard to the portfolio – invest, abandon, etc. The most popular framework is that proposed by the Boston Consulting Group (BCG Growth Share Matrix). Other analytical frameworks have subsequently been developed, deploying different composite variables, but essentially, they all have the same objective.

❖ Lewis, B. R. and Littler, D. (eds), *Blackwell's Encyclopaedic Dictionary of Marketing* (1999).

37.   *Positioning and Perceptual Mapping*
Positioning is the act of designing a company's offering and image in order to occupy a meaningful and distinct competitive position in the mind of its target audience. As such, it refers to the 'position' held by the product in the mind of the consumer. Psychological positioning must be supported by product reality, as otherwise, use experience will undermine the perceptions created by other elements of the marketing mix, and the product will lack sustainability over the longer-term. In developing a positioning strategy, it is crucial to understand product differentiation. Kotler suggests a range of factors that achieve this end:

1) importance to a sufficient number of buyers
2) distinctiveness
3) superiority to other products in achieving the same/more benefit
4) communicability and visibility to buyers
5) difficulty in replication
6) affordability for the target market
7) possibility for the company to engineer – few products are superior to their competitors in all their attributes, but it is often important that they differ in their key dimensions

Many companies advocate promotion of only one benefit to the target market, developing a *unique selling proposition* for each brand. The most commonly promoted 'number-one positions' are 'best quality,' 'lowest price,' 'best value,' 'safest,' 'fastest,' 'most customised,' 'most convenient,'

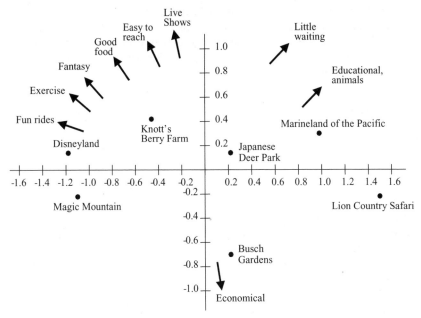

Figure 4.7 Perceptual Map
Source: Kotler, Philip, Marketing Management: Analysis, Planning, Implementation and Control,
9th Edition, © 1997. Reprinted by permission of Pearson Education, Inc., Upper Saddle River, NJ.

and 'most advanced technology.' *Double-benefit positioning* sometimes becomes necessary if two or more firms are claiming superiority of performance in relation to the same attribute. Market analysis is capable of depiction on a perceptual map (Figure 4.7).

This example applies to a competitor desirous of setting up a new theme park. The seven dots represent tourist attractions, and the closer together, the more similar they are in a tourist's mind. The arrows indicate nine elements of satisfaction demanded by consumers in their use of these attractions. Analysing the information provided by this map, the company can determine its options in terms of potential positioning strategies.

❖ Kotler, P., *Marketing Management* (1997).
❖ Lewis, B. R. and Littler, D. (eds), *Blackwell's Encyclopaedic Dictionary of Marketing* (1999).

38. *Price Elasticity*

Similar to the concept of price sensitivity, this term refers to the effect on demand of changes in price. Within elastic (or price sensitive) markets, small changes in price can exert a substantial influence on demand, whereas the inelastic (or price insensitive) market will see relatively little alteration in demand, even as a result of major changes in price. 'Basic' needs like food, health, and housing have traditionally fallen within the inelastic demand category. Availability of product alternatives, variants, and substitutes, and of product prerequisites, can exert a significant impact on the degree of elasticity within a market. The formula for determining this measure is as follows:

Price elasticity of demand = % change in demand/% change in price

❖ Lewis, B. R. and Littler, D. (eds), Blackwell's Encyclopaedic Dictionary of Marketing (1999).

39.   *Pricing Models*
These provide a means of deciding the pricing for a particular product or service. Distinction is usually drawn between decisions relating to existing and new offerings. Substantial market data is often available for existing (or 'established') products, so setting the price is relatively simple. For new products, however, pricing is likely to be an unfamiliar process, and hence, decision-making regularly operates on an intuitive and heuristic basis.

◆ Cost-plus Pricing/Mark-up
With deceptive simplicity, the cost-plus pricing method sums production and distribution costs, adds a suitable profit margin (or mark-up) in line with company policy, and generates an appropriate price. Providing a slight variation, target-return pricing works the cost of capital investment into these calculations, aiming to fix a price that will yield a targeted rate of return. Assumptions with regard to demand and competitive response are the primary problem with such an approach. Cost-plus pricing is certainly not above criticism:

• It is difficult to allocate all relevant costs to individual product variants.
• It takes no account of the discounting and competitive flexibility that provide the area of discretion necessary for negotiating contracts in organisational markets.
• It takes no account of competitive offerings, or the price sensitivity of demand.
• Costs can vary considerably over time, but it is both impractical and undesirable to constantly vary price.

❖ Lewis, B. R. and Littler, D. (eds), *Blackwell's Encyclopaedic Dictionary of Marketing* (1999).

◆ Demand-based Pricing

Using a mixture of market research, managerial experience, and intuition, this technique arrives at a price that is assumed to reflect demand. However, demand-based pricing exhibits several problems:

- It often reflects demand prior to introduction of the new product (though this can be compensated by certain market research techniques).
- Difficult assumptions are necessary with regard to future responses, not only concerning demand, but also in relation to the company's competitors.
- Demand is often influenced by qualitative factors (self-image and risk tolerance), factors that are not easily registered in the quantitative terms necessary for pricing decisions.
- Demand-based prices in consumer markets can only reflect an aggregate assessment of demand, as it would be impractical to vary prices on a case-by-case basis.

❖ Lewis, B. R. and Littler, D. (eds), *Blackwell's Encyclopaedic Dictionary of Marketing* (1999).

◆ Discounted Pricing

Discounts are offered to encourage customers to purchase when it is thought they might not otherwise do so. Discounting is also widely practised in organisational markets, since price is more a matter for negotiation than in the consumer arena. The reasons behind discounting are as follows:

- to encourage purchase in greater quantity than normal
- as a response to competitive developments
- to accelerate sales of outdated stock
- to encourage purchase at 'unpopular' times
- to reduce the customer's perceived risk
- to provide incentives for another product
- to drive out competition with a view to achieving a monopoly (illegal)

❖ Lewis, B. R. and Littler, D. (eds), *Blackwell's Encyclopaedic Dictionary of Marketing* (1999).

◆ Discriminatory Pricing

Price discrimination sees different prices charged to different customers. This practice sometimes seems inequitable, and hence, tends be resisted by customers and avoided by suppliers, but there are plenty of legitimate reasons why it might be necessary to vary price in this manner.

❖ Lewis, B. R. and Littler, D. (eds), *Blackwell's Encyclopaedic Dictionary of Marketing* (1999).

◆ Going-rate Pricing

This approach, also known as initiative pricing, seeks to minimise competitive disruption by setting prices that reflect what might be the going-rate for a parallel product or service. Relatively few new offerings are entirely differentiated in their appeal to the marketplace, and thus, most will compete with existing alternatives or substitutes. By setting prices in line with these established offerings, it is possible to side-step the problems of assessing price sensitivity, whilst also perhaps avoiding immediate competitive response. As with other pricing methods, this technique reflects the three principal problems of determining new-product price – uncertainty about costs, demand, and competitive response.

❖ Lewis, B. R. and Littler, D. (eds), *Blackwell's Encyclopaedic Dictionary of Marketing* (1999).

◆ Marginal Pricing

This technique is utilised on those occasions when a price is calculated to cover only the variable costs of production and distribution, with little or no contribution required towards fixed costs or profit margins. It may be used during a temporary fall in demand (an economic recession, or price war), keeping assets 'ticking over' pending the return of more normal trading conditions.

❖ Lewis, B. R. and Littler, D. (eds), *Blackwell's Encyclopaedic Dictionary of Marketing* (1999).

◆ Penetration Pricing

This is a pricing strategy whereby an organisation uses low-price marketing in order to develop substantial market share very quickly. It can be used by a new entrant to enhance its competitive position in a market dominated by established rivals. Alternatively, it could be used to launch a new product when the initial barriers to competitive entry were thought to be low, and the risk of rival development of imitative products subsequently quite high. Sometimes, a penetration pricing strategy only constitutes a temporary discount, price levels raised in the wake of successful entry into a market. More commonly, however, prices remain largely unchanged, profits achieved by decreasing unit costs in line with economies of scale. Penetration pricing often accelerates the early stages of the product life-cycle.

❖ Lewis, B. R. and Littler, D. (eds), *Blackwell's Encyclopaedic Dictionary of Marketing* (1999).

◆ Perceived-value Pricing

Hedonic or perceived-value pricing regards products and services as 'clusters of desirable attributes'. Each of these is allocated a 'price' component, subsequently combined to generate the total price. A washing machine, for example, might merit different price components according to such variables as spin speed, the time taken by its wash cycles, the availability of economy settings, the strength of its brand, the ease of servicing, etc.

❖ Lewis, B. R. and Littler, D. (eds), *Blackwell's Encyclopaedic Dictionary of Marketing* (1999).

◆ Predatory Pricing
This approach involves heavy discounting in a deliberate attempt to drive out competition, the aim being to achieve a monopoly situation whereby prices can be raised to exploitative levels. Predatory pricing is illegal in most countries, but it is sometimes difficult to distinguish unambiguously between vigorous discounting (price war) and more unethical practices.

❖ Lewis, B. R. and Littler, D. (eds), *Blackwell's Encyclopaedic Dictionary of Marketing* (1999).

◆ Promotional Pricing
Price promotions demand short-term adjustment in the price of an existing product/service. They are often prompted by disappointing sales resulting from an economic downturn, competitor activities, or seasonal trends. Such adjustment must take into account an estimate of price elasticity in order to ensure that the alteration of prices is worthwhile.

❖ Lewis, B. R. and Littler, D. (eds), *Blackwell's Encyclopaedic Dictionary of Marketing* (1999).

◆ Regulated Pricing
This is the practice of setting prices externally, and is usually applied by regulatory agencies (legal fines, wage councils), and political decision-makers (prescription charges).

❖ Lewis, B. R. and Littler, D. (eds), *Blackwell's Encyclopaedic Dictionary of Marketing* (1999).

40. *Product Idea Rating Device*
Most companies require ideas to be described on a standard form that can be reviewed by their new-product committee. This will outline the product idea, the target market, the time and costs, and the rate of return. Market opportunity can then be assessed in terms of the company's objectives and resources by asking certain prescribed questions (Figure 4.8). Surviving ideas are rated using a weighted-index method (Figure 4.9).

Factors for a successful product launch having been listed, the management assign a weight to reflect their relative importance, and score the

112

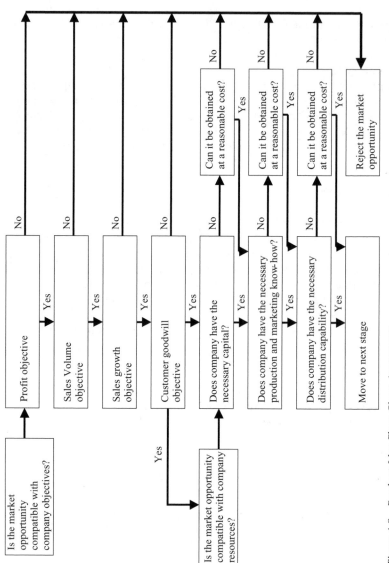

Figure 4.8 Product Idea Flow-Chart Assessment
Source: Kotler, Philip, Marketing Management: Analysis, Planning, Implementation and Control, 9th Edition, © 1997. Reprinted by permission of Pearson Education, Inc., Upper Saddle River, NJ.

Product Requirements	Success	(1) Relative Weight	(2) Product Score	(3 = 1*2) Product Rating
Unique or superior product		0.4	0.8	0.32
High performance-to-cost ratio		0.3	0.6	0.18
High marketing dollar support		0.2	0.7	0.14
Lack of strong competition		0.1	0.5	0.05
TOTAL		1.0		0.69*

* Rating scale: 0– 0.3 poor; 0.31– 0.6 fair; 0.61– 0.8 good. Minimum acceptance rate: 0.61

Figure 4.9   Product Idea Rating Device
Source: Kotler, Philip, Marketing Management: Analysis, Planning, Implementation and Control, 9th Edition, © 1997. Reprinted by permission of Pearson Education, Inc., Upper Saddle River, NJ.

product on each factor (0–1). Each factor's importance is then multiplied by the product score to obtain an overall rating of the company's ability to launch the product successfully. As the product moves through development, however, the company must constantly revise its estimate of the overall probability of success using the following formula:

Overall probability of success	=	Probability of technical completion	×	Probability of commercialisation given technical completion	×	Probability of economic success given commercialisation

❖ Kotler, P., *Marketing Management* (1997).

41. *Product-line Analysis*
In order to determine which items to build, maintain, harvest, and divest, the line manager must fully evaluate each of his products, considering a range of aspects:

<u>Product-line Sales and Profits</u> – the percentage of total sales and profits contributed by each item (Figure 4.10):

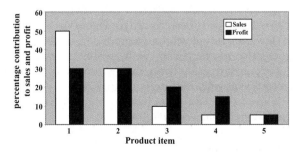

Figure 4.10   Product-Line Sales and Profits
Source: Kotler, Philip, Marketing Management: Analysis, Planning, Implementation and Control, 9th Edition, © 1997. Reprinted by permission of Pearson Education, Inc., Upper Saddle River, NJ.

<u>Product-line Market Profile</u> – positioning of the product-line in relation to those of its competitors (Figure 4.11):

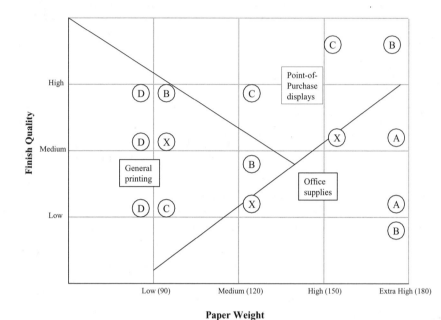

Paper Weight

Figure 4.11   Product Map for a Paper Product-Line
Source: Kotler, Philip, Marketing Management: Analysis, Planning, Implementation and Control, 9th Edition, © 1997. Reprinted by permission of Pearson Education, Inc., Upper Saddle River, NJ.

<u>Product-line Length</u> – the optimum and appropriate length of the product-line needs to be considered. Company objectives are influential – those seeking high market share or market growth will carry longer lines, exhibiting less concern when items fail to contribute to profits, whilst those emphasising high profitability will carry shorter lines consisting of more carefully chosen items. Product-lines tend to lengthen over time, either by *line-stretching* or *line-filling*. The former occurs when a company lengthens the product-line beyond its current range (Figure 4.12), either by downward stretch (lower-quality, lower-price products), upward stretch (higher-quality, higher-price products), or two-way stretch (both of the above). Line-filling, by contrast, sees the existing product-line lengthened by addition of more items within its present range.

❖ Kotler, P., *Marketing Management* (1997).

42.   *Product-mix Decisions*
A product-mix is the set of items that a particular firm offers for sale, characterised by a certain width, length, depth, and consistency. It will consist

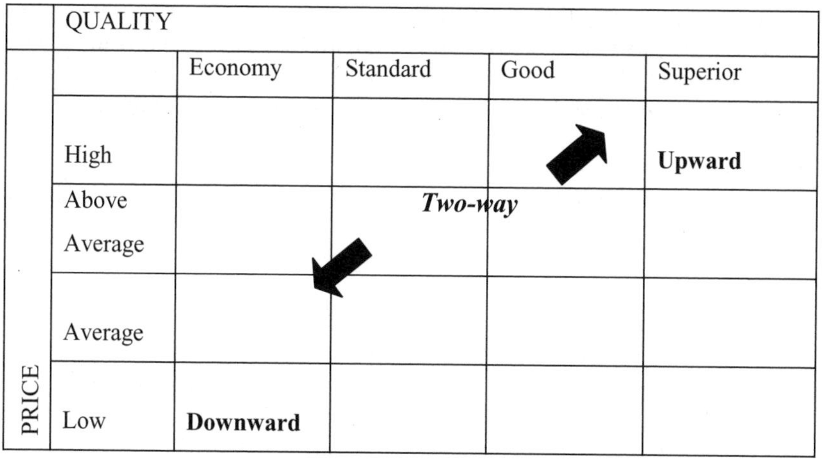

QUALITY				
	Economy	Standard	Good	Superior
High				Upward
Above Average		*Two-way*		
Average				
Low	**Downward**			

(PRICE — vertical axis label)

Figure 4.12   Product-Line Stretching
Source: Kotler, Philip, Marketing Management: Analysis, Planning, Implementation and Control, 9th Edition, © 1997. Reprinted by permission of Pearson Education, Inc., Upper Saddle River, NJ.

of various product lines, groups of product that are closely related because they perform a similar function, are sold to the same customer group, marketed through the same channel, or fall within a given price range.

❖ Kotler, P., *Marketing Management* (1997).

43.   *Project Management Techniques*
See the reference in strategy tools and techniques (chapter 2).

44.   *Promotion Evaluation System*
Essentially, this involves evaluating the success of a promotional campaign. It may demand testing before launch with a trial run, or piloting to a sub-group of the customer base. This can prove crucial in increasing a campaign's effectiveness, and may generate cost savings by improving the campaign itself, or by pinpointing particular market segments as likely targets. If the evaluation is conducted after the campaign's completion, the information may prove useful for future campaigns.

45.   *Relationship Marketing*
This notion has emerged owing to dissatisfaction with the traditional marketing literature when applied to business-to-business and services marketing. Rather than taking a 'one sale at a time' approach, relationship marketing means adopting a longer-term approach to marketing strategy that sees the development and maintenance of relationships with individual customers as fundamental in its importance. Such an approach is particularly relevant in relation to business customers, since long-term relations

are more likely, and the customer base is smaller. However, relationship marketing has also gained advocates as regards the general consumer. The rationale forwarded for its use is the high degree of correlation between retention and profitability. Established customers tend to buy more, are more predictable, and usually cost less to service than new customers. They also tend to be less price-sensitive, and may provide free word-of-mouth advertising and referral. Retaining customers makes it more difficult for competitors to enter the market or increase share, and furthermore, avoids the considerable cost of recruiting new buyers.

46.   *Reverse Engineering*
In order to break down and understand a competitor's cost structure, their products are dismantled in reverse engineering. By ascertaining build cost and technology utilised, a firm can identify potential efficiency improvements of its own.

47.   *Scenario Planning*
See reference in strategy tools and techniques (chapter 2).

48.   *Service Quality Model*
Parasuraman, Zeithaml and Berry have formulated a service-quality model (Figure 4.13) that identifies the five gaps responsible for unsuccessful service delivery:

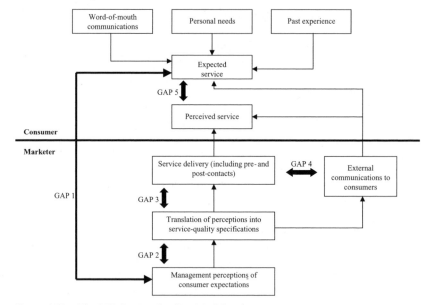

Figure 4.13   The PZB Service Quality Model
Source: Reprinted with permission from *Journal of Marketing*, published by the American Marketing Association, Kotler, P., Fall 1985, p. 44.

1) <u>Gap between consumer expectation and management perception</u> – management does not always perceive correctly what customers want.
2) <u>Gap between management perception and service-quality specifications</u> – managers may accurately perceive customer wants, but fail to set the appropriate performance standards.
3) <u>Gap between service-quality specifications and service delivery</u> – personnel may be poorly trained, incapable, or unwilling to meet the required standards, and sometimes, they are held back by conflicting demands.
4) <u>Gap between service delivery and external communications</u> – affected by advertising and the statements of company representatives, customer expectations may be distorted by external communication.
5) <u>Gap between perceived service and expected service</u> – occasionally, as a result of misinterpretation, the consumer may misconstrue the level of service.

The same researchers also recognised five determinants of service quality. These are presented in order of importance as rated by customers (from an allocation of 100 points):

1) <u>Reliability</u> – the ability to perform the promised service dependably and accurately (32)
2) <u>Responsiveness</u> – the willingness to help customers and provide prompt service (22)
3) <u>Assurance</u> – the knowledge and courtesy of employees, and their ability to inspire trust and confidence (19)
4) <u>Empathy</u> – the provision of caring, individualised attention to customers (16)
5) <u>Tangibles</u> – the appearance of physical facilities, equipment, personnel, and materials of communication (11)

Service companies that are managed to a high standard of excellence have been seen to exhibit the following common features:

- a strategic concept
- a history of top-management commitment to quality
- high standards
- a system for monitoring service performance
- a system for satisfying customer complaints
- an emphasis on employee satisfaction

❖ Kotler, P., *Marketing Management* (1997).

49.   Seven 'S' Framework
Strategy is only one of the elements present in the best-managed companies. A seven 'S' framework is recommended for achieving competitive

advantage. The first three elements – strategy, structure, and systems – are the 'hardware' of success. The next four – style, staff, skills, and shared values – are the supportive 'software' for strategy implementation.

❖ Kotler, P., *Marketing Management* (1997).

50.　SMART Targets
For the purpose of performance measurement, the 'SMART' technique is used to set objectives and targets that are specific and quantifiable.

51.　Sponsorship
An element of the marketing communications mix, sponsorship is the provision of assistance by an organisation, financial or in kind, for the purpose of achieving its commercial objectives. The objectives of sponsorship are as follows:

- keeping the company name in the public eye
- building or altering perceptions of the organisation, and thus gaining goodwill
- portraying a socially concerned and community-involved company
- identifying with a target market, and thus promoting products and brands
- countering adverse publicity
- aiding with recruitment

Sponsorship is typically associated with the arts, sport, and community activities, and hence, companies are seen to be supporting these 'events'. The sponsoring organisation aims to establish high visibility, to gain credibility through its association with the development and success of a venture. A major problem with sponsorship, however, is measurement of its cost-effective performance.

❖ Lewis, B. R. and Littler, D. (eds), *Blackwell's Encyclopaedic Dictionary of Marketing* (1999).

52.　Statistical Analysis Techniques

♦ Bivariate Analysis
This technique is concerned with quantitative analysis of data when analysing a pair of variables. Data can be displayed using a scatter diagram, and numerically, using simple correlation and regression – the product-moment correlation coefficient measures the strength of a linear relationship between the variables. If variables are measured using an ordinal scale then Spearman's rank or Kendall's tau may be used to indi-

cate the strength of the relationship. A range of hypothesis tests are available to determine if the relationship obtained is significant (chi-squared, t-test, F-test, etc).

◆ Cluster Analysis
This is the body of techniques used to identify similar objects and individuals. Using measurements on several variables for a number of cases, a small number of exclusive and exhaustive groups are formed.

◆ Conjoint Analysis
This set of techniques allows a researcher to determine the relative importance placed by respondents on different attributes, and the utilities assigned to different values of each attribute, when selecting from amongst several brands.

◆ Descriptive Statistics
Unless the sample in a market research project is very small, the data is tabulated and analysed by a computer. The simplest kind of statistical analysis involves summarising the data and describing the results for the sample. A more complicated alternative employs statistical inference, and may also incorporate confidence intervals and hypothesis testing.

◆ Discriminant Analysis
This technique is utilised when there are observations from a sample of population on many variables for cases that belong to two or more known groups. The purpose of discriminant analysis is to use this data about individuals whose group membership is known to facilitate the classification of individuals whose membership is unknown to one or other of the groups.

◆ Factor Analysis
This type of multivariate analysis is concerned with the inter-relationships within a set of variables. The procedure involves construction of a number of factors to explain variation in the measured variables. Data reduction is the result, as the number of factors created is less that the number of variables.

◆ Forecasting
Strategists rely upon long-term forecasting of changes in the environment, and of demand for both current and potential products in different markets and segments. However, marketing managers also apply medium-term forecasting to support their decision-making in relation to pricing and the allocation of resources.

♦ Graphical Representation
The results of marketing research can be presented in a graphical format as part of the reporting procedure.

♦ Multi-dimensional Scaling
This is the generic name given to a number of procedures related to attitude and image research. Its main uses in marketing are in attribute mapping, product positioning, and the identification of ideal brand points. It may also enable gaps in the customer offering to be spotted, providing motivation for the design of new products.

♦ Multivariate Analysis
This involves consideration of the relationships between more than two variables, and hence, operates as an extension of univariate and bivariate analysis.

♦ Principal Component Analysis
This is a multivariate statistical technique, similar to factor analysis, which attempts to represent the inter-relationships within a set of variables. Its first step is to identify the linear function of the variables with the largest variance, so that this newly created artificial (or latent) variable represents as much as possible of the variability of the original data. It then chooses a second linear function, independent of the first principal component, which explains as much as possible of the remaining variability. This process continues until one chooses to call a halt, the idea being to obtain some economy in the representation of data.

♦ Regression and Correlation
The possibility of a relationship between a pair of variables can be investigated using a scatter diagram. Simple correlation measures the strength of a relationship between two variables – the best measure is the product-moment correlation coefficient, which ranges from –1 to +1. A correlation coefficient whose magnitude is equal to 1 indicates a perfect linear relationship, while a value of 0 indicates no relationship at all. Bivariate regression measures the relationship between a pair of variables, fitting a straight line to the scatter of points.

♦ Structural Equation Models
These bring together research methods in a holistic way. Hypothetical relationships between variables are represented in a network of causal and functional paths.

♦ **Univariate Analysis**
This technique is concerned with the quantitative analysis of data, each variable considered in isolation. It often provides the basis for preliminary analysis of a survey.

❖ Lewis, B. R. and Littler, D. (eds), *Blackwell's Encyclopaedic Dictionary of Marketing* (1999).

53. Succession Planning
See reference in strategy tools and techniques (chapter 2).

54. SWOT Analysis
See reference in strategy tools and techniques (chapter 2).

55. Technology Watch
See the reference in strategy tools and techniques (chapter 2).

56. TQM Techniques
Total quality management is an approach that seeks to improve the quality of the value proposition that the organisation delivers to the customer in the most effective and efficient way possible. Based on the ideas of continuous improvement it requires the whole organisation to embrace the concept and cannot be undertaken by a department or group of managers alone. It requires the company to work as one team to focus on quality improvement in all systems and processes. Some times referred to as the Deming philosophy.

❖ Deming, W. E., Quality, *Productivity and Competitive Position* (1982).

57. VALS (2)
Introduced in 1978, SRI International's Values and Lifestyles (VALS) framework has been the only commercially available psycho-graphic segmentation to gain widespread acceptance. Revised in 1989, VALS 2 focuses more explicitly on explaining and understanding consumer behaviour. It classifies adults into eight consumer groups based on their answers to 35 attitudinal and 4 demographic questions (Figure 4.14). In 1996, the smallest two groups, Fulfilleds and Strugglers, each accounted for about 10% of the adult population, while the other segments each represented between 12 and 16%. The four groups with 'greater resources' display the following tendencies:

Actualisers – successful, sophisticated, active, 'take-charge' people. Purchases often reflect cultivated tastes for relatively up-scale, niche-oriented products.

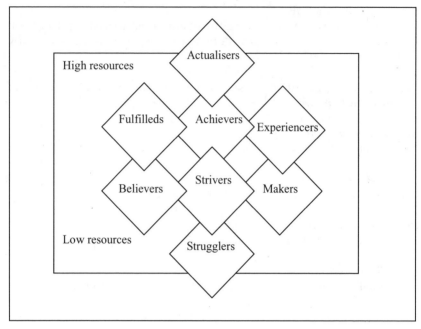

Figure 4.14   VALS (2) Consumer Groups
Source: SRI International, Menlo Park, CA VALS™ 2 is a trademark of SRI International.

Fulfilleds – mature, satisfied, comfortable, and reflective. Favour durability, functionality, and value-for-money in their products.

Achievers – successful career- and work-oriented people. Favour established prestige products that demonstrate success to their peers.

Experiencers – young, vital, enthusiastic, impulsive, and rebellious. Spend a comparatively high proportion of their income on clothing, fast food, music, movies, and videos.

The major tendencies of the four groups with 'fewer resources' are outlined below:

Believers – conservative, conventional, and traditional. Favour familiar products and established brands.

Strivers – uncertain, insecure, approval-seeking, resource-constrained people. Favour stylish products that emulate the purchases of those with greater material wealth.

Makers – practical, self-sufficient, traditional, and family-orientated. Favour products with a functional purpose.

Strugglers – elderly, resigned, passive, concerned, resource-constrained. Cautious consumers, loyal to their favourite brands.

❖ Kotler, P., *Marketing Management* (1997), London: Prentice-Hall.

58.   *Value Based Management*
See reference in strategy tools and techniques (chapter 2).

59.   *Value Chain Analysis*
See reference in strategy tools and techniques (chapter 2).

5
The Use of Marketing and Sales Management Tools and Techniques

For students or managers exposed to the marketing and sales arena for the first time it can be like entering a different country, with a language all of its own. It is a world of dogs, cows, wildcats and problem children. It is a world where practitioners talk about above-the-line and below-the-line, use E-metrics and undertake probability samples. For this reason marketing has given rise to so many different tools and techniques that it would come as something of a surprise if practitioners did not make extensive use of codified management practices.

However, the abundance of marketing tools and techniques is not the only reason why the function might have 'scientific' pretensions. Marketing decisions are often amongst the most important that firms have to take, and frequently under the most difficult of circumstances. First, in many areas the distinction between strategy and marketing is so blurred as to be meaningless. When a marketer considers the markets in which the firm should position, he or she is actually raising questions about corporate strategy (Kotler, 1994). Nothing could be more important to the firm. Second, even in those areas where the two functions do not fully overlap – like promotions, for example – many of the decisions are business critical. Companies like Cadburys-Schweppes, BMW, Virgin Atlantic and Tesco rely as much on branding as on products and services for success (Macrae, 1991).

At the same time, the background against which many of these decisions are taken can be challenging to say the least. In the area of IT and the Internet, for example, the turnover of new technologies is very quick and the product life cycle is very short (Evans & Wurster, 2000). A marketing strategy developed in one month might be redundant in the next due to the introduction of a new product by a competitor. Often two competitors are racing to introduce similar products into the same market. How the two products are positioned relative to one another can make the difference between success and failure. The competition between VHS and to Betamax technologies in the early video recording market is now well known. The promoters of Betamax technologies attempted to sell their products. VHS manufacturers, by contrast, brought their product to market through rental. Betamax, although generally regarded as having a superior product technically, failed and VHS became the industry standard.

The combination of key decisions being taken under high levels of market uncertainty means that for this function the need for codified tools and techniques ought to dovetail neatly with supply. At the same time, however, the acute uncertainties in the environment in which the tools and techniques have to be implemented may also impact on their effectiveness and also act as a deterrent to their use. The marketing survey, therefore, examines the use of marketing and sales tools and techniques in their widest sense.

Rather than just focusing on the use of promotional tools like the 4Ps, or key marketing philosophies such as relationship marketing, it also examines the use of strategic tools like PEST analysis and Porter's five forces. The first two groups of tools and techniques considered, therefore, consist of those that marketing and sales has in common with the strategy function (*market and environmental analysis* and *product and competence development*). Thereafter, the remaining business activities group tools and techniques that are peculiar to marketing and sales like *promotion and relationship management* and *pricing*, with the generic functional grouping of tools and techniques related to *performance management* and *IT and Internet applications* as well.

The chapter is arranged in the same manner as the other analytic chapters. It reports the survey findings by assessing the general use of tools and techniques in marketing and sales, and the uses related to specific business activities within the function. The use of these tools and techniques across industry sectors and industry sector groupings is also reported, as is their overall performance. The chapter concludes with a discussion of the barriers to successful implementation and some tentative arguments are provided to explain the pattern of use and performance.

1. The general use of tools and techniques in marketing and sales

The discussion that follows provides a description of the general use of marketing and sales tools and techniques in total, and across the 6 business activities outlined earlier in chapter 1. The analysis then focuses on the use of tools and techniques across the 16 industry sectors and the 6 industry sector groupings also outlined in chapter 1.

The use of tools and techniques in general

The survey was conducted in 116 companies (as outlined in Appendix C) and, as Table 5.1 indicates, 48 tools and techniques were discovered to be in use, with 465 total usages across the companies surveyed. This compares

Table 5.1 The Total Use of Marketing Tools and Techniques (*48 Tools with 465 Tool Usages in Total Recorded*)

Tool	Incidence	%	Tool	Incidence	%
Pricing Models	88	18.81	4Ps Analysis	3	0.65
Market Research	56	11.98	Activity Based Costing	3	0.65
Consumer Profiling	45	9.63	Audience Share Research	3	0.65
SWOT Analysis	23	4.93	Balanced Scorecard	3	0.65
E-Business-Seller Side Software	22	4.71	Core Competence Thinking	3	0.65
Benchmarking	20	4.28	Plan o Grams	3	0.65
Competitor Analysis	19	4.07	TQM Techniques	3	0.65
Relationship Marketing	19	4.07	Sponsorship	3	0.65
Brand Management	13	2.79	Capture Planning	2	0.44
Focus Groups	13	2.79	BCG Competitive Adv. Matrix	2	0.44
Porter's Five Forces	13	2.79	Decision Gates	2	0.44
Portfolio Matrix	11	2.36	E-Business-Buy Side Software	2	0.44
Promotion Evaluation System	11	2.36	Product Mix Decisions	2	0.44
PEST Analysis	9	1.93	Scenario Planning	2	0.44
Gap Analysis	7	1.51	Succession Planning	2	0.44
New Product Development	7	1.51	Value Chain Analysis	2	0.44
E-Business-Internal Applications	6	1.29	Brand Equity Analysis	1	0.24
Key Performance Indicators	6	1.29	Business Stream Analysis	1	0.24
Knowledge Management	6	1.29	Competitive Advantage Mapping	1	0.24
Price Elasticity	6	1.29	Contact Management System	1	0.24
Direct Marketing	5	1.07	Reverse Engineering	1	0.24
Key Account Management	4	0.87	SMART Targets	1	0.24
Marketing Information System	4	0.87	Technology Watch	1	0.24
Project Management Techniques	4	0.87	Value Based Management	1	0.24

with a total of 61 tools and techniques itemised in the literature search (see chapter 4) and indicates that only 11 tools and techniques were discovered not to be in use in one company or another. The full listing of the tools and techniques in use is provided in Table 5.1; Table 5.2 lists the 11 tools and techniques not found to be in use in this survey. Interestingly, virtually all of the tools and techniques not found to be in use were those that might be characterised as specific to the marketing and sales function, rather than those that are well known and that might also be seen of direct relevance to the strategy function. This indicates, perhaps, that there may be something of a 'herding instinct' within the strategy and marketing and sales functions when it comes to tool and technique use. On the other hand, it could mean that some of the more esoteric marketing and sales tools and techniques may not be well known within the function and, therefore, rarely implemented.

As one might expect the marketing and sales function tends to use more tools and techniques than any other function (although only slightly more than the strategy function), and this is a measure of the criticality of what this function does for the survival and success of the firm in generating revenue, as well as an indication of the uncertainty that must be managed as well. The most commonly used tool and technique, as one might expect, is pricing models (18.81% of total usages). This is unsurprising because firms cannot really operate effectively against their competition, or in transactions with their customers, unless they have thought through in a rigorous and robust way what their strategy ought to be in relation to the pricing of their products and/or services. Thus the use of demand and value based, discounted or marginal and penetration pricing approaches was common amongst respondents. What is perhaps more surprising is that only 86% (88 from 116) of our respondents were utilising structured pricing strategy models. This meant that 14% did not think this through formally at all.

Table 5.2 **The 11 Marketing and Sales Tools and Techniques Not Found in Use**

AIO Framework
Buy-grid Framework and Buy-flow Maps
Consumer-Adoption Process/Innovation-Adoption Model
Importance-Performance Analysis
Positioning and Perceptual Mapping
Product Idea Rating Device
Product-line Analysis
Service Quality Model
Seven 'S' Framework
Statistical Analysis Techniques
VALS (2)

The second most popular tool or technique was market research (11.98% of total usages), closely followed by consumer profiling (9.63%) and SWOT Analysis (4.93%). Each of these tools and techniques for *market and environmental analysis* were also used in the strategy function survey, as was E-Business Seller-side software (4.71%), benchmarking (4.28%), competitor analysis (4.07%), Porter's five forces (2.79%) and the portfolio matrix (2.36%). These findings reinforce the view that the marketing and sales function is often duplicating the activities of the strategy function. Whether this is a good or bad practice is not possible to ascertain from the survey results available. We merely record the fact that there is such. a duplication of effort within the functions.

After these findings the marketing and sales specific tools and techniques (alongside the most popular pricing models) start to appear in use. Thus relationship marketing scores 4.07 total usages, brand management 2.79%, focus groups 2.79%, promotion evaluation systems 2.36%, new product development processes 1.51%, price elasticity analysis 1.29%, direct marketing 1.07% and key account management 0.87%. Despite this it is clear that, as in the strategy function, companies appear to rely quite extensively on a small number of tools and techniques that are used extensively. Thus, the findings show that the top eight tools and techniques account for 62.48% of total tool and technique usage overall. Furthermore, of these eight only two can be regarded as specific to the marketing and sales function (pricing models with 18.81% of total usages and relationship marketing with 4.07%). This means that tools and techniques that are also in regular use in the strategy function appear to account for 40.60% of total major tool and technique usage, while only 22.88% is accounted for by marketing and sales specific tools and techniques.

As Table 5.1 also indicates there is a very long tail of tools and techniques – most of which are specific to the marketing and sales functional role – which have only one or two recorded usages. This finding reinforces what was discovered in the strategy survey and this is that, while most tools and techniques that have been isolated in the literature are in use they are not always in use by very many companies. This means that only a few popular tools and techniques appear to be used by most firms most of the time, and these are often duplicates of those used more regularly in the strategy function.

The use of tools and techniques by business activity

As indicated above it is clear that the marketing and sales function tends to share many of the same tools and techniques as those found to be in use in the strategy function. Thus, as Table 5.1 indicates, 25 of the tools and techniques found to be in use in marketing and sales were also reported to be in use by respondents in the survey of the strategy function. Despite this fear of a duplication of effort in the use of tools and techniques for *market and environmental analysis* and *product and competence development* business activities (see Table 5.3 and compare it with Table 3.3), there is clear evidence that the marketing and sales function does use tools and techniques that are not primarily found in the strategy function. These non-duplicated tools and techniques are normally those that are used for the *pricing* and *promotion and relationship management business* activities in marketing and sales. Many, if not all, of the tools and techniques used for the *performance management* and *IT and Internet applications* business activities are, however, also similar to those found in other functions (i.e. benchmarking, KPIs, activity based costing, the balanced scorecard and E-Business seller, buyer and internal applications).

As Table 5.3 demonstrates the most popular business activities in terms of total tool and technique usage were *market and environmental analysis* (49.21%) and *product and competence development* (33.72%). These are the two business activity areas that use very similar tools and techniques as those in the strategy function. It is not, however, until the third and fourth business activity groupings that the more functionally specific marketing and sales tools and techniques begin to appear in use. The third most popular business activity for total usage was *pricing* (29.34%). In this business activity pricing models and price elasticity analysis tools were being used regularly. The fourth most popular business activity *promotion and relationship management* had 26.65% of total usages. It is in this business activity that one also sees the use of many of the most functionally specific tools and techniques – like relationship marketing, brand management, focus groups, promotion evaluation, direct marketing and key account management – being used.

The total usage of these functionally specific tools and techniques slipped some way from the usage rates recorded in the areas that are also addressed by the strategy function (like *market and environmental analysis* and product and *competence development* activities). There is also evidence that few of these functionally specific tools and techniques for marketing and sales are being used extensively across the respondent companies. The more operational, *performance management* (13.14% of total usages) and the *IT and Internet application* (6.44%) business activities are also not apparently used as extensively as one might have expected. This is all somewhat surprising given the relatively large budgets normally granted to marketing and sales functions to develop their capabilities compared with other functions. Once again this appears to provide evidence that, rather than managers being the gullible dupes of self-interested academics and consultants, there is either a lack of awareness of the availability of tools and techniques or there is a genuine reluctance or scepticism about using them in most of the companies surveyed.

Table 5.3   The Use of Marketing and Sales Tools and Techniques by Business
Activity

(The total % figures do not sum to 100% because some tools and techniques can be
used for more than one business activity)

Rank Order of Tools and Techniques by Business Activities	Tools and Techniques	% of Total Usage Recorded	Total Business Activity Usage Score
1 Market & Environmental Analysis	Market Research	11.98	
	Consumer Profiling	9.63	
	Swot Analysis	4.93	
	Benchmarking	4.28	
	Competitor Analysis	4.07	
	Focus Groups	2.79	
	Porter's Five Forces	2.79	
	Portfolio Matrix	2.36	
	Pest Analysis	1.93	
	Marketing Information Systems	0.87	49.21%
	4ps Analysis	0.65	
	Audience Share Research	0.65	
	Competitive Advantage Matrix	0.44	
	Scenario Planning	0.44	
	Value Chain Analysis	0.44	
	Brand Equity Analysis	0.24	
	Business System Analysis	0.24	
	Competitive Advantage Mapping	0.24	
	Technology Watch	0.24	
2 Product and Competence Development	Consumer Profiling	9.63	
	Benchmarking	4.28	
	Competitor Analysis	4.07	
	Brand Management	2.79	
	Focus Groups	2.79	
	Portfolio Matrix	2.36	
	Gap Analysis	1.51	
	New Product Development Process	1.51	33.72%
	Knowledge Management	1.29	
	Project Management Techniques	0.87	
	Core Competence Thinking	0.65	
	TQM Techniques	0.65	
	Capture Planning	0.44	
	Decision Gates	0.44	
	Product Mix Decisions	0.44	

Table 5.3 **The Use of Marketing and Sales Tools and Techniques by Business Activity** – *continued*

(The total % figures do not sum to 100% because some tools and techniques can be used for more than one business activity)

Rank Order of Tools and Techniques by Business Activities	Tools and Techniques	% of Total Usage Recorded	Total Business Activity Usage Score
3 Pricing	Pricing Models	18.81	
	Benchmarking	4.28	
	Competitor Analysis	4.07	29.34%
	Price Elasticity	1.29	
	Activity Based Costing	0.65	
	Value Based Management	0.24	
4 Promotion and Relationship Management	Consumer Profiling	9.63	
	Relationship Marketing	4.07	
	Brand Management	2.79	
	Focus Groups	2.79	
	Promotion Evaluation System	2.36	
	Direct Marketing	1.07	
	Key Account Management	0.87	26.65%
	Audience Share Research	0.87	
	Planograms	0.65	
	Sponsorship	0.65	
	Product Mix Decisions	0.44	
	Value Chain Analysis	0.44	
	Contract Management System	0.24	
5 Performance Measurement	Benchmarking	4.28	
	Competitor Analysis	4.07	
	Key Performance Indicators	1.29	
	Marketing Information Systems	0.87	
	Activity Based Costing	0.65	13.14%
	Balanced Scorecard	0.65	
	Quality Management Techniques	0.65	
	Value Chain Analysis	0.44	
	Smart Targets	0.24	
6 It and Internet Applications	E-Susiness – Seller Side Software	4.71	6.44%
	E-Business – Internal Applications	1.29	
	E-Business – Buyer Side Software	0.44	

The use of tools and techniques by industry sector and by industry sector groupings

The overall average use of tools and techniques in the marketing and sales area is 4.01 compared to 3.65 in the strategy area (compare Table 3.4 with Table 5.4), and this indicates that the marketing and sales function tends to use tools and techniques only slightly more than the strategy function. Across industry sectors there is some communality with what occurs in the strategy area also. The top four industry groups in both the strategy and marketing and sales areas are Basic Chemicals, Aerospace, Transport Equipment and Power & Water. The only difference is that Power & Water (7.67 average uses) is the most frequent user of tools and techniques in marketing and sales, but is the fourth most frequent user in strategy. These positions are reversed for Basic Chemicals, which is first in usage for strategy but fourth (with 5.75 average uses) in marketing and sales. Aerospace (with 6.00) and Transport Equipment (with 5.86%) are the third and fourth most frequent users respectively in both functional areas. This appears to support the view, developed from the strategy survey, that *high strategic risk* industries, with heavy capital investment requirements for product and/or service level delivery, facing fierce competition and regulation, are likely to have within the companies that see a need to monitor market and environmental circumstances rigorously and continuously.

Thus, companies that face relatively *low strategic risk*, like Media & Entertainment (1.50 average uses) and Tourism and Leisure (1.88 average

Table 5.4   **The Rank Order Use of Marketing and Sales Tools and Techniques by Industry Sector**

Industry	Total Tools	No. of Firms	Average
Power & Water	46	6	7.67
Aerospace	42	7	6.00
Transport Equipment	41	7	5.86
Basic Chemicals	46	8	5.75
Confectionery	45	8	5.63
Retail & Distribution	35	7	5.00
Publishing	25	6	4.17
Retail Financial Services	29	7	4.14
Computer Hardware	45	11	4.09
Healthcare	32	8	4.00
IT Solutions	28	8	3.50
Construction	6	3	2.00
Tourism & Leisure	15	8	1.88
Oil & Gas	8	5	1.60
Media & Entertainment	12	8	1.50
Telecommunications	10	9	1.11
Overall Average	**465**	**116**	**4.01**

uses), where it is not normal to 'bet the business' on the development of a particular product or services, were once again some of the least frequent users. Similarly, those industries characterised in chapter 3 as relatively *medium strategic risk* – like Retail and Distribution (with 5.00 average uses), Retail Financial Services (4.14), Computer Hardware (4.09), Healthcare (4.00), IT Solutions (3.50) and Construction (2.00) – once again appear to be in the middling ranks of users. The three industry sectors that appear out of character in this regard were the *low strategic risk* industry of Publishing (with 4.17 average uses) and the high strategic risk industries of Oil & Gas (with 1.60 uses) and Telecommunications (with 1.11 average uses).

The Telecommunications responses were low and out of character in the survey findings and this may be a function of the fact that the survey covered both older more established industry players like Advent, Cannon, Orange and Motorola and also some of the new and emerging start-up companies in this sector. For some of these firms there may be lower strategic risks than for others and this may be the explanation of the anomaly in the findings expected. The Oil & Gas anomaly is relatively more easily explained and appears to be a function of the fact that many of the respondent companies were located in the upstream or exploration and production side of the Oil & Gas sector.

Companies in this part of the Oil & Gas supply and value chain face very different market circumstances than those operating in the chemical refining and/or downstream businesses. In the upstream exploration and production business there is no effective market other than a spot market. In the upstream businesses all that is, and can be, produced is sent to market and receives the prevailing market price. This means that continuous analysis of market and environmental circumstances is much less important than in other industry sectors and, indeed, when compared with what is required in the chemical refining and downstream businesses in this industry. Given that many of our respondents came from the exploration and production side of the industry (Agip, Amerada Hess, BG, BP, Enterprise, Lasmo, Ranger and Shell) this probably accounts for this apparent anomaly in the results.

The Publishing findings appear to contradict the view that relatively *low strategic risk* industries are unlikely to use marketing and sales tools and techniques extensively. The reason for this (and the anomaly with the findings for Publishing in the strategy survey) may well be a result of the fact that publishing firms do not worry too much about the competition strategically, but do spend a great deal of time thinking about their customers and their channels to markets for sales, as well as the authors that they intend to work closely with. Interestingly most publishing companies tend to see author relationships as part of marketing and sales rather than as part of procurement and supply, and this may in part account for the anomaly in the expected results in this area.

Overall however, notwithstanding these slight anomalies, the findings in marketing and sales seem broadly to confirm those from the strategy survey about high, medium and low strategic risk industries. This borne out in Figure 5.1, which indicates what the tool usage scores were when the industry sectors are segmented into industry sector groupings. As the Table shows the highest average usage scores were recorded in *Project/Manufacturing* (5.34) and *Process/Manufacturing* (5.16), followed by *Process/Services* (4.57) and *Process/Combined* (4.26), the lowest scores were recorded by the *Project/Combined* (2.37) and *Project/Services* (1.69) industry sector groupings. These rank order results are very similar to the findings reported in the strategy survey (reported in Figure 3.1), where the relative scores were *Project/Manufacturing* (5.04), *Process/Manufacturing* (5.03), *Process/Combined* (3.71), *Process/Services* (2.02), *Project/Combined* (2.89) and *Project/Services* (1.36) respectively. These findings appear to confirm that industry groupings with high levels of strategic risk appear to use tools and techniques much more than those with medium and low levels of strategic risk.

2.   The performance of the tools and techniques used in marketing and sales

Having seen that there is some clear duplication of effort within the strategy and the marketing and sales functions when it comes to the use of tools and techniques, and that the function does not appear to use marketing and sales specific tools and techniques as extensively as one might have expected, it is now possible to asses the performance of those that were found to be in use. In this part the objectives behind the use of tools and techniques are described and their impact on both the firm and the function. This is followed by an analysis of their impact by industry sector and by industry sector grouping. Finally there is a discussion of the major barriers to effective implementation.

The corporate and functional objectives for implementing tools and techniques

Table 5.5 provides an overview of the major firm-level objectives behind the use of marketing and sales tools and techniques. As the Table indicates 52% of usages were for strategic purposes, with a surprisingly high figure of 48% focused on operational effectiveness objectives. One might have expected the marketing and sales function to see its role primarily as one focused overwhelmingly on the development of marketing strategy but this is not borne out by the survey findings. While assisting with the development of corporate and marketing strategy is clearly a major concern the function also appears to understand that they should be focusing just as much on the operational delivery of strategy and ensuring its efficient and effective performance management. These findings reinforce similar

TYPE OF OPERATIONAL DELIVERY	PROCESS/ MANUFACTURING	PROCESS/ MANUFACTURING & SERVICES	PROCESS/ SERVICES	
	Group Average Usage 5.16	Group Average Usage 4.26	Group Average Usage 4.57	*Total Process Average Usage:*
PROCESS	Basic Chemicals (5.75) Computer Hardware (4.09) Confectionery (5.63)	Healthcare (4.00) Power & Water (7.67) Telecommunications (1.11)	Retail & Distribution (5.00) Retail Financial Services (4.14)	*4.66*
	PROJECT/ MANUFACTURING	PROJECT/ MANUFACTURING & SERVICES	PROJECT/ SERVICES	*Total Project Average Usage:*
	Group Average Usage 5.34	Group Average Usage 2.37	Group Average Usage 1.69	
PROJECT	Aerospace (6.00) Publishing (4.17) Transport Equipment (5.86)	Construction (2.00) IT Solutions (3.50) Oil & Gas (1.60)	Media & Entertainment (1.50) Tourism & Leisure (1.88)	*3.90*
	Total Manufacturing Average Usage 5.25	Total Combined Average Usage 3.32	Total Service Average Usage 3.13	
	MANUFACTURING	COMBINED MANUFACTURING & SERVICES	SERVICES	

TYPE OF GOODS AND/OR SERVICES

Figure 5.1 The Use of Marketing and Supply Tools and Techniques by Industry Groups

Table 5.5 Overall Objectives for Introducing Marketing Tools and Techniques

Group	Industry	Strategic Objectives			
		Unique Products %	Cost Advantage %	Repositioning %	Operational Effectiveness %
Process/Manufacturing Group	Basic Chemicals	0	4	4	92
	Computer Hardware	2	4	7	87
	Confectionery	24	5	0	71
	Group Average	*9*	*4*	*4*	*83*
Process/Combined Group	Healthcare	31	8	45	16
	Power and Water	4	0	24	72
	Telecommunications	20	5	28	47
	Group Average	*18*	*5*	*32*	*45*
Process/Services Group	Retail and Distribution	13	0	11	76
	Retail Financial Services	15	4	33	48
	Group Average	*14*	*2*	*22*	*62*
Project/Manufacturing Group	Aerospace	33	7	33	27
	Publishing	57	0	11	32
	Transport Equipment	35	16	33	16
	Group Average	*42*	*7*	*26*	*25*
Project/Combined Group	Construction	14	29	14	43
	IT Solutions	7	0	14	79
	Oil & Gas	36	10	27	27
	Group Average	*19*	*13*	*18*	*50*
Project/Services Group	Media and Entertainment	79	7	7	7
	Tourism & Leisure	0	32	47	21
	Group Average	*39*	*20*	*27*	*14*
Overall Average (%)		23	8	21	48

findings in the strategy survey, where the relative scores were 56% for strategic and 44% for operational effectiveness objectives (see Table 3.5 and compare with Table 5.5).

When disaggregating the data it is clear that, while the marketing and sales function is concerned with operational delivery, it is not really interested in cost leadership strategies. The function as a whole appears to be more interested strategically in providing differentiation through the development of unique products (23% of total recorded objectives) and/or market and value chain repositioning through branding and relocation (21%) than it does cost leadership (8%). That said, when one disaggregates by industry sector there are some unusual findings. The Tourism & Leisure sector appears to be the most keenly interested in cost leadership (32% of total reported objectives), although it also appears to be the most interested in repositioning through branding and relocation (47% of total reported objectives). This may largely be a function of the fact that the industry often finds it difficult to provide unique products and services and must seek alternative ways of differentiating than many other industry sectors.

Of the other industry sectors Media & Entertainment demonstrated the strongest interest in the development of unique products (79% of total recorded objectives). This is a relatively unsurprising finding in an industry where being first to market with unique products and services is one of the key mechanisms for corporate success. The fact that Publishing also scored very highly (with 57% of total recorded objectives) for the development of unique products and/or services reinforces this point. As do the relatively high scores recorded for unique products and services in the Aerospace (with 33%), Healthcare (31%), Transport Equipment (with 35%) and Confectionery (with 24%) industries. These are all industries where the development of new supply offerings in dynamic markets is a key requirement of success.

Once again the data supports the view that, rather than there being no pattern at all for tool and technique use, practitioners appear to have objectively defined reasons for many of the decisions they take. Thus, it is also not surprising that the Construction industry places a great premium on cost leadership (29% of objectives) and operational effectiveness (43%). In an industry with fierce competition and low margins it is inevitable that the marketing and sales sides of the business will understand the need to focus on the key requirements that allow for corporate survival and success in an industry in which differentiation is so difficult to achieve on a permanent basis. Similarly, it is not surprising that Basic Chemicals reported that 92% of its tool and technique objectives were related to operational effectiveness, a figure that is closely followed by other process related industries like Computer Hardware (87%), Confectionery (71%), Power & Water (72%) and Retail & Distribution (76%). These are all industries that may search for differentiation but normally have to recognise that operational effectiveness and efficiency is critically important to bottom-line performance.

This rational basis for the pattern of tool and technique usage is further reinforced when one considers that it was the highly contested and low margin process-related industries that score much higher on operational effectiveness objectives (with a combined average across the three process-industry sector groupings of 63% compared with 37% for strategic objectives). This is contrasted with an average operational effectiveness score of 30%, with 70% for strategy objectives, across the three combined project-industry sector groupings. Clearly, the process-related industries have a different external reality to manage than in the more dynamic project environment, in which differentiation (even if only in the short-term) is more often possible than for the more mature and heavily contested low margin process-industry sectors.

When considering the functional objectives behind the use of marketing and sales tools and techniques the findings are very similar to those obtained in the strategy survey. In the strategy survey (see Table 3.6) the major functional objectives for tool and technique use were, first, the provision of information to allow the function to make better decisions (31% of functional objectives reported). Second came the desire to improve the functional service level of delivery (24%) and, third, the desire to improve communication within the business about functional issues and opportunities (16%). As Table 5.6 demonstrates although the figures are slightly different the scores reported for marketing and sales follows the same general rank ordering as those reported in the strategy survey. Thus, the first priority functionally was the provision of information to make better decisions (34% of total recorded objectives). Second came improving the functionality of service level delivery (22%) and, third, was improving communication (20%).

These figures demonstrate that there appear, once again, to be rational functional reasons for tool and technique use. These appear to be focused primarily on reducing bounded rationality in decision-making and improving functionality and communication in the business. Interestingly, just as in the strategy survey, it is clear from the findings for marketing and sales that there was also little interest in using tools and techniques either to increase the number of staff employed in the function (0%), or to increase flexibility (5%) or reduce costs of operations (7%). More worrying perhaps was the finding related to the desire to use tools and techniques to improve skill sets within the function. The objectives score for this category was only 3%, which is even worse than the low score for this category reported in the strategy survey at 7%. Once again there is a concern in these findings that managers do not appear to understand that the use of tools and techniques is also a way of improving the competence of staff by forcing them to ask necessary questions

Table 5.6 The Functional Objectives for Introducing Marketing Tools and Techniques (%)

Industry	Functionality	Cost	Communication	Information	Flexibility	Skill Sets	Number Employed	Other	No Data
Process/Manufacturing									
Basic Chemicals	6	11	15	39	0	4	1	23	1
Computer Hardware	0	2	29	41	0	1	0	26	1
Confectionery	6	11	22	51	0	0	0	0	10
Group Average	*4*	*8*	*22*	*44*	*0*	*2*	*0*	*16*	*4*
Process/Combined									
Healthcare	11	4	26	55	0	2	0	0	2
Power & Water	43	10	9	29	2	0	0	4	3
Telecommunications	28	10	22	7	13	3	0	5	12
Group Average	*27*	*8*	*19*	*30*	*5*	*2*	*0*	*3*	*6*
Process/Services									
Retail & Distribution	47	19	7	26	0	0	0	0	1
Retail Financial Services	34	12	22	25	6	1	0	0	0
Group Average	*41*	*16*	*14*	*26*	*3*	*0*	*0*	*0*	*0*
Project/Manufacturing									
Aerospace	6	3	35	45	0	10	0	1	0
Publishing	49	4	0	43	0	0	0	0	4
Transport Equipment	17	4	31	47	0	1	0	0	0
Group Average	*24*	*4*	*22*	*45*	*0*	*4*	*0*	*0*	*1*

Table 5.6 The Functional Objectives for Introducing Marketing Tools and Techniques (%) – *continued*

Industry	Functionality	Cost	Communication	Information	Flexibility	Skill Sets	Number Employed	Other	No Data
Project/Combined									
Construction	0	8	38	15	23	8	0	8	0
IT Solutions	0	2	31	44	0	3	0	20	0
Oil and Gas	33	0	4	26	15	7	4	11	0
Group Average	*11*	*3*	*24*	*29*	*13*	*6*	*1*	*13*	*0*
Project /Services									
Media & Entertainment	42	3	6	33	0	12	0	0	4
Tourism & Leisure	33	8	22	14	17	6	0	0	0
Group Average	*38*	*5*	*14*	*24*	*8*	*9*	*0*	*0*	*2*
Overall Average	22	7	20	34	5	3	0	7	2

and to focus on key firm and functional issues in a rigorous way and on a regular, codified basis.

The impact of tools and techniques by industry sector and industry sector grouping

It had been expected in the strategy function that tools and techniques would be used primarily for their impact on firm rather than functional level performance. This view was shown to be invalid in chapter 3, where the overall performance score for firm impact was lower at 0.63 than that recorded for functional impact or performance at 0.69. Similar findings were reported for marketing and sales. The satisfaction scores for marketing and sales tools and techniques reported in Table 5.7 (again using a subjectively evaluated scoring system between +1, zero and –1) show that performance satisfaction levels were lower overall when compared with the

Table 5.7   The Use and Impact of Marketing and Sales Tools and Techniques by Industry Sector and Groupings

Rank Order of Most Usages by Industry Sector	Performance Score			No Data %	
	Firm	Function	Average Combined Score	Firm	Function
Power & Water (7.67)	0.56	0.66	0.61	26	12
Aerospace (6.00)	0.62	0.64	0.63	2	2
Transport Equipment (5.86)	0.51	0.59	0.55	9	4
Basic Chemicals (5.75)	0.69	0.91	0.80	10	9
Confectionery (5.63)	0.64	0.76	0.70	8	8
Retail & Distribution (5.00)	0.57	0.66	0.62	23	6
Publishing (4.17)	0.71	0.67	0.69	13	4
Retail Financial Services (4.14)	0.64	0.64	0.64	20	3
Computer Hardware (4.09)	0.63	0.83	0.73	0	0
Healthcare (4.00)	0.52	0.67	0.60	2	2
It Solution (3.50)	0.60	0.77	0.69	0	0
Construction (2.00)	0.58	0.64	0.61	1	0
Tourism & Leisure (1.88)	0.72	0.72	0.72	0	0
Oil & Gas (1.60)	0.22	0.35	0.29	1	0
Media & Entertainment (1.50)	0.80	0.22	0.51	10	6
Telecommunications (1.11)	0.44	0.32	0.38	14	8
Overall Average	**0.59**	**0.63**	**0.61**	**9**	**4**
Project/Manufacture (5.34)	0.61	0.63	0.62	8	3
Process/Manufacture (5.16)	0.65	0.83	0.74	6	6
Process/Services (4.57)	0.61	0.65	0.63	22	5
Process/Combined (4.26)	0.51	0.55	0.53	1	0
Project/Combined (2.37)	0.47	0.59	0.53	14	7
Project/Services (1.69)	0.76	0.47	0.62	5	3
Overall Average	**0.59**	**0.63**	**0.61**	**9**	**4**

strategy function (the combined firm and function performance satisfaction score was 0.66 in strategy but only 0.61 in marketing and sales). Furthermore, the marketing and sales performance satisfaction score for functional impact at 0.63 was also (as in the strategy survey) higher than that recorded for impact on the firm at 0.59.

Despite this the scores in Table 5.7 generally show that managers were broadly satisfied with the use of tools and techniques in this function with no negative scores reported at all. There was also a strong sense that managers in marketing and sales were objectively aware of the performance of their tool and technique usage. This was indicated by the fact that few respondents reported a lack of robust data about performance. This is in contrast to the strategy function that had a very large number of respondents without robust data to analyse performance at all (see Table 3.7).

When disaggregating the data it is clear that some industry sectors have a much higher performance satisfaction rating than others. The most satisfied firm-level score by industry sector was reported by the Media & Entertainment sector (0.80) and then by Tourism & Leisure (0.72) and by Publishing (0.71). This is compared with the lowest firm-level performance satisfaction scores reported by Oil & Gas (0.22), Telecommunications (0.44) and Transport Equipment (0.51). These figures are interesting because they confirm some of the expectations derived from the initial analysis of usage. It was noted earlier that some industries use marketing and sales tools and techniques much less than others, and the findings here also appear to demonstrate that those that use them least also appear to be those that report the lowest performance or impact satisfaction scores. This conclusion is confirmed when one links the data in Table 5.7 with that presented in Table 5.8.

Table 5.8 reports the total usage figures by industry sector relative to the average combined (firm and function) performance scores for each industry. As the figures show Telecommunications was the lowest (16th) total user of tools and techniques (1.11) and the second lowest (15th) in the performance league table, with a reported combined firm and function satisfaction score of 0.38. Media & Entertainment was the 15th in the usage league table (1.50) and 14th in the performance league (0.51). Oil & Gas, a sector that we saw does not necessarily need to use marketing and sales tools and techniques extensively (especially upstream), was 14th in usage (1.60) and 16th (and last in performance) with a combined satisfaction score of 0.29. These figures demonstrate conclusively that overall those firms in sectors using marketing and sales tools and techniques the least are also those that appear to derive the least satisfaction from using them. This general conclusion does, however, mask some interesting findings when one disaggregates the data to the industry sector and industry sector grouping levels.

There are firms in industry sectors where the use of tools and techniques are highly valued. At the firm level, as Table 5.7 demonstrates, Media &

Table 5.8 Rank Order Comparisons for Usage and Impact

Rank Order Usage Scores	Industry Sector	Rank Order Combined Impact Scores
1 (7.67)	Power & Water	10= (0.61)
2 (6.00)	Aerospace	8 (0.63)
3 (5.86)	Transport Equipment	13 (0.59)
4 (5.75)	Basic Chemicals	1 (0.80)
5 (5.63)	Confectionery	4 (0.70)
6 (5.00)	Retail & Distribution	9 (0.62)
7 (4.17)	Publishing	5= (0.69)
8 (4.14)	Retail Financial Services	7 (0.64)
9 (4.09)	Computer Hardware	2 (0.73)
10 (4.00)	Healthcare	12 (0.60)
11 (3.50)	It Solutions	5= (0.69)
12 (2.00)	Construction	10= (0.61)
13 (1.88)	Tourism & Leisure	3 (0.72)
14 (1.60)	Oil & Gas	16 (0.29)
15 (1.50)	Media & Entertainment	14 (0.51)
16 (1.11)	Telecommunications	15 (0.38)

Entertainment (0.80), Tourism & Leisure (0.72), Publishing (0.71) and Basic Chemicals (0.69) were the most positive about the impact of tools and techniques on the performance of the firm. At the functional level Basic Chemicals (0.91), Computer Hardware (0.83), IT Solutions (0.77) and Confectionery (0.76) were the most positive industry sectors about performance. Once again a pattern appears to emerge that is echoed in the strategy function survey. Sometimes, and especially at the firm level, industry sectors that do not normally use tools and techniques extensively – like Media & Entertainment, Publishing and Tourism & Leisure – are the very ones that report the highest levels of performance satisfaction when compared with those that use the tools and techniques extensively.

The explanation for this apparent contradiction of the general trends reported above was explained in the strategy chapter as being due to the fact that the extensive use of tools and techniques is normally occasioned by high levels of strategic risk and in circumstances where there are often only limited opportunities for significant market differentiation. In such circumstances it is likely that managers will be somewhat dissatisfied with tools and techniques that fail to solve all of their problems. On the other hand in some industries, where there is scope for differentiation, the use of tools and techniques – especially those that might assist the firm in developing unique products and/or provide opportunities for market repositioning – may often provide much higher levels of satisfaction with performance. This will be partly a result of the fact that, since many firms in the market do not operate in such a scientific manner, a more rigorous approach to marketing and sales strategy is likely to pay significant dividends in an industry where a 'gentleman's club' attitude often prevails.

It would appear that Media & Entertainment, Publishing and Tourism & Leisure have many of the preconditions for this type of approach and, therefore, opportunities for the successful use of tools and techniques that support *market and environmental analysis* and *competence and product development* marketing and sales business activities. In other words, the opportunities for tools and techniques to delight managers may in fact be industry specific.

This conclusion appears to be borne out by the findings related to functional level performance satisfaction levels. The industry sectors reporting the highest levels of satisfaction with tool and technique use related to functional improvements were Basic Chemicals (0.91), Computer Hardware (0.83), IT Solutions (0.77) and Confectionery (0.76). It would appear that these are sectors in which the level of competition is severe and the opportunities for 'mould breaking' initiatives strategically are limited. In such an environment it is likely that tool and technique usage will be heavily weighted in favour of those that improve operational effectiveness and functional improvement.

The figures generally appear to confirm this explanation because, as Table 5.8 demonstrates, the four major users of tools and techniques also have reasonably high performance satisfaction scores at the functional level. Thus, Power & Water, which is the major user of marketing and sales tools and techniques (7.67 average uses), has a positive view of functionally focused tools and techniques (0.66). Aerospace, the second most frequent user, with an average score of 6.00, also has a positive view of functional tools and techniques (0.64). Transport Equipment, the third most frequent user with 5.86 average uses, has a positive view of performance with a score of 0.59. Basic Chemicals, the fourth highest user at 5.75, has an extremely positive view of functional tools and techniques reporting a performance satisfaction score of 0.91.

When disaggregating the data by industry sector groupings it is also clear that those firms using marketing and sales tools and techniques the most do not always report the highest performance satisfaction levels. The most frequent user of marketing and sales tools and techniques is the *Project/ Manufacturing* sector (5.34 average usages), but this grouping only reports a middle level satisfaction rating at the firm (0.61), function (0.63) and combined (0.62) levels. Interestingly enough, however, the *Process/ Manufacturing* grouping is the second highest user of tools and techniques in this area and the most positive about their use. This grouping scores the second highest performance score at the firm impact level (0.65); the highest impact score at the functional level (0.83); and, the highest combined score (0.74). These findings appear to confirm the view developed earlier in the strategy chapter that industries that have a continuous process requirement operationally are likely to use tools and techniques more extensively than those that do not, and that they will also have a very high regard for those tools and techniques that allow them to optimise their operational effectiveness.

The industry sector grouping data also reinforces the findings above about industry sectors least using the tools and techniques reporting, ironically, some of the highest performance satisfaction scores. The *Project/Services* grouping (which includes Tourism & Leisure and Media & Entertainment) is the lowest user of tools and techniques in this area overall (as it was in the strategy function) but reports the highest positive performance score for firm-level impact (0.76). Once again this seems to confirm that industries that do not see a need for extensive operational and functional use of marketing and sales tools and techniques may still derive considerable benefit from a more structured approach at the firm level.

Overall, however, even for those industries that do not use tools and techniques for marketing and sales extensively there is still considerable evidence from the survey that most managers have a reasonably positive view of the impact of the tools and techniques that they use in this functional area. The use and performance scores may not be quite as high as those reported in the strategy function but, nevertheless, the general view is one that is positive about tool and technique use. This once again contradicts the more jaundiced views of those who argue that practitioners are just the unwitting dupes of academics and consultants selling shoddy goods. The evidence seems to indicate that when managers use tools and techniques in this area they use those that are tried and tested (they do not innovate radically with new and esoteric offerings) and, when they use them, they are fairly positive about the experience.

The barriers to successful implementation of tools and techniques

Although managers may be broadly positive about the use of tools and techniques there is still considerable evidence from the survey results that managers experience problems in implementing them successfully within their businesses. This final part analyses, therefore, the major barriers that respondents reported hindered successful implementation when they adopted particular tools and techniques. Once again the results, presented in Table 5.9, show very similar findings to those that were reported by managers in the strategy survey.

Table 5.9 was constructed by asking respondents what were the proximate causes of failure when tools failed to be implemented successfully. The two major options provided were either problems with the integrity and utility of the tools and techniques (they were not capable of delivering what was promised), or there was nothing wrong with the tool or technique but there were barriers internally to successful implementation. A third category – the respondent did not know why the application had

146

Table 5.9 The Barriers to Effective Implementation in the Marketing and Sales Function

Industry	Causes of Failure 100%			Types of Barriers 100%						
	No Data (%)	Tool (%)	Barriers (%)	Culture	Wrong Performance Measure	Insufficient Resource	Senior Management	Disruptive Internal Reorganisation	Unrealistic Expectations	Other
Process/Manufacturing										
Basic Chemicals	10	65	25	42	0	20	5	20	10	3
Computer Hardware	2	86	12	27	5	27	0	0	32	9
Confectionery	21	38	41	50	0	36	0	0	0	14
Group Average	*11*	*63*	*26*	*40*	*1*	*28*	*1*	*8*	*14*	*8*
Process/Combined										
Healthcare	20	27	53	38	0	13	0	0	33	16
Power and Water	2	44	54	7	0	23	0	10	32	28
Telecoms	12	45	43	15	0	38	10	0	22	15
Group Average	*11*	*39*	*50*	*20*	*0*	*25*	*3*	*3*	*29*	*20*
Process/Services										
Financial Services	7	31	62	13	0	63	0	0	21	3
Retail and Distribution	0	67	33	0	0	73	0	0	27	0
Group Average	*4*	*49*	*47*	*6*	*0*	*68*	*0*	*0*	*24*	*2*
Project/Manufacturing										
Aerospace	14	55	31	44	0	20	6	6	13	11
Publishing	0	74	26	0	0	57	0	0	43	0
Transport Equipment	16	43	41	38	0	24	10	10	18	0
Group Average	*10*	*57*	*33*	*27*	*0*	*34*	*5*	*5*	*25*	*4*

Table 5.9 The Barriers to Effective Implementation in the Marketing and Sales Function – *continued*

Industry	Causes of Failure 100%			Types of Barriers 100%						
	No Data (%)	Tool (%)	Barriers (%)	Culture	Wrong Performance Measure	Insufficient Resource	Senior Management	Disruptive Internal Reorganisation	Unrealistic Expectations	Other
Project/Combined										
Construction	0	86	14	13	0	46	10	21	5	5
IT Solutions	9	70	21	43	14	0	0	14	29	0
Oil and Gas	0	58	42	40	0	0	0	40	20	0
Group Average	*3*	*71*	*26*	*32*	*5*	*15*	*3*	*25*	*18*	*2*
Project/Services										
Media & Entertainment	0	87	13	0	0	50	50	0	0	0
Tourism & Leisure	5	79	34	33	0	33	0	0	34	0
Group Average	*3*	*83*	*14*	*16*	*0*	*42*	*25*	*0*	*17*	*0*
Overall Average	7	60	33	25	1	33	6	8	21	6

failed – was also provided for in a no-data category. For those answering that the cause of failure was an internal barrier rather than tool or technique failure a series of further options were provided to ascertain what the major internal barriers to successful implementation might be. Finally, a "other" category was provided to capture any causes that were not initially isolated by the research team.

As the findings demonstrate the major cause of failure in implementation was problems with the integrity and utility of the tool or technique itself (60% of all respondents reported this failing). Only a third (33%) of respondents felt failure occurred as result of internal barriers. The findings were very similar to those reported by strategy managers (58% compared with 32%, see Table 3.9). These findings raise interesting questions about the integrity and utility of tools and techniques in general. Anecdotally, from the interviews conducted, it appears that many managers felt that the tools and techniques that are provided are often far too complex and require far too much resource, time and effort to utilise in the fast moving and head count reduced environment within which most practitioners operate today. This led them to argue that the problems reside primarily with the integrity and utility of the tools and techniques.

It is, however, debatable whether this is in fact a reasonable view for managers to take since tools and techniques are normally developed on a fairly rigorous and robust basis, but it is normal that those who frame them require that managers collect the information required to use them rigorously. The fact that managers rarely have the time or resources to do so is, arguably, not an indictment of the tool or technique but of senior managers who will not, or do not, understand what is required to analyse problems properly. That said, from the point of view of a manager, if a tool or technique is potentially available but they do not have the time and resource to use it properly, then it is reasonable, from their perspective, to argue that there is, therefore, something wrong with the tool or technique. Unfortunately there is clearly a tension here between the desire by managers for simplicity and speed and the desire by academics and consultants for rigour and robustness.

Unfortunately there is little that either side can do about this dilemma, and one can only focus on trying to resolve the key internal barriers to implementation that arise within firms (rather than the problem of non-commensurable goals between practitioners and their advisers) when a tool or technique may have value for managers. It is interesting to note, however, that it is the industry sectors and industry sector groupings that least use tools and techniques that find them of most limited utility. The *Project/Services* industry sector grouping reports that 83% of the causes of failure were associated with inappropriate tools and techniques. The *Project/Combined* grouping also reported a 71 % score related to tool and technique failure. These findings confirm the view that in the project environment, with high levels of uncertainty and scope for innovative entrepreneurial activity, the use of standardised tools and techniques (requiring robust and rigorous data collection and analysis) may not be as appropriate as it is in more stable process environment. The fact that many of the process based industry groupings report lower tool and technique failure scores is partial evidence to support this view.

When considering the internal barriers to successful implementation the findings for marketing and sales are very similar to those reported in the strategy survey (compare Table 3.9 with Table 5.9). This is perhaps not surprising given that the problems facing those who seek to innovate in companies tend to be the same whatever functional area they are in. All innovation that involves the implementation of tools and techniques involves some element of change management. This is because in the absence of the new tool or technique there must be an existing standard operating procedure (or a lack of it) that supports particular power structures internally within the firm. Given this the introduction of any new tool or technique will of necessity challenge existing internal power structures to some extent. In this light it is interesting that the second most commonly reported internal barrier was culture, with 25% of managers specifying this as a major problem. In this survey culture refers to the existing power structures within the organisation and the mindset of individuals around standard operating procedures that stop the implementation of new tools and techniques. The 25% score reported in marketing and sales is very similar to the 24% reported in the strategy area.

The single biggest obstacle to implementation was not culture, however, but insufficient resource (33% of respondents). This was also the first obstacle reported in the strategy survey (30%). Insufficient resource refers to the inability of managers to find the time and/or personnel to implement a tool or technique effectively and, as we argued above, it is a barrier that this volume demonstrates very many managers experience in all functions. The third highest scoring obstacle or barrier was unrealistic expectations, with 21% of respondents reporting this problem. This compares with a comparative score of 14% in the strategy area. Beyond these major obstacles only disruptive internal reorganisation (8%) and senior management opposition (6%) figure prominently at all.

When disaggregating by industry sector and groupings it is clear that most sectors follow these broad patterns, but there are one or two anomalies. Thus, the *Process/Combined* grouping stands out as the one sector that places internal barriers (50%) over tool and technique inadequacy (39%) as the major cause of failure. This grouping also stands out as the one that places unrealistic expectations ahead of all of the other internal barriers. When it comes to internal barriers the *Process/Manufacturing* and the *Project/Combined* sectors both place culture (40% and 32% respectively) as the major barrier ahead of insufficient resource (28% and 15 respectively).

Despite these slight anomalies, in general the findings reinforce those from the strategy survey and indicate that the problems are either inadequate tools and techniques or the need to implement them with a properly resourced and communicated change management approach firmly in hand before implementation begins.

3.   Conclusions: the appropriateness of the use of tools and techniques in marketing and sales management

Perhaps the most striking conclusion that one can make about the use of tools and techniques in the marketing and sales function is the duplication of effort that appears to occur between this function and the strategy function. Whether this duplication of effort is sensible or not is not easy to decide on the basis of the survey evidence reported here. One could take the view that it is a criminal waste of scarce and valuable corporate resource to have two separate functions undertaking very similar analyses to those being undertaken elsewhere within the same company. On the other hand it can be argued that, since each function has slightly different remits, the fact that different individuals within a company are using the same tools and techniques provides a useful basis for comparison and may add to the rigour and robustness of what is done.

Of course it has to be said that this counter argument is only really valid if the firms concerned rigorously compare and contrast and share the findings from these duplicated studies of SWOT, core competence thinking, market research, benchmarking and Porters' Five Forces etc. This process, if undertaken correctly, ought to result in the creation of a centrally owned and communicated codified repository for knowledge management in the company. The evidence from the survey interviews undertaken here is that this rarely occurs in practice and one has to conclude, therefore, that the duplication of effort reported may well be a waste of valuable and scarce corporate resources.

Despite this the managers surveyed appear to be broadly happy with the performance of most of the tools and techniques that were being used, even though the survey results show that they tend to focus their efforts on a few that are well known and tried and tested. This is hardly a surprising finding given the benchmarking mentality that prevails in most corporate thinking. Many managers do not appear to understand that benchmarking only allows firms to catch up with what innovators are doing, and this rarely provides them with opportunities for differentiation and competitive advantage (Cox, 1997). Given this it is not surprising that most managers were using very similar tools and techniques most of the time. This is always likely to be the case given that most practitioners are taught very similar things when they undertake marketing and sales training or courses of academic study.

It is not surprising also, given the risk averse nature of many practitioners, that rather than a large and diverse number of tools and techniques being used (as one might suspect from some critiques of management consulting practice) the truth appears to be that marketing and sales managers can be criticised not for using too many, but rather for not using them very much at all. As the figures reported here show, while there were 48 tools and techniques found to be in use, with 465 usages, by 116 companies, the vast bulk of the usage (67% or two thirds) was confined to the top eight tools and techniques (pricing models, market research, consumer profiling, SWOT analysis, e-business seller software, benchmarking, competitor analysis and relationship marketing).

More surprising, perhaps, was the fact that while 75% of companies were using structured pricing models, 25% were not. Similarly, while 48% of firms were undertaking structured market research, 52% were not. 20% of firms undertook SWOT analyses but 80% did not. 16% of firms undertook relationship marketing but 84% did not. 11% of companies undertook brand management but 89% did not. All of these figures demonstrate what is perhaps one of the major findings from this survey overall and this is that rather than managers using tools and techniques indiscriminately they tend to use them relatively sparingly, if at all.

Two final issues need to be addressed in assessing the performance of marketing and sales tools and techniques. The first issue relates to whether or not managers, when they do use tools and techniques are using them appropriately. The second relates to whether or not there is any overall explanation for the pattern of tool and technique usage and performance reported. The appropriateness issue is difficult to decide upon because of the duplication problem with the strategy function. Clearly, the strategy related tools and techniques that are being used within the marketing and sales function must be appropriate, in the sense that it is not possible to decide on marketing and sales strategies in the absence of an understanding of market and environmental circumstances, and how these impact on new product and organisational and personnel competence development issues. Thus, it is sensible that firms use such strategically relevant tools and techniques extensively (which the survey shows they do and more so than most of the functionally specific tools and techniques). The issue is then not one of whether or not these tools and techniques are appropriate but, rather, whether or not they should be duplicated. The findings here seem to indicate that they should not and that firms need to address this duplication issues as soon as possible.

When assessing the other major tools and techniques it is clear that the use of those that assist with *pricing* and *promotional and relationship management* business activities is highly appropriate for the marketing and sales function to do. The fact that pricing models figure so prominently is a clear demonstration of this understanding. The use of those for *promotional and relationship management* activities is, however, less clear-cut. This is because these tools and techniques – especially those associated with brand and relationship management – are those that one might expect most marketing and sales functions to specialise in. The evidence seems to indicate, however, that this is in fact rarely the case. Only a few companies appear to use these tools and techniques extensively.

Thus, as we saw above, only 16% of firms were using relationship marketing techniques and only 11% were using brand management tools. More surprising perhaps was the fact that only 6% of firms appeared to involve marketing and sales directly in new product development processes, and only 11% used focus groups to understand customer wants and needs. Most surprising of all only 3% were undertaking structured approaches to key account management. The evidence reported here shows overwhelming, therefore, that firms do not use many of the specific tools and techniques for marketing and sales purposes very much at all. Whether this is appropriate is debatable. Most of the firms interviewed appear to survive without an extensive array of tools and techniques in place. The key question must be, therefore, although it is not one that can be answered in the context of the survey findings reported here, is whether there is any correlation between those using tools and techniques more than others and better marketing and sales performance. The answer to this question must, unfortunately, await further research.

The final question to be addressed was discussed at the end of chapter 3 on strategy usage and this is whether there is any way of explaining the overall patterns of use and performance described here. Since marketing and sales shares many of the same tools and techniques as those found in the strategy area, and since there was evidence of quite high levels of similarity in the findings reported, it is interesting to see whether the strategic risk categorisation used in the strategy chapter provides any useful insights in to the data from the marketing and sales survey. The findings from this analysis are presented in Table 5.10.

As was made clear in the strategy area it is useful to differentiate between industries that experience different levels of strategic risk. Thus, *high strategic risk* industries are those in which companies face severe competition and regulation, as well as having high levels of uncertainty and heavy sunk costs in capital investment for operational delivery processes and systems, that face severe operational and financial risks if their chosen strategy fails. In this category are found the Aerospace, Basic Chemicals, Confectionery, Oil & Gas, Power & Water, Telecommunications and Transport Equipment industries.

Low strategic risk industries are at the other extreme and comprise those that do not face fierce competition or regulation, do not have heavy sunk capital costs in operational processes and systems, do not face severe financial and operational risks from the failure of a particular strategy and

Table 5.10   The Use and Performance of Marketing and Sales Tools and Techniques in High, Medium and Low Risk Sectors

Type of Industry Sectors	Indicators of Use And Performance			
	Average Tool Usage	Performance Impact Scores		
		Firm	Function	Average Combined Score
High Strategic Risk				
Aerospace	6.00	0.62	0.64	0.63
Basic Chemicals	5.75	0.69	0.91	0.80
Confectionery	5.63	0.64	0.76	0.70
Oil & Gas	1.60	0.22	0.35	0.29
Power & Water	7.67	0.58	0.65	0.61
Telecommunications	1.11	0.44	0.32	0.35
Transport Equipment	5.86	0.51	0.59	0.55
Group Average	*4.80*	*0.53*	*0.60*	*0.57*
Medium Strategic Risk				
Computer Hardware	4.09	0.63	0.83	0.73
Construction	2.00	0.58	0.64	0.61
Healthcare	4.00	0.52	0.67	0.60
IT Solutions	3.50	0.60	0.77	0.69
Retail & Distribution	5.00	0.57	0.66	0.62
Retail Financial Services	4.14	0.64	0.64	0.64
Group Average	*3.79*	*0.59*	*0.70*	*0.65*
Low Strategic Risk				
Media & Entertainment	1.50	0.80	0.22	0.51
Publishing	4.17	0.71	0.67	0.69
Tourism & Leisure	1.88	0.72	0.72	0.72
Group Average	*2.52*	*0.74*	*0.54*	*0.64*

do not have to 'bet the business' on any particular product or service offering. In this category are located the Media & Entertainment, Publishing and Tourism & Leisure industries. In the *medium strategic risk* category are located the Computer Hardware, Construction, Healthcare, IT Solutions, Retail & Distribution and Retail Financial Services industry sectors. These are sectors in which firms face some of the high strategic risks but not all of them, or on as regular a basis.

Using these three categories for analysis Table 5.10 demonstrates that the firms located in the *high strategic risk* category were much more likely to use tools and techniques than those in the medium or low categories. The high-risk categories reported an average usage score of 4.80 compared with 3.79 for the medium risk and 2.52 for the low risk categories. These findings, which are mirrored in the strategy results reported in chapter 3 (where the scores were 5.51, 2.64 and 1.45 respectively), demonstrate that the degree of strategic risks appears to explain why it is that some firms use marketing and sales tools and techniques more than others.

When considering performance scores across risk categories the findings do not, however, exactly replicate those in the strategy survey. The *medium strategic risk* category is the most satisfied with the performance of the tools and techniques being used for marketing and sales with a combined performance score of 0.65. This is a similar finding to that reported for the strategy function, where this category also led in performance with a score of 0.70 (see Table 3.10). In the marketing and sales function, however, the second performance score is with the *low strategic risk* category, with a score of 0.64, followed by the *high strategic risk* category, with a score of 0.57. This apparent anomaly is easily explained however. It was argued earlier that the Oil & Gas sector has a relatively unique position when it comes to marketing and sales requirements, and this clearly distorts the findings for the high-risk category. As we saw the Oil & Gas sector does not need to use marketing and sales tools and techniques extensively (especially in its upstream exploration and production businesses) because of the presence of a spot market for all oil and gas produced. Given this the utility of marketing and sales tools and techniques is generally perceived to be low and this probably explains the fact that the performance scores for the high-risk category are lower for this function than in the strategy area, where finding the right production assets is obviously critical for Oil & Gas companies forcing them to use strategy tools and techniques extensively.

Despite this major difference the findings in marketing and sales are broadly consistent with those in strategy. The findings here also demonstrate that *high strategic risk* industries tend to use tools and techniques more often (5.51 average uses), and that they do not always value their performance as highly as the other sectors (0.66), especially the *medium strategic risk* category industries (2.64 average uses and 0.70 performance). The reason for this, it was argued in chapter 3, is that the extensive need to use tools and techniques may not always lead to satisfaction – especially if they cannot resolve all of the problems that firms face in the high-risk category. This ensures that while tools and techniques are used more their performance is likely to be judged more critically. On the other hand the firms using tools and techniques less extensively but in medium risk industries may be somewhat more satisfied with performance (as the findings indicate) because the problems to be managed are less taxing and expectations, as result, may be relatively lower.

When assessing the *low strategic risk* category industries and firms it is clear that, not only do they use tools and techniques less (1.45 average uses), but they also have a tendency to value them less as well (recording a 0.60 combined performance score). Despite this there is evidence (reinforcing similar findings in the strategy survey) that, when it comes to the use of tools and techniques that impact on firm-level performance, there is sometimes a high level of performance satisfaction in the low risk category (0.74 for firm performance compared with 0.54 for functional performance). The reason for this, as was also argued in chapter 3, is because these types of industries – which have a more project rather than process based approach operationally and financially – tend to value unique products and services that allow them to differentiate their offerings much more than they do functional improvement initiatives. This is, of course, the opposite for many of the firms operating in the medium and high risk categories that must focus on functional improvement to achieve bottom-line results in highly contested and mature industry sectors.

Once again, therefore, it can be argued that, while there may be evidence of some duplication of effort and a lack of use of marketing and sales specific tools and techniques in general, there is clear evidence that managers in this function were generally positive about the tools and techniques they use. It is also clear that the general pattern of use can be broadly explained based on an understanding of the level of strategic risk that has to be managed by the function. This once again demonstrates that managers, while not always radical innovators, appear to use tried and tested tools and techniques on the basis of fairly rational calculations.

References

Cox, A. (1997), *Business Success*, Helpston, UK: Earlsgate Press.

Evans, P. & Wurster, T. S. (2000), *Blown to Bits*, Boston, Mass: Harvard Business School Press.

Kotler, P. (1994), *Marketing Management*, Englewood Cliffs, NJ: Prentice Hall.

Macrae, C. (1991), *World Class Brands*, Reading, MA: Addison Wesley.

Part III

Operations and Production Management

6
Tools and Techniques for Operations and Production Management

The 73 tools and techniques listed below are not definitive but they do provide a comprehensive listing of some of the major tools and techniques regularly used by managers in the production and operations function, as well as some of the most recently developed by academics and consultants. When appropriate a reference source is provided for further reading. These tools and techniques provide a basis for comparison with the actual tools and techniques found to be in use by operations and production managers in the research survey. These findings are reported in chapter 7.

1. Activity Based Costing
See the reference in Strategy Tools and Techniques (chapter 2).

2. Agile
This concept refers to an approach associated with the development of a responsive and flexible approach to manufacturing and production processes and systems. The approach is based on a rejection of lean principles in favour of an approach that focuses on companies developing operating systems that allow them to be flexible and responsive to rapidly changing consumer demand requirements. In this approach waster reduction is less important that responsiveness and flexibility.

❖ Fisher, M. L. (1997) 'What is the Right Supply Chain for Your Product?', *Harvard Business Review* (May–June).
❖ Christopher, M. (2000), 'The Agile Supply Chain', *Industrial Marketing Management*, Vol. 29.

3. Balanced Scorecard
See the reference in Strategy Tools and Techniques (chapter 2).

4.   *Batch Production*
In terms of process type, batch production is an approach characterised by medium volume and medium variety, enabling labour and general-purpose equipment to be shared across the range of products. It involves the transformation of predetermined quantities of a product known as a batch. Each stage of manufacturing tends to be clearly separated. This means that periods of added value processing will be separated by periods of non-added value movement and delay. The result is an intermittent flow of materials, conditioning high levels of work-in-progress. Throughput efficiency is often low, which may result in a slow response from order to delivery. In spite of such delays, batch processing remains the most common form of process in manufacturing. Its main advantage is the flexibility it allows to produce a wide range of outputs in differing volumes.

❖ Slack, N. (ed.), *Blackwell's Encyclopaedic Dictionary of Operations Management* (1999).

5.   *Behavioural Models*
Behavioural models of job design aim to understand an individual's attitude towards their work. Those jobs that fulfil personal needs of self-esteem and personal development are more likely to achieve satisfactory work performance, and hence, an approach such as vertical job loading (job enrichment) might be used to provide greater opportunities for self-actualisation in the workplace. This technique seeks to create more satisfying jobs by adding work at a different level of responsibility rather than increasing the total amount of work carried out. The result tends to be a more motivated and flexible workforce. Job rotation is another method of increasing job satisfaction – workers move from one job to another as a way of extending the scope and variety of tasks in a form of horizontal job loading.

❖ Slack, N. (ed.), *Blackwell's Encyclopaedic Dictionary of Operations Management* (1999).

6.   *Benchmarking*
See the reference in Strategy Tools and Techniques (chapter 2).

7.   *Blueprinting Techniques*
There are a variety of techniques designed to facilitate process documentation. All have two primary features – they indicate the flow of materials, people, and information through an operation, and identify the different activities that make up that process. The following tools might be utilised:

• Simple flow charts.

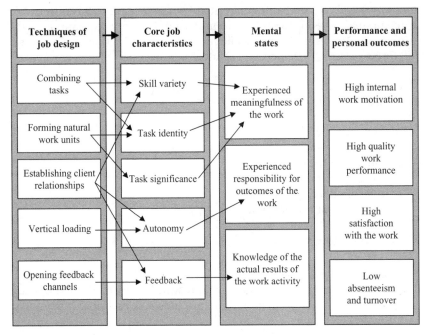

Figure 6.1 A Typical 'Behavioural' Job Design Model
Source: *Operations Management*, Slack, N., Chambers, S., Harland, C., Harrison, A., and Johnston, R., Pearson Education Limited © 1998, London: Pitman Publishing.

- Routing sheets, which describe the activity, and list the tools and equipment required.
- Flow process charts, which use different symbols to identify activity types, allowing a more detailed design and evaluation.
- A customer-processing framework, which identifies the key activities in 'processing' customers through an operation – selection, point of entry, response time, point of impact, delivery, point of departure, and follow-up.

❖ Slack, N. (ed.), *Blackwell's Encyclopaedic Dictionary of Operations Management* (1999).

8. *Brainstorming*
See the reference in Strategy Tools and Techniques (chapter 2).

9. *Business Excellence Model*
The Business Excellence model was established in 1992 as part of the European Foundation for Quality Management's European Quality Awards. The basic approach of the model is to allow companies to self-assess their organisational capabilities. This is achieved by providing a self-assessment

framework to help companies understand what the path to business excellence in quality terms looks like, to understand current gaps and provide stimulation for resolution of problems. Basic principles that are measured fall into two types – enablers and results – and include:

- customer focus;
- results orientation;
- leadership and constancy of purpose;
- management by processes and facts;
- people development and involvement;
- continuous learning;
- innovation and improvement;
- partnership development; and,
- corporate social responsibility.

❖ Contact: info@efqm.org

10.   Business Operating Model
This is basically a procedural framework relating to the method of operating within a particular firm, providing the guidelines that shape day-to-day running of the business.

11.   Business Process Re-engineering (BPR)
See the reference in Strategy Tools and Techniques (chapter 2).

12.   Capability Maturity Model
Developed at Carnegie University in the US, this idea for systems/software engineering sees 'best in class' design practices measured against the industry benchmarks of the CMM. It looks at five levels of maturity – initial, repeatable, defined, managed, and optimising. Each level has key process areas of best practice. The model's value is its provision of a structure for improvement – firms can attempt to gain different levels of accreditation. There have been efforts to incorporate its use with return on investment, but this is obviously very difficult.

❖ Slack, N. (ed.), *Blackwell's Encyclopaedic Dictionary of Operations Management* (1999).

13.   Capacity Management
Operational capacity is the maximum level of value-adding activity that a process can achieve over a given period under normal operating conditions. Measuring capacity is problematic owing to the complexity of resources. Input and output measures are those most commonly utilised. In practical terms, it

is not always possible to achieve an operation's *theoretical/design capacity*. Hence, one may need to calculate *effective capacity* by subtracting the losses that result from change-over and maintenance. Queuing theory is often used to set capacity levels. In the process of capacity planning and control, managers are usually faced with a forecast of demand that is neither certain nor constant. Though they may have an idea of their own ability to meet this demand, accumulation of quantitative data on capacity and demand is advisable prior to decision-making. Having measured aggregate demand and capacity levels for the planning period, they can then identify alternative capacity plans that could be adopted in response to demand fluctuations, and choose the most appropriate for their circumstance. The dynamics of capacity management demand both a long- and short-term outlook (Figure 6.2):

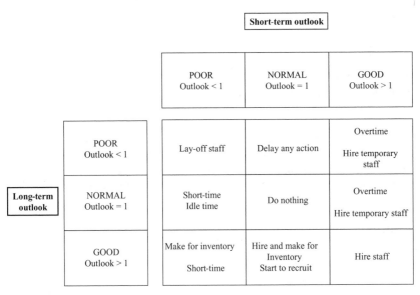

		Short-term outlook		
		POOR Outlook < 1	NORMAL Outlook = 1	GOOD Outlook > 1
Long-term outlook	POOR Outlook < 1	Lay-off staff	Delay any action	Overtime Hire temporary staff
	NORMAL Outlook = 1	Short-time Idle time	Do nothing	Overtime Hire temporary staff
	GOOD Outlook > 1	Make for inventory Short-time	Hire and make for Inventory Start to recruit	Hire staff

Figure 6.2 The Outlook Matrix
Source: *Operations Management*, Slack, N., Chambers, S., Harland, C., Harrison, A., and Johnston, R., Pearson Education Limited © 1998, London: Pitman Publishing.

❖ Bleuel, W. H., 'Management science's impact on service strategy', *Interfaces* (1975).
❖ Chaiken, J. M. & Larson, R. C., 'Methods for allocating urban emergency units survey', *Management Science* (1972).
❖ Holt, C., Modigliani, C. F. & Simon, H., 'A linear decision rule for production and employment scheduling', *Management Science* (1955).
❖ Lee, W. B. & Khumwala, B. M., 'Simulation testing of aggregate production planning models in an implementation methodology', *Management Science* (1974).

14. *Cell Layout and Production Flow Analysis (PFA)*

A cell layout is a hybrid facility arrangement based on the combination of principles of fixed position and product layout. It involves the grouping together of dissimilar machines according to the design of the product being made, or the operations required for its production. It differs from product layout, however, in its potential for variation of the operation sequence and flow. Workers also tend to be multi-skilled. Predominately utilised for intermittent batch operations, it generates whole product families rather than single products, operating on principles of 'group technology.' Overcoming many of the disadvantages associated with product layout, it also has the benefit of providing a single planning point. Production flow analysis provides the most popular means of allocating tasks and machines to cells. Its matrix format provides simultaneous analysis of both product requirements and process grouping.

❖ Slack, N. et al., *Operations Management* (1998).

15. *Computer-Aided Design (CAD)*

Providing the ability to create and modify product drawings, CAD systems allow conventionally used shapes to be added to a computer-based representation of the product. Incorporated into the design, these "entities" can subsequently be copied, rotated, magnified, etc. Though capable of configuration with a range of computers, large mainframe through to single PC, degree of sophistication and modelling ability will vary in relation to the software deployed. The ability to store and retrieve design data quickly, and to manipulate its details, clearly increases both the productivity and flexibility of design activity. CAD, moreover, is more than simply a drafting device, since it also performs a prototyping function.

❖ Slack, N. et al., *Operations Management* (1998).

16. *Continuous Improvement (Kaizen)*

This approach to improving operational performance promotes an ongoing process that sees frequent, incremental steps towards improvement in contrast to the breakthrough improvements that emphasise immediate creativity. 'Kaizen' is the Japanese word for 'improvement' – use of this term stresses adaptability, teamwork, and attention to detail.

❖ Slack, N. (ed.), *Blackwell's Encyclopaedic Dictionary of Operations Management* (1999).

17. *Continuous Production*

This type of production tends to involve relatively inflexible, capital-intensive technologies with highly predictable flow. There is usually little labour input, the worker focused on process control and monitoring. High volume, low variety, and an extended operating period are all typical features.

❖ Slack, N. (ed.), *Blackwell's Encyclopaedic Dictionary of Operations Management* (1999).

18. Design Chain Management
This is a specific form of supply chain relating to the transfer of information between organisations in the interests of product design and development. It focuses on management by those participants, both internal and external to a focal firm, who contribute the capabilities necessary for product development. The chain involves all contributors from product conceptualisation through to prototype manufacture and beyond.

❖ Slack, N. (ed.), *Blackwell's Encyclopaedic Dictionary of Operations Management* (1999).

19. Design for Manufacture
This approach demands reassessment of the design requirements for particular projects. Particularly useful in project-based industries, the aim is to focus on manufacturing issues at an early stage in the design cycle.

❖ Slack, N. (ed.), *Blackwell's Encyclopaedic Dictionary of Operations Management* (1999).

20. Design to Cost
This technique aims to develop solutions fitted to client need. It requires that firms closely monitor the costs of each aspect of a project, providing an important check, particularly within project-based industries.

❖ Slack, N. et al., *Operations Management* (1998), London: Pitman Publishing.

21/22/23. E-Business Applications
See the references to the three types of E-Business Applications (Seller/Internal/Buyer) in Strategy Tools and Techniques (chapter 2).

24. Economic Order Quantity (EOQ) Formula
When stock needs replenishing, the EOQ formula provides a common means of deciding how much of any particular item to order. It is the quantity that will keep the sum of total annual ordering and stockholding costs at a minimum (Figure 6.3).

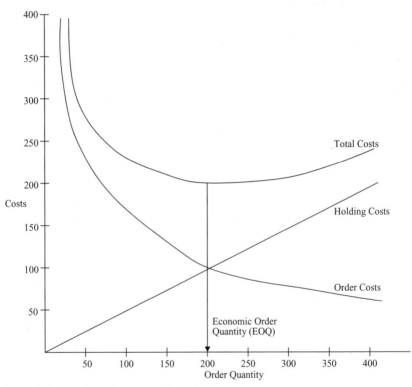

$$EOQ = \sqrt{\frac{2SD}{IV}}$$

S = cost of raising a single order
D = annual demand
I = annual stockholding fraction
V = value of one unit of stock

Figure 6.3   Graphical Representation of EOQ
Source: *Operations Management*, Slack, N., Chambers, S., Harland, C., Harrison, A., and Johnston, R., Pearson Education Limited © 1998, London: Pitman Publishing.

The EOQ formula does, however, have its limitations:

- the ordering cost (S) and stockholding fraction (I) are very difficult to estimate accurately
- mechanical application of the formula can generate order quantities representing several years of usage (though this can be overcome by setting an upper limit)
- unit value is assumed to be constant and unaffected by order quantity, which means that no account is taken of bulk discounts, a fairly

major omission given that these may be far in excess of any other costs
- application of the formula to every stock item may demand an unacceptable change in the size of the purchasing department, or in the amount of storage space required
- for manufacturing decisions on batch size, it is more important to balance capacity than set-up and stockholding costs.

❖ Slack, N. (ed.), Blackwell's *Encyclopaedic Dictionary of Operations Management* (1999), Oxford: Blackwell.

25. Empowerment
In its application to job design, this principle concentrates on increasing individual autonomy to shape the nature of daily activities. This thinking can be fed into autonomous work teams – staff with overlapping skills collectively perform a defined task, granted a high degree of discretion over how they actually achieve their objectives. There are three levels of empowerment – suggestion involvement, job involvement, and high involvement.

❖ Slack, N. (ed.), *Blackwell's Encyclopaedic Dictionary of Operations Management* (1999).

26. Ergonomics
Considering the physiological aspects of job design, ergonomics examines both how the human body fits into its workplace, and how it copes with its immediate environment, particularly in terms of heating, lighting, and noise characteristics.

❖ Slack, N. (ed.), Blackwell's Encyclopaedic Dictionary of Operations Management (1999), Oxford: Blackwell.

27. ERP Systems
Enterprise Resource Planning systems are relatively new and are associated with the development of IT and Internet applications. The basic idea of ERP systems is that they provide management information systems that reduce the 'data rich information poor' situation often found in companies due to the proliferation of IT systems that cannot speak to one another effectively. One of the most common applications is SAP, although there are many others including those offered by Oracle and Microsoft etc.

28. Failure Analysis
This activity aims to identify the root cause of failure in order to gain an understanding and take steps to prevent a future occurrence. Different mechanisms can be utilised to seek out failure in a proactive way – process

checks, complaint cards, surveys, etc. Further tools and techniques are available to provide analysis in the wake of failure. Using cheap and readily available information, complaint analysis is perhaps the most common means of assessment, but the following methods are also frequently applied:

- *Blueprinting* – systematic documentation and evaluation of processes enables potential problems to be identified and their causes investigated prior to implementation
- *Failure Mode and Effect Analysis (FMEA)* – mostly used in the design stage of products, this checklist procedure not only identifies potential problems, but also assess their likelihood and the consequences of failure
- *Fault Tree Analysis* – working backwards from a failure or potential failure, this logical procedure identifies all the possible causes, and hence, the origins of that failure. The fault tree consists of branches connected by AND and OR nodes – all the branches below an AND node need to coincide for the event above the node to occur, but only one of the branches below an OR node is required to condition the same. In these terms, a cause-effect 'map' of failure is constructed. The advantage of such analysis is that it codifies a common understanding of the intrinsic logic of failure possibility.
- *Critical Incident Technique (CIT)* – this service quality technique attempts to identify critical incidents in order to understand customer-perceived quality and engineer its improvement. Critical incidents are events that contribute towards, or detract from, perceived service/product performance in a significant way, either positively or negatively. CIT analysis usually comprises two questions, asking customers to think of a time when:

a) they felt pleased with the service/product received, and why
b) they were dissatisfied with the service/product, and why.

The value of CIT is that it provides an understanding of quality from the customer's point-of-view. However, the fact that incidents may have occurred long before the collection of data, subsequently reinterpreted in the light of further events, is an obvious weakness. The time-consuming nature of the technique, moreover, tends to condition a low response-rate from customers.

❖ Slack, N. et al., *Operations Management* (1998).

29.   *Failure Mode and Effect Analysis (FMEA)*
Aiming to identify the product/service features that are critical to different types of failure, FMEA provides a means of recognising symptoms before a

problem becomes unmanageable. It operates through a checklist procedure built around three key questions:

- What is the likelihood that failure will occur?
- What would be the consequences of failure?
- How likely is such a failure to be detected before it affects the customer?

Quantitative evaluation of these three questions enables generation of a risk priority number (RPN) for each potential cause of failure. Causes whose RPN warrants priority attention can then be addressed with corrective action. FMEA basically constitutes a seven-step process:

1) identify all the component parts of the products/service
2) list all the possible ways in which the components could fail (the failure modes)
3) identify the possible effects of failure (down-time, safety, repair requirements, effect on customers)
4) identify all the possible causes of failure for each failure mode
5) assess the probability of failure, the severity of the effects, and the likelihood of detection (rating scales can be used to quantify these three factors)
6) calculate the RPN by multiplying all three ratings together
7) instigate corrective action on failure modes exhibiting a high RPN

❖ Slack, N. (ed.), *Blackwell's Encyclopaedic Dictionary of Operations Management* (1999), Oxford: Blackwell.

30. Five 'S' Strategy Analysis
See the reference in Strategy Tools and Techniques (chapter 2).

31. Fixed-Position Layout
This technique of facility arrangement sees a stationary product or person transformed by appropriate transfer of resources around a place of work. Such a layout usually features in batch production or jobbing operations. Most crucially, it provides product flexibility, since machines are general-purpose, workers are multi-skilled, and several different products can be produced simultaneously. Resource location analysis is often employed to decide upon the location of work-centres within a stable fixed-position arrangement. Using criteria associated both with the site itself and the interaction of its resources, this method of evaluation examines the effects of locating transforming resources at all available site locations. The aim is to minimise cost and inconvenience as transforming resources are moved in relation to the transformed product or person.

❖ Gaither, N., Frazier, B. V., and Wei, J. C., 'From job shops to manufacturing cells', *Production and Inventory Management Journal* (1990).

❖ Hyer, N. L. and Wemmerlov, U., 'Group technology and productivity', *Harvard Business Review* (1984).

32.   *Gap Analysis*
See the reference in Strategy Tools and Techniques (chapter 2).

33.   *Hazard Analysis*
Such analysis is undertaken in the assessment of potential risk. It involves carrying out a series of technical tests on those materials in use. Specific testing will depend on a firm's product criteria.

❖ Slack, N. (ed.), *Blackwell's Encyclopaedic Dictionary of Operations Management* (1999), Oxford: Blackwell.

34.   *Hill Methodology*
This approach to the formulation of operations strategy was devised by Professor Terry Hill of London Business School. His five-step procedure (Figure 6.4) attempts to provide a link between different levels of strategic thinking:

1) Understand the long-term corporate objectives of the organisation.
2) Understand how marketing strategy has been developed to achieve corporate objectives – develop knowledge of the product/service market, and the characteristics (range, mix, and volume) that the operation must satisfy.
3) Integrate marketing strategy with the "competitive factors" of customer requirement – examine for any mismatch between organisation strategy and operational potentialities.
4) Define an appropriate and consistent set of structural characteristics for operational best practice (process choice).
5) Define the infra-structural features of operation.

Rather than envisaging a sequential movement through these steps, Hill sees the process as an iterative one. Thus, operations managers are expected to combine an understanding of the long-term strategic requirements of an operation with an awareness of the specific resource developments necessitated by this strategy.

❖ Slack, N. (ed.), Blackwell's *Encyclopaedic Dictionary of Operations Management* (1999), Oxford: Blackwell.

35.   *Importance-Performance Matrix*
First proposed by Martilla and James in 1977, this matrix provides an effective means of judging the relative performance priorities that need to be applied to competitive criteria (Figure 6.5). Its strength in utility is the ability to bring

Step 1	Step 2	Step 3	Step 4	Step 5
Corporate Objectives	Marketing strategy	How do products or services win orders?	Operations Strategy	
			Product choice	Infrastructure
• Growth rates • Profitability • Return on net assets • Cash flow • Financial 'gearing'	• Product/ service markets and segments • Range of products/ services • Mix of specifications • Volumes • Standardisation or customisation • Rate of innovation	• Price • Quality • Delivery Speed • Delivery dependability • Product/ service range • Product/ service design • Brand image • Supporting services	• Process technology • Trade-offs embodied in the process • Role of inventory • Capacity, size, timing, location	• Functional support • Operations planning and control systems • Work structuring • Payment systems • Organisational structure

Figure 6.4   The Hill Methodology of Operations Strategy Formulation
Source: *Operations Management*, Slack, N., Chambers, S., Harland, C., Harrison, A., and Johnston, R., Pearson Education Limited © 1998, London: Pitman Publishing.

together both a customer (importance) and competitor (performance) perspective. The matrix itself is divided into zones representing different improvement priorities. Below the 'lower boundary of acceptability' (AB), there is a need to improve, but it is only in the zone below line CD that urgent action is required. Line EF provides a further boundary between performance regarded as 'appropriate', and that characterised as 'excessive'. In the case of excess performance, it is recommended that one assess to see whether it might be possible to divert resources to a more needy factor.

❖ Slack, N. (ed.), *Blackwell's Encyclopaedic Dictionary of Operations Management* (1999).

36. Improvement Analysis

This is the process of quantifying action, of measuring performance. It recognises that the level of performance a business attains is a function of the efficiency and effectiveness of the actions undertaken by its management. Discredited by their focus on the short-term and lack of strategic focus, traditional cost-accounting performance measures have tended to be

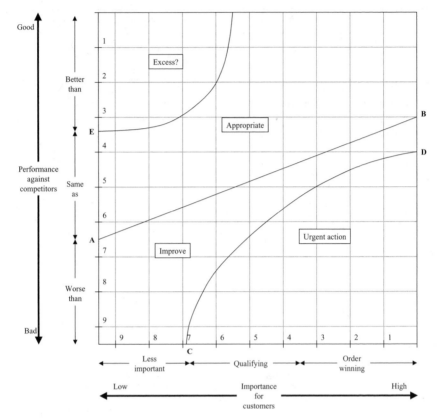

Figure 6.5 Importance-Performance Matrix
Source: *Operations Management*, Slack, N., Chambers, S., Harland, C., Harrison, A., and Johnston, R., Pearson Education Limited © 1998, London: Pitman Publishing.

replaced by newer methods that not only monitor performance, but also assess the company's health, stimulate learning, and improve communication. This approach is perhaps best illustrated by Kaplan and Norton's balanced scorecard, which provides a measurement system aimed at answering the following questions:

- How do we look to our shareholders? (financial perspective)
- Where must we excel? (internal business perspective)
- What are customer perceptions? (customer perspective)
- How can we improve and create extra value? (innovation and learning perspective)

The value of measurement is that it tends to stimulate action and improve communication. However, a range of factors must be considered in the implementation of an effective measure, factors that are incorporated in the following ten-step procedure:

1) Measure – fix self-explanatory title
2) Purpose – specify underlying rationale
3) Business Objectives – identify the company aims to which the measure relates
4) Target – specify the level of performance to be achieved and a time-scale for its realisation to enable ongoing assessment
5) Formula – determine the way performance is to be measured
6) Frequency – determine how often performance is to be measured
7) Responsibility – identify who is to collect and report the data
8) Source – specify derivation of the data
9) Response – identify who is to act on the data
10) Action – define the management processes that should be followed depending upon the level of performance identified

❖ Slack, N. et al., *Operations Management* (1998).

37. ISO Quality System

Establishing the requirements for a company's quality management systems, the ISO 9000 series provides a set of world-wide standards. Listing the features and characteristics required in the documented policies, manuals, and procedures of an organisation, its aim is to support a process of systematic quality assurance and control. However, rather than outlining the specific methods by which to achieve control, these standards represent a codification of the principles of control, enabling alternate interpretation and application across a wide range of environments. The series encompasses five individual standards:

- *ISO 9000* – guidelines for selection and use of quality assurance standards
- ISO 9001 – model for quality assurance in design/development, production, installation, and servicing
- ISO 9002 – model for quality assurance in production and installation
- ISO 9003 – model for quality assurance in final inspection and testing
- ISO 9004 – guidelines for quality management systems

❖ Slack, N. (ed.), *Blackwell's Encyclopaedic Dictionary of Operations Management* (1999).

38. Just-In-Time Techniques (Lean Manufacturing)

The primary objective of JIT, according to Taiichi Ohno (1988), is to make the time between customer order and cash collection as short as possible.

Three broad approaches characterise the quest for superior performance manufacturing that is a hallmark of JIT philosophy:

1) use of techniques to identify and reduce all causes of waste
2) an inclusive concept of 'total' worker involvement
3) processes of continuous improvement (kaizen)

A further feature is the progressive removal of (surplus) resources, educating the operation in a more streamlined approach. JIT has been broken down by Bicheno (1991) into 'stage one' techniques (of simplification), and 'stage two' techniques (of integration):

Stage One
- *Design for manufacture* – the aim is for simplicity in both design and manufacture.
- *Focus* – operational tasks are limited to a consistent and achievable set of goals.
- *Use of small machines* – less subject to bottlenecks, lengthy maintenance, and the build up of inventories, several of these tend to be used in preference to a single, large one.
- *Simple layout and flow* – machines and processes are moved closer together in line with layout principles, reducing wasted effort in the transport of materials.
- *Total productive maintenance (TPM)* – the aim is to assure maximum equipment up-time at minimum cost, and to drive dependability of operations.
- *Set-up reduction (SUR)* – reducing equipment change-over time between batches is crucial to the objective of improving flexibility without loss of capacity. Traditional thinking has been constrained by the economic batch quantity formula, with its perceived trade-off between the carrying cost of inventory and a fixed set-up cost. However, it is increasingly recognised that reduced set-up times are capable of translation into reduced batch sizes. This enables early discovery of defects, means that less inventory is required, and results in the reduction of throughput times.
- *Team preparation* – within a total quality environment, workers are assigned to particular product work areas, but the ultimate aim is to develop operators who are both multi-skilled and multi-functional.

Stage Two
- *Flow scheduling* – materials are kept moving in line with the 'direction' of a factory assembly schedule.
- *Inventory reduction* – a product of the reduced batch sizes and buffer stocks that result from improvements in set-up time, productive maintenance, and flow scheduling.

- *Visibility* – charts and fulfilment check-sheets record the status of operation processes and improvement projects, providing transparency of operation within a culture of shared information.
- *Enforced improvement* – deliberately creating pressure for change, the motivation is a further identification and reduction of waste.
- *Co-makership* – joint development programmes, partnership agreements, integrated systems, and mutual investments tend to emerge given an understanding of dependencies within the supply chain.

JIT is operationalised through the use of *kanbans* and application of *heijunka*:

◆ Kanban
Delegating routine material control transactions to the shop floor, this simple to operate, visible control system provides a means to organise supply as appropriate, to synchronise part movements during the course of manufacture. 'Pull scheduling' sees parts pulled from preceding processes in line with demand. Kanban can be classified into three basic categories:

a) *conveyance* – signals to a previous stage that material can be withdrawn from inventory and transferred to a specific destination
b) *production* – signals to a production process that it can begin manufacture of a specific inventory item
c) *vendor* – signals to an external supplier that material/parts must be sent to a specific process stage

◆ Heijunka (Levelled scheduling)
Following levelling, it is possible to co-ordinate scheduled material movements when work cycles repeat. This approach can be extended throughout the supply chain. It involves the even distribution of volume and mix over a given production time-span (Figure 6.6).

The weekly production schedule for a range of products (A, B and C) runs at 200, 120, and 80 respectively. Even product usage across the range tends to lead to production peaks, imposing excessive work on each process team. Hence, it is advisable to level the finished product schedule as much as possible, and furthermore, to down-date that levelling to production of sub-assemblies and components. Batch sizes might be reduced (5A, 3B, 2C), but even greater levelling would be achieved by scheduling in the sequence AABABCABCA. Such a mixed-model assembly sequence achieves maximum repetition in the shortest cycle. However, its production system requirements are demanding – the capability to switch quickly between product mixes, and the harmonisation of machine processing capacities.

❖ Henricks, J. A., 'Performance measures for a JIT manufacturer', *Industrial Engineering* (1994).

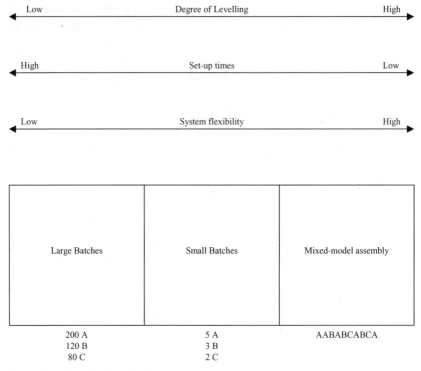

Figure 6.6   Levelled Scheduling
Source: Slack, N., (ed), *Blackwell's Encyclopaedic Dictionary of Strategic Management* (1999) Blackwell Publishing.

- ❖ Jordan, H. H., 'Inventory management in the JIT age', *Production and Inventory Management Journal* (1988).
- ❖ Slack, N. (ed.), *Blackwell's Encyclopaedic Dictionary of Operations Management* (1999).

39.   Johnson's Rule
Used to organise the scheduling of n jobs through two work centres, this rule first determines the smallest processing time. If that time applies to the first work centre, then that job should be scheduled first, or as near first as possible. If the next smallest time applies to the second work centre, then that job should be scheduled last, or as near last as possible. This process is continued until all the jobs have been scheduled.

- ❖ Slack, N. (ed.), *Blackwell's Encyclopaedic Dictionary of Operations Management* (1999).

40.   Key Performance Indicators (KPIs)
See the reference in the Strategy Tools and Techniques (chapter 2).

41.   Knowledge Management
See the reference in Strategy Tools and Techniques (chapter 2).

42.   Location Techniques
Systematic and quantitative techniques can provide assistance in the process of location decision-making:

- *Weighted-score method* – having identified the criteria of evaluation, these are weighted to indicate relative importance, and each location is rated in accordance with these measures.
- *Centre-of-gravity method* – operating on the principle that all potential locations have a 'value' which is the sum of transportation costs to and from that site, this technique aims to minimise those costs. A weighted centre of gravity for all transportation points represents the best possible location.

- ❖ Baker, B. N. and Wileman, D. L., 'A summary of major research findings regarding the human element in project management', *IEEE Engineering Management Review* (1981).
- ❖ Randolph, W. A., and Posner, B. Z., 'What every project manager needs to know about project manager needs to know about project management', *Sloan Management Review* (1988).

43.   Maintenance Techniques

◆ Condition-Based Maintenance (CBM)
This approach involves intervention to repair or replace parts on the basis of an ongoing monitoring activity. CBM aims to perform facility maintenance only when required, and can involve study of any equipment characteristic that might indicate its condition.

◆ Preventive Maintenance (PM)
By servicing facilities at pre-planned intervals, it is hoped to either eliminate or reduce the chances of failure.

◆ Reliability-Centred Maintenance (RCM)
RCM recognises that if maintenance can't either predict or prevent failure, and such failure has important consequences, efforts need to be directed at reducing impact. The approach adopted in maintenance is dictated by the pattern of failure exhibited by the different failure modes for each part in a system.

◆ Run to Breakdown (RTB)
Facilities continue operating until they fail, and only then is maintenance work performed.

♦ Total Productive Maintenance (TPM)

Defined by Nakajima as 'productive maintenance carried out by all employees through small group activities', TPM aims to establish good maintenance practices by the fulfilment of five basic goals:

1) improve equipment effectiveness
2) achieve autonomous maintenance
3) plan maintenance
4) train all staff in relevant maintenance skills
5) achieve early equipment management

❖ Slack, N. (ed.), *Blackwell's Encyclopaedic Dictionary of Operations Management* (1999), Oxford: Blackwell.

44. *Management Information Systems (MIS)*

See the reference in Strategy Tools and Techniques (chapter 2).

45. *MRP Systems*

There are normally two different types of MRP system, sometimes known as MRPI and MRPII.

♦ Material Requirements Planning (MRPI)

Utilising a master production schedule (MPS) in conjunction with inventory status data, lead-time information, and a bill of materials (the recipe for each product assembly), this computer-based set of planning techniques establishes the requirements for all sub-assemblies, components, and raw materials that contribute to a finished product. It recommends replenishment ordering of materials when necessary, and highlights a need to reschedule open orders when due dates/need dates are out of phase. Designed for a dependent demand environment, MRPI basically aims to provide the right parts at the right time. Through a company's MPS, it is committed to producing certain volumes of finished product within a particular time period, which drives MRP. In line with management policies and objectives, and the resources of the business, this master production schedule can be drawn together through a planning process that assesses both customer orders and forecast demand. An outgrowth of material requirements planning and the intermediary stage before MRPII, closed-loop MRP allows for the checking of plans against capacity to determine whether they are realistic and achievable. Closing of the loop at planning stage is achieved by this review of aims in relation to resources, and by the feeding back of necessary alterations.

♦ Manufacturing Resources Planning (MRPII)

This is a structured approach to manufacturing management that deploys an integrated business system for effective closed-loop planning of all company resources. Functional areas of the business are linked by the shared information of a central database, use of which encourages inter-departmental interaction. MRPII provides a comprehensive approach to business management, but in order to succeed, it requires thorough under-standing of its underlying philosophy and discipline, top management support, stable implementation, and the commitment of resources to support education and training.

❖ Slack, N. (ed.), *Blackwell's Encyclopaedic Dictionary of Operations Management* (1999).

46. *Network Analysis*

Project network techniques provide a means to determine the sequence of activities and their subsequent scheduling. Through a network analysis process, also referred to as CPM (critical path method) or PERT (programme evaluation review technique), constituent project activities are assembled into a logical, diagrammatic model, and then analysed in terms of time and resource. The planning sequence runs as follows:

1) determine all the activities required to complete the project
2) produce a diagram that models their logical sequence
3) assign a duration to each activity
4) calculate the total duration of the project, and the timings of each activity

Future success of a project is often dependent on the production of an acceptable plan, and this demands consensus amongst the whole team. Updated regularly with activity progress, this plan is also re-analysed to produce revised scheduling. There are two diagrammatic standards in network analysis:

• *Arrow* (activity on arrow, or AOA)
• *Precedence* (activity on node, AON)

Both achieve the same purpose in modelling the project, but the *precedence* method tends to be more appropriate for complex interactivity relation-ships. It is drawn in conventional fashion from left to right (Figure 6.7), encompassing:

• *Activities* – represented by a nodal rectangle
• *Constraints* – relationships between activities, represented by an arrow
• *Milestone Activities* – important nodal points in the plan (START or END), represented by a different shape as a means of distinction, since no time is consumed

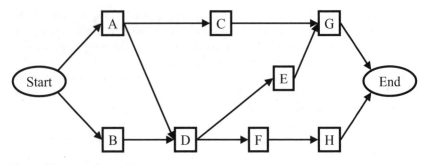

Figure 6.7   Precedence Diagram
Source: Slack, N., (ed), *Blackwell's Encyclopaedic Dictionary of Strategic Management* (1999) Blackwell Publishing.

❖ Slack, N. (ed.), *Blackwell's Encyclopaedic Dictionary of Operations Management* (1999).

47.   New Product Development Process
See the reference in Marketing and Sales Tools and Techniques (chapter 4).

48.   Optimised Production Technology (OPT)
This computer-based tool enables scheduling of production systems to the pace dictated by the most heavily loaded resources (bottle-necks). Use of OPT is a recognition that if the rate of system activity exceeds that of a bottle-neck, item production surpasses capacity, but if the rate falls below bottle-neck pace, the entire system is under-utilised. The principles of OPT are as follows:

1) Flow must be balanced rather than capacity.
2) The level of utilisation of a non-bottleneck is determined by other constraints in the system, not by its own capacity.
3) Utilisation and activation of a resource are not the same.
4) An hour lost at a bottle-neck is an hour lost forever by the entire system.
5) An hour saved at a non-bottleneck is a mirage.
6) Bottle-necks govern both the throughput and inventory of the system.
7) The transfer batch does not always equal the process batch.
8) The process batch should be variable.
9) Lead-times are the result of a schedule, and can't be predetermined.
10) Schedules should be established by examining all constraints simultaneously.

❖ Jacobi, M. A., 'How to unlock the benefits of MRP II and just-in-time', *Hospital Maternity Management Quarterly* (1994).
❖ Miller, J. G., and Sprague, L. G., 'Behind the growth in materials requirements planning', *Harvard Business Review* (1975).
❖ Porter, K., Little, D., Kenworthy, J., and Jarvis, P., 'Finite capacity scheduling tools: observations of installations offer some lessons', *Integrated Manufacturing Systems* (1996).

49. *Pareto Analysis*

This provides a means to assess the relative importance of items, events, and activities for the purpose of classification. Within the context of inventory management, it is used to arrange stock item groups on the basis of total annual expenditure. Given the impracticality of giving detailed attention to every item, it increasingly constitutes an essential element of organisational arrangements. Analysis begins with an identification of those factors that might make a high degree of control appropriate – high rate of usage, and high unit value, for example. These factors can be assessed for each stock item by calculating the total value of annual usage, or annual requirement value (ARV), ascertained by multiplying unit value by annual usage. Cumulative ARV can be plotted against item numbers to produce a Pareto curve (Figure 6.8). The first 20% of items typically account for 80% of cumulative ARV, and demand fairly sophisticated methods of control.

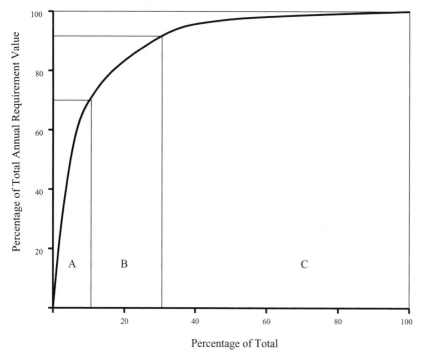

Figure 6.8   Pareto Curve
Source: Slack, N., (ed), *Blackwell's Encyclopaedic Dictionary of Strategic Management* (1999) Blackwell Publishing.

❖ Austin, L. M., 'Project EOQ: a success story in implementing academic research', *Interfaces* (1977).
❖ Nakane, J. and Hall, R., 'Management Specs for Stockless Production', *Harvard Business Review* (1983).

❖ Slack, N. (ed.), *Blackwell's Encyclopaedic Dictionary of Operations Management* (1999).

50.   Partnership Sourcing
See the reference in Procurement and Supply Tools and Techniques (chapter 8).

51.   Platts Gregory Procedure
This three-stage procedure was developed by Ken Platts and Professor Mike Gregory of Cambridge University:

Stage One – assess the opportunities and threats of the competitive environment in order to understand an organisation's market position. By comparing 'profiles' of market requirement and achieved performance, gaps in operational strategy can be highlighted.

Stage Two – assess operational capabilities, identifying current practice and the extent to which it enables effective performance.

Stage Three – develop new operational strategies by reviewing options and selecting those most suitable for facilitating current capabilities and overcoming identified gaps.

❖ Bhattacharya, A. K., Jina, J. & Walton, A. D., 'Product market turbulence and time compression: three dimensions of an integrated approach to manufacturing systems design', *International Journal of Operations and Production Management* (1996).
❖ Chyr, F., 'The effect of varying set-up costs', International Journal of Operations and Production Management (1996).
❖ Hayes, R. H. and Pisano, G. P., 'Beyond world class: the new manufacturing strategy', *HBR* (1994).
❖ Slack, N. (ed.), *Blackwell's Encyclopaedic Dictionary of Operations Management* (1999).

52.   Problem Solving and Improvement Techniques
There are many problem solving and improvement tools and techniques. The most common are root cause or cause and effect diagrams (also known as fish-bone or Ishikawa diagrams). Other techniques include: flow charts, input-output analysis, scatter diagrams and why-why analysis.

❖ Slack, N. et al. (1998), *Operations Management*, London: Pitman.

53.   Process Layout
This approach to facility arrangement sees all similar production processes grouped together in the same area. It is utilised most commonly in batch operations that see a single production operation, or

limited number, carried out on parts routed from one process area to another. Batch priority can be changed as they progress through the production system, providing a degree of flexibility, and the opportunity for specialised supervision is a further advantage. Unfortunately, high work-in-progress levels, frequent set-ups, extensive material movements, and long throughput times, mean that this type of layout is not without its weaknesses. Designed to offer the best efficiency, to ensure that total material movement is minimised, CRAFT (computerised relative allocation of facilities technique) and CORELAP (computerised relationship layout planning) are computer software packages that can be used to optimise process layout. However, these only offer the solution to a static problem, and in reality, problem-solving is very much a dynamic process. Hence, 'simulation' is becoming an increasingly popular tool for analysis of layout design, enabling the instantaneous assessment of modifications.

❖ Slack, N. (ed.), *Blackwell's Encyclopaedic Dictionary of Operations Management* (1999).

54. Process Mapping
By outlining the different stages of a work process, usually using a flow diagram, it is not only possible for a company to ensure adherence to the correct procedure, but it can also identify potential areas for improvement, and thus, streamline its operations.

55. Product Design Evaluation Stage
This stage analyses a preliminary design for possible improvements before the product is introduced to the market for testing:

♦ Quality Function Deployment (QFD)
Developed at Mitsubishi in Japan, this structured procedure aims to translate the expressed or perceived needs of the customer into specific product or service design characteristics, with subsequent impact on process and operational characteristics. Prioritising design process requirements (the whats), the principal objective is to reconcile these with design solution attributes (the hows) via the 'what-how' matrix. The procedure to operationalise this mechanism is as follows:

1) *House of quality matrix* – customer requirements (vertical axis) are matched with design attributes (horizontal axis), and a coding scheme is used to indicate the degree and direction of influence.
2) *Design matrix* – design attributes are transposed to form the 'whats', which must be reconciled with the specific design features of the product or service.

3) *Process matrix* – design features are transposed to form the 'whats', which must be reconciled with the process design attributes that create the product or service.
4) *Operational matrix* – process design attributes are transposed to form the 'whats', enabling design of the most effective operational control system.

QFD has advantages in its requirement that designers be analytical and explicit in their assessment of both design objectives and solutions. Unfortunately, the extreme complexity of QFD often restricts its usage. Unless the number of factors used in both axes of the matrix is kept under control, the whole process becomes unmanageable.

♦ Taguchi Methods
These are used to test the robustness of a design, to check the performance of a product or service in extreme conditions.

♦ Value Engineering (VE)
Aiming to eliminate those unnecessary costs that contribute neither to the value nor performance of a product, value-engineering programmes are usually conducted by project teams consisting of designers, purchasing specialists, operations managers and financial analysts. Following a process of identification, often using Pareto analysis, the most notable elements of the product package are subjected to rigorous scrutiny.

❖ Slack, N. (ed.), Blackwell's *Encyclopaedic Dictionary of Operations Management* (1999).

56.   *Product–Process Matrix*
Originally devised by Hayes and Wheelwright (1979), this model links product characteristics of volume and variety with the attendant processes of creation (Figure 6.9). It is indicative of both the operational needs of products with different competitive characteristics, and of the consequences of failing to match product and process characteristics. Points on the volume-variety continuum (horizontal dimension) range from low volume, one-off products through to high volume, high standardisation products. The manufacturing continuum (vertical dimension) ranges from jobbing processes, through batch and mass, to continuous production.

The matrix is used by Hayes and Wheelwright to illustrate three important points:

1) For all points on the volume-variety continuum, there is a corresponding position on the process continuum, represented by the 'natural' diagonal of the matrix.

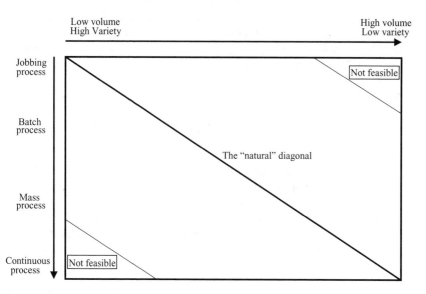

Figure 6.9   The Product-Process Matrix
Source: Slack, N., (ed), *Blackwell's Encyclopaedic Dictionary of Strategic Management* (1999) Blackwell Publishing.

2) Companies can move away from the 'natural' diagonal in order to achieve a competitive advantage, or as a result of drift into inappropriate processes. Moving into the upper right segment means that a process is more flexible than strictly necessary, while moving towards the bottom left is indicative of less flexibility. Either move can incur extra costs.
3) Companies can focus their manufacturing resources more effectively by using the matrix to define product groups, and distinguish between those that require different processes.

❖ Slack, N. (ed.), *Blackwell's Encyclopaedic Dictionary of Operations Management* (1999).

57.   Production Information System
Inferior to MRP and ERP, this is a basic system employed by companies to monitor the production process. Often, it is specifically designed by the company itself.

❖ Slack, N. (ed.), *Blackwell's Encyclopaedic Dictionary of Operations Management* (1999).

58.   Programmable Logic Controllers (PLCs)
Used to control production processes, PLCs are integrated, multi-functional devices that support a wide range of applications. These computer-based

systems are capable of digital and analogue signal processing, and include high level languages for simpler programming and communication with other PLCs. Operating as a low-cost, general-purpose controller, this technology can move up from simple, stand-alone material handling and packing, or monitoring applications, through sequential and interlocking control of processes, right up to complex, integrated machine control.

❖ Slack, N. (ed.), *Blackwell's Encyclopaedic Dictionary of Operations Management* (1999).

59. Project Management Techniques

Emphasising team-working across functional boundaries, process orientation, and strong leadership, project management involves co-ordinating all those parties contributing to a particular undertaking. It not only encompasses planning and scheduling techniques, but also the detailed management and control of cost, resources, quality, and performance. Projects tend to be either developmental, or related to organisational improvement and change. Successful schemes generally demand the following:

- Clearly defined goals
- A competent project manager
- Top-management support
- A competent project team (staff continuity)
- Sufficient resource allocation
- Adequate communication and feedback capabilities
- Control and trouble-shooting mechanisms

❖ Slack, N. et al., *Operations Management* (1998).

60. Project Teams

Cross-functional teams are increasingly popular, particularly for the purpose of new product development. Their aim is to encourage harmonious relations across corporate units. Many companies have not operated in this manner historically, so implementation often requires substantial cultural change.

❖ Slack, N. (ed.), *Blackwell's Encyclopaedic Dictionary of Operations Management* (1999).

61. Quality Management Techniques

Supporting a process of continuous improvement, quality management techniques need to be carefully attuned with a company's requirements. The basic tools of quality control are as follows:

- *Checklists* – highlight key features that require attention, and ensure that procedure is correctly observed

- *Flow charts* – enable process mapping by providing a diagrammatic picture that indicates all the steps in a process
- *Check-sheets* – indicate non-conformities, machinery breakdown, and non-value-adding activities through a simple recording of data
- *Tally charts, graphs, and histograms* – identify patterns of data
- *Pareto analysis* – enables problem prioritisation, indicating where improvement efforts can be directed for greatest impact
- *Cause-and-effect diagrams* – determine the main causes of a given problem
- *Brainstorming* – generates creative ideas through synergistic group effort
- Scatter diagrams – examine the correlation between two variables

Professor D. Garvin has defined five approaches to quality management:

1) Transcendent – views quality as synonymous with innate excellence
2) Manufacturing-based – aims to make products, or provide services, that are free of errors, and conform precisely to their design specification
3) User-based – aims to provide a product or service that is fit for purpose
4) Product-based – views quality as a precise and measurable set of characteristics that must be fulfilled in order to satisfy the customer
5) Value-based – defines quality in terms of cost and price

❖ Garvin, D. A., 'Quality on the line', *Harvard Business Review* (1983).
❖ Garvin, D. A., 'Competing on the eight dimensions of quality', *HBR* (1987).
❖ Schonberger, R. J., 'Human resource management lessons from a decade of TQM and re-engineering', California Management Review (1994).

62. *Risk Analysis Tools*
See the reference in Strategy Tools and Techniques (chapter 2).

63. *Scheduling Tools*
These are tools that assist with the determination of the dates and timing schedule by which jobs should commence and be completed. The aim of scheduling is to optimise the timing and the performance of operations. It can involve forward (when it arrives) and backward (only when required) scheduling.

❖ Conway, R. W. et al. (1967), *Theory of Scheduling*, Reading, MA: Addison Wesley.

64. *Simulation*
This predictive technique enables designers to explore the consequences of their decisions without actually constructing the product, service, or

process under development. Design models can be tested, and results used to either confirm or adjust an original design.

❖ Slack, N. et al., *Operations Management* (1998).

65.   Six Sigma

Six Sigma is a philosophy relating to defects based on a normal distribution but has become synonymous with the development of structured approach to the improvement of organisational systems and processes, using total quality management techniques. Staff can be trained as black belt facilitators of the six sigma approach.

66.   Statistical Quality Techniques

♦ Acceptance Sampling

On the basis of batch sample analysis, this inspection method supports a decision to either accept or reject a product. Based on the mathematical theory of probability, it is employed in situations of continuous flow between supplier and customer. The objective of a statistically designed sampling plan is to ensure that batches of the acceptable quality level (AQL) have a high probability of acceptance, while those with high non-conformity levels will almost certainly be rejected. All decisions are based on the systematic analysis of a random sample. The economic and psychological pressure that results from lot non-acceptance encourages suppliers to maintain a process average at least as good as the specified AQL, and sampling also minimises the risk to the consumer of accepting the occasional poor lot. Acceptance sampling basically constitutes a screening technique based on after-the-event detection.

♦ Statistical Process Control (SPC)

SPC is a form of process management utilising statistical methods. It can be used for the following purposes:

- to achieve process stability
- to provide guidance on process improvement through the reduction of variations
- to assess process performance
- to provide information to assist with management decision-making

❖ Slack, N. (ed.), *Blackwell's Encyclopaedic Dictionary of Operations Management* (1999).

67.   Supply Chain Management

This refers to a process by which a company manages all of the suppliers in the extended supply chain from raw materials through the buying company to the end customer. The process normally involves the company making extensive dedicated investments in long-term collaborative relationships with all of the supply chain tiers in order to improve value for money in sourcing. The model was developed initially in the lean manufacturing and supply principles established by Toyota. It has been emulated outside of Japan in some manufacturing process industries.

❖ Cox, A. et al., *Supply Chain Management: A Guide to Best Practice*, London: Financial Times/Prentice Hall.

68. Target Based Costing
See the reference in Procurement and Supply Tools and Techniques (chapter 8).

69. Technology Watch
See the reference in Strategy Tools and Techniques (chapter 2).

70. Value Based Management
See the reference in Strategy Tools and Techniques (chapter 2).

71. Value Stream Management
See the reference in Procurement and Supply Tools and Techniques (chapter 8).

72. Variance Analysis
See the reference in Strategy Tools and Techniques (chapter 2).

73. Work Study

♦ **Method Study**
This is a systematic approach to job design that follows six basic steps:

1) Select the work to be studied
2) Record all the relevant facts relating to the present method
3) Examine those facts critically, and in sequence
4) Develop the most practical and economic method
5) Install the new method
6) Remain pro-active through periodic method checking

The recording stage utilises simple process charts that analyse the flow of materials or information through a job, or the sequence of activities performed by a particular member of staff. These are often supplemented, however, by motion studies that use photography and video recording to determine specific work sequences.

♦ **Work Measurement**
This is the process of establishing the time taken to perform a specified task by a 'qualified worker' operating at a 'defined level of performance.' Both of these measures are difficult to define, and hence, the process is quite controversial. Nevertheless, basic procedure involves three distinct phases – analysis, measurement, and synthesis. Measurement techniques like time study and analytical estimating usually demand direct observation. An understanding of work-time consequences is unquestionably crucial to job design.

❖ Slack, N. (ed.), Blackwell's *Encyclopaedic Dictionary of Operations Management* (1999).

7
The Use of Operations and Production Management Tools and Techniques

Operations and production is the management function concerned with the design, planning, control and improvement of production and operating systems in both manufacturing and service organisations. Operations and production involves such diverse activities as process design and work; inventory planning and control; project planning and control; service operations management; and quality planning and control. Operations and production strategies encompass customer service management; manufacturing systems and processes; inventory and stock management; and, planning and distributional operations. Operational and production tools and techniques, which impinge directly on internal administrative and organisational structures, are used to facilitate the smooth day-to-day running of a business. Firms obviously depend upon the successful management of these operational and production activities to achieve their overall corporate objectives both operationally and strategically.

In many ways one might expect operations and production to be the most formalised of any of the management functions. As it focuses on production and operational processes it can be argued that a large number of the activities performed within the function are likely to be highly repetitive. Given this, one might expect that the introduction of tools and techniques within the production and operations environment would be extremely cost effective. Furthermore, the idea that structured systems and processes would prove of significant benefit to the productivity of this function, has a lineage that is hardly new and can be traced back at least to the ideas of Taylor about principles of scientific management (Taylor, 1911). Indeed, since these early insights the end of the twentieth century has witnessed the growth of lean manufacturing and production ideas based initially on the quality ideas developed by Deming, that were implemented originally most assiduously within Japanese business management practice (Deming, 1982, 1986; Womack and Jones, 1996).

At the same time there has been a significant effort in the later half of the twentieth century by consultants and academics to convince managers to adopt total quality management and business process re-engineering tools and techniques to reorganise and restructure the internal operational processes and systems of companies (Crosby, 1979; Dale & Cooper, 1992; Hammer & Champy, 1993). Given all of this pressure to improve operational delivery and reform production processes and systems it was expected that the operations and production function would be one of the heaviest users of tools and techniques. This was also expected because, in the last ten years there has also been a boom in the development of internal IT and Internet based tools and techniques to provide operational improvement through the creation of management information systems like MRP and ERP (Farmer & van Amstel, 1991; Vollman, et al., 1992).

Despite this, as the findings reported here show, the operations and production functions in the companies surveyed did not demonstrate any marked proclivity to use tools and techniques more than any of the other functions surveyed. In fact, as the data presented here demonstrates, while the operations and production function had the highest number of tools and techniques to choose from, with 73, and had 50 tools and techniques in use, it was not the heaviest average user. The marketing and sales function, with an average usage score of 4.01 per company surveyed, scored slightly higher than operations and production, with an average score of 3.78 per company surveyed (compare Table 5.4 with Table 7.4).

1. The general use of tools and techniques in operations and production

The discussion that follows provides a description of the general use of operations and production tools and techniques in total, and across the 5 business activities outlined in chapter 1. The analysis then focuses on the use of tools and techniques across the 16 industry sectors and the 6 industry sector groupings also outlined in chapter 1.

The use of tools and techniques in general

As Table 7.1 indicates the operations and production survey covered 114 companies (see Appendix D) and 50 tools and techniques were found to be in use, with 431 total uses. This meant that, when compared with the 73 tools and techniques discovered in the literature survey (reported in chapter 6) there were 23 operations and production tools and techniques that were not found to be in use at all (see Table 7.2). This was the highest incidence of non-usage, a distinction that was shared with the procurement and supply function. This clearly indicates that, while the operations and production function has a wide range of tools and techniques to choose from, the function either chooses not to, or is not able to, use all of those available. Many of the tools and techniques not found to be in use focus on the *product and competence development* and/or the *planning, design and work*

Table 7.1 **The Total Use of Operations and Production Tools and Techniques (50 Tools with 431 Tool Usages in Total Recorded)**

Tool	Incidence	%	Tool	Incidence	%
Quality Management Techniques	40	9.28	Five 'S' Strategy	4	0.93
Project Management Techniques	31	7.20	Brainstorming	4	0.93
ISO Quality Standards	28	6.50	E-Business-Seller Side	4	0.93
Business Process Reengineering	24	5.57	Maintenance Techniques	4	0.93
Continuous Improvement(Kaizen)	24	5.57	E-Business-Seller Side	3	0.70
Just-in-Time (Lean)	21	4.87	Continuous Production	3	0.70
Key Performance Indicators	21	4.87	Failure Analysis	3	0.70
MRP Systems	21	4.87	Process Layout	3	0.70
Process Mapping	20	4.64	Cell Layout and PFA	2	0.47
ERP Systems	19	4.41	Gap Analysis	2	0.47
E-Business-Internal Applications	14	3.25	Knowledge Management	2	0.47
New Product Development	12	2.78	Activity Based Costing	1	0.23
Risk Analysis Tools	12	2.78	Agile	1	0.23
Benchmarking	11	2.55	Capability Maturity Model	1	0.23
Business Excellence Model	11	2.55	Design for Manufacture	1	0.23
Statistical Quality Techniques	11	2.55	Design to Cost	1	0.23
Management Information System	10	2.32	Hazard Analysis	1	0.23
Balanced Scorecard	9	2.09	Pareto Analysis	1	0.23
Problem Solving Techniques	8	1.86	Partnership Sourcing	1	0.23
Batch Production	7	1.62	Project Teams	1	0.23
Business Operating Model	7	1.62	Target Based Costing	1	0.23
Six Sigma	6	1.39	Technology Watch	1	0.23
Supply Chain Management	6	1.39	Value Based Management	1	0.23
Production Information System	5	1.16	Value Stream Mapping Mgmt	1	0.23
Scheduling Tools	5	1.16	Variance Analysis	1	0.23

Table 7.2 **The 23 Tools and Techniques Not Found in Use**

Behavioural Models
Blueprinting Techniques
Capacity Management
Computer-Aided Design (CAD)
Design Chain Management
Economic Order Quantity (EOQ) Formula
Empowerment
Ergonomics
Failure Mode and Effect Analysis (FMEA)
Fixed-Position Layout
Hill Methodology
Importance-Performance Matrix
Improvement Analysis
Johnson's Rule
Location Techniques
Network Analysis
Optimised Production Technology (OPT)
Platts Gregory Procedure
Product Design Evaluation Stage
Product–Process Matrix
Programmable Logic Controllers (PLCs)
Simulation
Work Study

organisation rather than on the *process and system improvement* and *performance measurement* business activities. This is interesting because it is clear that, when compared with the strategy and marketing and sales functions, where there was considerable use of the same tools and techniques, the operations and production function stands out in using tools and techniques that are primarily function-specific.

As Table 7.1 indicates there are some tools and techniques that are in common use across the operations and production and strategy and marketing and sales functions. The tools and techniques that tend to be used most commonly were clearly those related to *performance measurement* and *IT and Internet* business activities. Thus, KPIs, E-Business applications, the balanced scorecard, benchmarking and activity based costing are all in use across the three functions. It is clear, however, that the operations and production function has a very high number of tools and techniques that it uses uniquely for its own purposes. This function-specificity is something that recurs when one considers the procurement and supply function.

The tools and techniques that stand out as uniquely relevant to the operations and production function are those focused on improvements in the design, planning and control of workflow processes and systems. Thus it is no surprise that some of the most heavily used tools and techniques are those focused on total quality management (9.28% of total usages), project management (7.20%), ISO quality standards (6.50%), BPR (5.57%), Kaizen (5.57%), JIT (4.87%) and process mapping (4.64%). Indeed, these seven tools and techniques alone account for almost a half (43.63%) of total recorded usages. What is also interesting is that information management tools and techniques are also used heavily. Thus, MRP systems (4.87% of total usages), ERP systems (4.41%), E-Business internal applications (3.25%), management information systems (2.32%) and product information systems (1.16%) combined account for 16.01% of total reported usages.

It is clear, therefore, that the operations and production function is very heavily focused in its tool and technique use on those that provide mechanisms for effective delivery of improvements in operating systems and processes. This explains the emphasis on improvements in the design, planning and control of processes and systems, and the need to have the management information to allow for effective decision-making. It also explains why a large number of the tools and techniques reported to be in use were also focused on performance measurement. Clearly, it is not possible to ascertain whether or not improvements occur unless there is data to allow performance to be measured accurately. Thus, many of the tools and techniques reported to be in use measure performance, such as: TQM (9.28% of total usages), ISO (6.50%), Kaizen (5.57%), KPIs (4.87%) benchmarking (2.55%), statistical quality techniques (2.55%), the balanced scorecard (2.09%), six sigma (1.39%) and the capability maturity model (0.23%).

Despite this obvious function-specific approach within operations and production it is also clear that the function does not as a whole use very many tools and techniques. The overall average figure reported for tool and technique usage across the function was 3.78. This is the second highest average score after marketing and sales (4.01) and just ahead of procurement and supply (3.74). Despite this it seems clear that the operation and production function suffers from many of the same problems as the other functions in this study. Over 57.78% of total tools and technique usage was accounted for by the top ten tools and techniques listed in Table 7.1. This indicates that, as in other functions, practitioners tend to rely on just a few tried and tested tools and techniques for the bulk of their usage. Indeed close to two–thirds (74.24%) of total usage was recorded by the top 16 applications.

To put this matter another way only 35% of respondents were using TQM techniques, only 27% were using project management tools, only 24% were applying ISO standards, only 21% were undertaking BPR or Kaizen, and a mere 18% of respondents were engaged in JIT, or introducing KPIs or MRP systems. What this clearly demonstrates is that, while there is a long tail of tools and techniques that two or three companies (or even only one) may be using, the bulk of the tool and technique usage was recorded by only a few applications, and that most companies do not use tools and techniques very much at all to improve their operational processes and systems. Once again this supports the conclusion that runs throughout this volume and this is that managers do not indiscriminately use tools and techniques. In fact they appear to innovate rarely and use those that are tried and tested quite sparingly, when they use them at all.

The use of tools and techniques by business activity

These findings are reinforced when one considers in more detail the use of tools and techniques across the five broad business activities defined earlier in chapter 1. There it was argued that in the operations and production function the major business activities can be sub-divided into: *product and competence development; planning, design and work organisation, process and systems improvement, performance measurement;* and, *IT and Internet solutions.* Clearly, there is necessarily some overlap between these activities, and this fact is captured in Table 7.3 where the tools and techniques found to be in use are listed by the relevant business activities. As is clear from this analysis some tools and techniques can be used in more than one business activity and, when this occurs, the tool or technique has been recorded under each relevant business activity. This also means that the figures do not sum to 100%.

When one analyses the use of tools and techniques used in the operations and production function this way it is clear that the function devotes a considerable amount of its effort to *planning, design and work organisation.* This business activity reports 67.75% of total usages. This is unsurprising but does demonstrate clearly that, when the function uses tools and techniques, they are used for key aspects of operational delivery within the firm. This view is reinforced when one considers that the second highest recorded usage by business activity is for *process and systems improvement* (52.20%). This underscores the clear operational focus of the function in improving the performance of the systems and processes that must be managed operationally. Furthermore, in order to achieve this the function also appears to recognise that it must use performance measurement tools and techniques to allow effective decisions to be made. The *performance measurement* business activity recorded 44.54% of total uses.

It is interesting to note that the operations and production function does not appear to be heavily involved in more strategic business activities. This conclusion is drawn because the *product and competence development* business activity recorded only 29.92% of total business activity usages. It would appear that, while the operation and production function understands that it must create effective and efficient operational processes and systems, that it is less involved in the development of new products or core competencies than other functions, like strategy and marketing and sales. This is a reassuring finding not least because, as we saw in our previous

Table 7.3 The Use of Operations and Production Tools and Techniques by
Business Activity

(The total % figures do not sum 100% because some tools and techniques can be
used for more than one business activity)

Rank Order of Tools and Techniques by Business Activities	Tools and Techniques	% of Total Usage Recorded	Total Business Activity Usage Score
1 Planning, Design and Work Organisation	Quality Management Techniques	9.28	
	Project Management	7.20	
	ISO Quality Standards	6.50	
	Business Process Re-Engineering	5.57	
	JIT (Lean)	4.87	
	MRP Systems	4.87	
	Process Mapping	4.64	
	ERP Systems	4.41	
	Benchmarking	2.55	
	Statistical Quality Techniques	2.55	
	Problem Solving Techniques	1.86	
	Batch Production	1.62	
	Business Operating Modle	0.02	
	Six Sigma	1.39	
	Supply Chain Management	1.39	67.75%
	Production Information Systems	1.16	
	Scheduling Tools	1.16	
	Brainstorming	0.93	
	Maintenance Techniques	0.93	
	Continuous Production	0.70	
	Process Layout	0.70	
	Cell Layout	0.47	
	Agile	0.23	
	Design For Manufacture	0.23	
	Design For Cost	0.23	
	Hazard Analysis	0.23	
	Partnership Sourcing	0.23	
	Project Teams	0.23	
2 Process and Systems Improvement	Quality Management Techniques	9.28	
	ISO Quality Standards	6.50	
	Business Process Re-Engineering	5.57	
	Continuous Improvement (Kaizen)	5.57	
	Process Mapping	4.64	
	Risk Management Tools	2.78	
	Benchmarking	2.55	

Table 7.3   The Use of Operations and Production Tools and Techniques by Business Activity – *continued*

(The total % figures do not sum 100% because some tools and techniques can be used for more than one business activity)

Rank Order of Tools and Techniques by Business Activities	Tools and Techniques	% of Total Usage Recorded	Total Business Activity Usage Score
*	Business Excellence Model	2.55	
	Statistical Quality Techniques	2.55	
	Problem Solving Techniques	1.86	
	Six Sigma	1.39	52.20%
	Supply Chain Management	1.39	
	Production Information System	1.16	
	Scheduling Tools	1.16	
	Maintenance Techniques	0.93	
	Continuous Production	0.70	
	Gap Analysis	0.49	
	Agile	0.23	
	Capability Maturity Model	0.23	
	Hazard Analysis	0.23	
	Value Based Management	0.23	
	Value Stream Mapping	0.23	
3 Performance Measurement	Quality Management Techniques	9.28	
	ISO Quality Standards	6.50	
	Continuous Improvement (Kaizen)	5.57	
	Key Performance Indicators	4.87	
	Risk Management Tools	2.78	
	Benchmarking	2.55	
	Business Excellence Model	2.55	
	Statistical Quality Techniques	2.55	
	Balanced Scorecard	2.09	
	Problem Solving Techniques	1.86	44.54%
	Six Sigma	1.39	
	Failure Analysis	0.70	
	Gap Analysis	0.47	
	Activity Based Costing	0.23	
	Capability Maturity Model	0.23	
	Hazard Analysis	0.23	
	Pareto Analysis	0.23	
	Target Based Costing	0.23	
	Variance Analysis	0.23	

Table 7.3 **The Use of Operations and Production Tools and Techniques by Business Activity – *continued***

(The total % figures do not sum 100% because some tools and techniques can be used for more than one business activity)

Rank Order of Tools and Techniques by Business Activities	Tools and Techniques	% of Total Usage Recorded	Total Business Activity Usage Score
4 Product and Competence Development	Quality Management Techniques	9.28	
	ISO Quality Standards	6.50	
	New Product Development Process	2.78	
	Risk Management Tools	2.78	
	Benchmarking	2.55	
	Statistical Quality Techniques	2.55	
	Production Information Systems	1.16	29.92%
	Five 'S' Strategy	0.93	
	Knowledge Management	0.47	
	Agile	0.23	
	Pareto Analysis	0.23	
	Technology Watch	0.23	
	Value Based Management	0.23	
5 It And Internet Solutions	MRP Systems	4.87	
	ERP Systems	4.41	
	E-Business – Internal Applications	3.25	16.48%
	Management Information Systems	2.32	
	E-Business – Seller Side Software	0.93	
	E-Business – Buyer Side Software	0.70	

discussion of the strategy and marketing and sales functions, there was clear evidence of a duplication of effort within these two functions. It would not be sensible if the operations and production and the procurement and supply functions were also attempting to replicate the activities of these two functions.

The conclusion must be, therefore, that operations and production as a function knows its place and what it should focus on. This view is reinforced when one considers that the fifth business activity – *IT and Internet solutions* – recorded a respectable 16.48% of total business activity usages. This is respectable because many of the tools and techniques in this activity set are relatively new (such as ERP systems and buyer and supplier side software applications). Given this it is clear that the impact of these types of applications can only be expected to increase in the future in this function of business (Cox, et al., 2001). This is because operational improvement can only occur if companies can be moved from their current 'data rich and management information poor' situation to one in which decisions can be made on the basis of objective information about processes and systems.

The use of tools and techniques by industry sector and industry sector grouping

If the function appears to be properly focused on the improvement of operating systems and processes the survey found that the use of tools and techniques is very different across industry sectors and industry sector groupings. As Table 7.4 indicates the overall average score for tool and technique use was 3.78, with the heaviest usage in the Confectionery (6.66 average uses), Transport Equipment (6.33) and Aerospace (5.57) industry sectors. Interestingly enough, each one of these three sectors is involved in manufacturing systems and processes. As are the fourth and sixth heaviest users – Basic Chemicals and Computer Hardware – with 4.86 and 4.22 average uses respectively. Of the top six users only Retail Financial Services (a sector with a significant need for the effective management of complex transactional processes and systems on a daily basis) is not drawn from the manufacturing sector.

The data indicates clearly that there is a correlation between the level of operational complexity that has to be managed and the use of tools and techniques. Thus, as Figure 7.1 demonstrates, the highest usage is in manufacturing industry sectors (4.85 average uses), followed by the

Table 7.4   The Rank Order Use of Operations and Production Tools and Techniques by Industry Sector

Industry	Total Tool Usages	No. Of Firms	Average
Confectionery	40	6	6.66
Transport Equipment	57	9	6.33
Aerospace	39	7	5.57
Basic Chemicals	34	7	4.86
Retail Financial Services	26	6	4.33
Computer Hardware	38	9	4.22
It Solutions	33	8	4.13
Oil & Gas	30	8	3.75
Healthcare	25	7	3.57
Telecommunications	26	8	3.25
Power & Water	30	10	3.00
Construction	20	7	2.86
Media & Entertainment	7	3	2.35
Retail & Distribution	12	6	2.00
Publishing	10	7	1.43
Tourism & Leisure	4	6	0.66
Overall Average	**431**	**114**	**3.78**

TYPE OF OPERATIONAL DELIVERY	PROCESS/ MANUFACTURING	PROCESS/ MANUFACTURING & SERVICES	PROCESS/ SERVICES	
	Group Average Usage 5.25	Group Average Usage 3.27	Group Average Usage 3.17	
PROCESS	Basic Chemicals (4.86) Computer Hardware (4.22) Confectionery (6.66)	Healthcare (3.57) Power & Water (3.00) Telecommunications (3.25)	Retail & Distribution (2.00) Retail Financial Services (4.33)	*Total Process Average Usage:* **3.90**
	PROJECT/ MANUFACTURING	PROJECT/ MANUFACTURING & SERVICES	PROJECT/ SERVICES	
	Group Average Usage 4.44	Group Average Usage 3.58	Group Average Usage 1.51	
PROJECT	Aerospace (5.57) Publishing (1.43) Transport Equipment (6.33)	Construction (2.86) IT Solutions (4.13) Oil & Gas (3.75)	Media & Entertainment (2.35) Tourism & Leisure (0.66)	*Total Project Average Usage:* **3.18**
	Total Manufacturing Average Usage 4.85	Total Combined Average Usage 3.43	Total Service Average Usage 2.34	
	MANUFACTURING	COMBINED MANUFACTURING & SERVICES	SERVICES	

TYPE OF GOODS AND/OR SERVICES

Figure 7.1 The Use of Operations and Production Tools and Techniques by Industry Groups

combined manufacturing and services sectors (3.43 average uses) and the services sectors (2.34 average uses). This demonstrates that the use of tools and techniques is likely to be higher when there is a complex manufacturing process, requiring detailed planning and design and workflow management, to be organised when compared with the less operationally complex service-based industries – like Media & Entertainment (2.35 average uses) and Tourism & Leisure (0.66 average uses). The combined manufacturing and services industry sectors – IT Solutions (4.13 average uses), Oil & Gas (3.75) Healthcare (3.57), Telecommunications (3.25), Power & Water (3.00) and Construction (2.86) – were in the middle usage range.

The frequency with which firms in an industry sector have to manage changes in the workflow that they are involved with, and whether or not what has to be done to make a product or service is done continuously or irregularly, also appears to have a major impact on tool and technique usage rates. Thus, as Figure 7.1 indicates, process-based industries that manage products and services on a regular continuous basis appear to have a higher average usage score (3.90) when compared with project-based industries. The project-based average usage score was only 3.18. These findings support the view, demonstrated elsewhere in this study, that regular process demand and operational delivery, especially with high levels of operational complexity in delivery processes and systems, and with high sunk costs in capital intensive infrastructure for delivery, tends to encourage the use of tools and techniques, whereas project-based industries with irregular demand, low capital intensive sunk costs and relatively simple operational delivery processes and systems tend to use tools and techniques far less. This pattern appears to be consistent across functions and is no different in the operations and production function.

Thus, the highest average usage score for operations and production tool and technique use was in the *Process/Manufacturing* industry sector grouping (5.25 average uses). This was closely followed by the *Project/Manufacturing* grouping (4.44 average uses). These findings seem to support the view that in the operations and production function it is not just the regularity (process) or irregularity (project) nature of what is done but rather the complexity of what is done–in the sense of having to manage highly integrated and multifaceted manufacturing and scheduling processes and systems with high levels of operational risk – that is one of the key determinants of tool and technique usage. This finding is partially borne out by the fact that the combined industry sector groupings – which arguably have somewhat less regular and continuous levels of manufacturing/production risk to manage – record the middling level average usage scores. Thus, the *Project/Combined* grouping recorded an average usage score of 3.58, while the *Process/Combined* score was 3.27.

In the combined industry groupings only the IT Solutions sector stands out as having a somewhat higher reported score than the others (with 4.13 average uses). This is probably explained by the fact that, for many of the firms operating in this industry, the manufacturing processes and systems that have to be managed alongside the services element are just as complex as those in the manufacturing industry sectors. The relatively lower level usage scores for the Construction (2.86 average uses) and the Power & Water (3.00 average uses) sectors is probably explained by the relatively simpler technologies that have to be managed in these sectors when compared with the other combined industry sectors.

The impact of technical and process complexity and its impact on operational risk is clearly a major factor in explaining why the *Process/Services* (with 3.17 average uses) and the *Project/Services* (with 1.51 average uses) are the lowest scoring industry sector groupings. Clearly, the Tourism & Leisure (0.66 average uses) and the Media & Entertainment (with 2.35 average uses) industry sectors that make up the *Project/Services* grouping have far less technical and process complexity and, therefore, operational risk to manage than most of the other industry sectors, and this must explain the relatively low usage rates in these industry sectors. The same can be said, ironically, for the Publishing industry and this sector also records a very low average usage rate at 1.43.

The *Process/Services* industries by and large have high levels of operational complexity to manage, even though they may not have a very high level of technical complexity and risk to deal with. This probably explains why the Retail Financial Services sector has such a high average usage score at 4.33. This is because of the massively complex level of small transactions that must be managed on a daily basis requiring extensive investment in operational management tools and techniques for process improvement. The Retail & Distribution sector on the other hand has lower levels of technical complexity and risk, and somewhat lower levels of regular transactional detail to manage. This helps to explain its relatively low average usage score of 2.00.

It would appear once again, therefore, that there are rational explanations for why the pattern of tool and technique use varies across different types of industry sector and industry sector grouping. This reinforces the general finding in this study that, rather than managers being the unthinking dupes of academics and consultants selling the latest fad (fashionable tool or technique), they are more likely to be highly sceptical of any new tool or technique. Furthermore, the analysis here seems to demonstrate that when they use any tools or techniques at all there tends to be a correlation between the levels of operational and process risks and capital intensive sunk costs that have to be managed in different industry sectors.

2.   The performance of tools and techniques used in operations and production

Having explained the underlying rationale for the use of tools and techniques across industry sectors it is now possible to analyse the performance of the tools and techniques that were found to be in use within the operations and production function. The first part of this analysis focuses on the objectives behind the use of operations and production tools and techniques and the impact of these on both the firm and the function. This is followed by an analysis of their impact by industry sector and by industry sector grouping. Finally, there is a discussion of the major barriers to effective implementation.

The corporate and functional objectives for implementing tools and techniques

Perhaps the most striking thing about the objectives behind the introduction of operations and production tools and techniques is the alignment between the broad role of the function and an understanding of what its objective should be. As Table 7.5 indicates the operations and production function generally understands that its key role is to deliver improvements in operational effectiveness for the firm. Thus, operational effectiveness was reported as the major objective behind the use of tools and techniques by 73% of respondents in this function, compared with 27% reporting strategic objectives. Of those reporting having strategic objectives 16 % were focused on the creation of new products, 7% on achieving cost leadership advantages and a mere 4% saw themselves as pursuing market repositioning opportunities. These findings are consistent with what one might expect from the key function managing the processes and systems for operational delivery within the firm.

Table 7.5 shows, however, that there are some differences across industry sectors and industry sector groupings that need to be explained. As one might expect the three industry sector groupings that reported the highest average use of tools and techniques (see Tables 7.4 and 7.5) were also the three industry sectors that reported the highest emphasis on operational effectiveness as their primary objective. Thus, the *Process/Manufacturing* grouping reported operational effectiveness as the primary objective for 83% of its tool and technique usage, *Project/Manufacturing* reported a score of 79% and *Process/Services* a score of 85%.

Only the *Project/Services* grouping stands out as the one industry sector grouping that places strategic objectives ahead of operational effectiveness in this function. In this grouping the operational effectiveness objective score was only 37% compared with 63% for strategic objectives. The explanation for this anomaly may well be a function of the corporate reliance on finding unique offerings in Media & Entertainment (36% of objectives)

Table 7.5 Overall Objectives for Introducing Operations and Production Tools and Techniques

Group	Industry	Strategic Objectives			Operational Effectiveness %
		Unique Products %	Cost Advantage %	Repositioning %	
Process/Manufacturing Group	Basic Chemicals	31	4	0	65
	Computer Hardware	15	0	0	85
	Confectionery	0	0	0	100
	Group Average	*16*	*1*	*0*	*83*
Process/Combined Group	Healthcare	18	3	3	76
	Power And Water	17	0	2	81
	Telecommunications	26	5	0	69
	Group Average	*20*	*3*	*2*	*75*
Process/Services Group	Retail And Distribution	14	0	0	86
	Retail Financial Services	6	0	10	84
	Group Average	*10*	*0*	*5*	*85*
Project/Manufacturing Group	Aerospace	20	5	8	67
	Publishing	0	0	0	100
	Transport Equipment	19	6	3	72
	Group Average	*13*	*4*	*4*	*79*
Project/Combined Group	Construction	20	9	3	68
	It Solutions	12	0	10	78
	Oil & Gas	11	28	7	54
	Group Average	*4*	*13*	*6*	*67*

Table 7.5 Overall Objectives for Introducing Operations and Production Tools and Techniques – *continued*

| Group | Industry | Strategic Objectives | | | |
		Unique Products %	Cost Advantage %	Repositioning %	Operational Effectiveness %
Project/Services Group	Media And Entertainment	36	14	21	29
	Tourism & Leisure	10	45	0	45
	Group Average	*23*	*30*	*10*	*37*
Overall Average (%)		16	7	4	73

and the need to find cost leadership advantages in Tourism and Leisure (45% of objectives). One other industry sector reports strategic objectives quite highly and that is Oil & Gas, with 46% for strategic objectives and only 54% for operational effectiveness. We saw earlier, in the analysis of the marketing and sales function, that Oil & Gas sometimes has anomalous results. The explanation for the sectors focus on cost leadership (28% of objectives) here may also be a function of the fact that reducing costs is one of the few opportunities to improve bottom line margin performance when there is an absence of opportunities to differentiate in the spot markets that many Oil & Gas companies have to sell into.

It is also interesting to note that in two industry sectors respondents – Confectionery and Publishing – claimed to have no strategic objectives whatsoever and that 100% of their objectives were directed towards operational effectiveness. High levels for operational effectiveness objectives were recorded in virtually all of the process-based industry sectors: Basic Chemicals (65%), Computer Hardware (85%), Confectionery (100%), Healthcare (76%), Power & Water (81%), Telecommunications (69%), Retail & Distribution (86%) and Retail Financial Services (84%).

There was a somewhat lower percentage for operational effectiveness objectives in the project-based industries: Aerospace (67%), Publishing (100%), Transport Equipment (72%), Construction (68%), IT Solutions (78%), Oil & Gas (54%), Media & Entertainment (29%) and Tourism & Leisure (45%). Part of the reason for the lower scores in the project-based industries may well be because in these types of environment there is a need to find unique product offerings to provide differentiation. It is interesting in this regard to note that many of the project-based industries sectors recorded reasonable scores for the strategic objective of finding unique products: Aerospace (20%), Transport Equipment (915), Construction (20%), IT Solutions (12%), Oil & Gas (11%), Media & Entertainment (36%) and Tourism & Leisure (10%).

All of this seems to indicate that there are, once again, fairly rational grounds behind the pattern of tool and technique use in the operations and production function, as well as a correlation with that usage pattern and the broad objectives that managers are endeavouring to achieve at the firm level. When turning to an analysis of the functional objectives behind tool and technique usage the operations and production function has a similar pattern of objectives to those found in the strategy and marketing and sales function, but it is perhaps more evenly spread across a number of different objectives. In the strategy and marketing and sales functions we saw that the primary objectives functionally were to improve functionality and to increase communication and information flow (See Table 3.7 and Table 5.7). As Table 7.6 demonstrates this is also true for the operations and production function overall (27% for functionality, 19% for communication and 20% for information flow), but this function also appears to place

Table 7.6 The Functional Objectives for Introducing Operations and Production Tools and Techniques (%)

Industry	Functionality	Cost	Communication	Information	Flexibility	Skill Sets	Number Employed	Other	No Data
Process/Manufacturing									
Basic Chemicals	5	13	19	12	8	14	0	26	3
Computer Hardware	0	10	20	30	0	5	0	34	1
Confectionery	21	18	27	29	2	2	0	0	1
Group Average	*9*	*14*	*22*	*23*	*3*	*7*	*0*	*20*	*2*
Process/Combined									
Healthcare	27	21	19	16	1	14	0	2	0
Power & Water	38	21	10	15	3	0	5	8	0
Telecommunications	36	2	19	25	7	9	2	0	0
Group Average	*34*	*15*	*16*	*19*	*3*	*8*	*2*	*3*	*0*
Process/Services									
Retail & Distribution	33	14	18	24	6	2	2	0	1
Retail Financial Services	35	18	12	11	12	5	3	0	4
Group Average	*34*	*16*	*15*	*18*	*9*	*4*	*2*	*0*	*2*
Project/Manufacturing									
Aerospace	32	20	11	20	7	10	0	0	0
Publishing	26	12	14	22	16	6	4	0	0
Transport Equipment	32	20	20	18	5	3	0	0	2
Group Average	*30*	*18*	*15*	*20*	*9*	*6*	*1*	*0*	*1*

Table 7.6 **The Functional Objectives for Introducing Operations and Production Tools and Techniques (%)** – *continued*

Industry	Functionality	Cost	Communication	Information	Flexibility	Skill Sets	Number Employed	Other	No Data
Project/Combined									
Construction	37	12	12	22	3	7	0	8	0
It Solutions	0	3	29	28	0	9	0	30	1
Oil And Gas	32	9	20	23	3	8	3	2	0
Group Average	*23*	*8*	*20*	*24*	*2*	*8*	*1*	*14*	*0*
Project /Services									
Media & Entertainment	30	5	25	10	0	25	0	0	5
Tourism & Leisure	45	0	20	20	15	0	0	0	0
Group Average	*38*	*2*	*23*	*15*	*7*	*13*	*0*	*0*	*2*
Overall Average	**27**	**12**	**19**	**20**	**6**	**7**	**1**	**7**	**1**

a major emphasis on cost reduction (12% of objectives) as well. This is, of course, entirely consistent with the functions focus on operational effectiveness overall at the firm level.

When disaggregating at the industry sector and industry sector grouping levels it is clear that there is a relatively consistency in the responses across both categories. Virtually all of the industry sector groupings have the same balance of functional objectives, apart that is from the *Process/ Manufacturing* grouping, where functionality objectives were of much lower significance than in all of the other groupings. Overall, the findings are consistent with a function that understands what its role is, and knows that its job is to improve the functionality of its product and service offerings. Furthermore, it is a function that understands that it needs tools and techniques to assist in the improvement of the processes and systems that deliver products and services. If this can be done at lower cost and by breaking down internal barriers to change through better communication and information flow, then so much the better.

This is, therefore, clearly an aligned function in terms of firm and function level objectives, but it is also one that suffers from the same apparent weakness as the other two functions analysed so far. As we saw the other two functions appear to under estimate the value that rigorous use of tools and techniques can provide in developing skill sets within the function. Once again the findings report only a very low percentage score for improved skill sets at 7% for functional objectives. This is disappointing and confirms the view developed earlier that managers appear to under value the impact on skill sets that can occur from the rigorous use of tools and techniques.

The impact of tools and techniques by industry sector and industry sector grouping

We saw that in the analysis of the strategy and marketing and sales functions that satisfaction with the performance of tools and techniques tended to be highest in regard to the impact of the tools and techniques on the function not at the firm level. This is also true for the procurement and supply function, and the operations and production function is no different in this regard. As Table 7.7 demonstrates, not only were respondents in the survey broadly satisfied with the use of tools and techniques, recording an overall combined impact score of 0.67 (which was the highest overall combined score across all of the four functions surveyed), but once again the most significant impact is reported to be at the function rather than the firm level. The respective overall scores were 0.61 for satisfaction with the impact of tools and techniques on the firm and 0.72 for impact on the function's objectives. Furthermore, in a function that we saw tends to understand that it should be delivering operational effectiveness and improved functionality to the business, the 0.72 overall score for impact on the function was the highest reported in the study as a whole.

Table 7.7 The Use and Impact of Operations and Production Tools and Techniques by Industry Sector and Groupings

Rank Order of Most Usages by Industry Sector	Performance Score			No Data %	
	Firm	Function	Average Combined Score	Firm	Function
Confectionery (6.66)	0.66	0.74	0.70	10	1
Transport Equipment (6.33)	0.51	0.62	0.57	10	6
Aerospace (5.57)	0.63	0.73	0.68	4	1
Basic Chemicals (4.86)	0.82	0.97	0.90	3	3
Retail Financial Services (4.33)	0.35	0.56	0.46	18	7
Computer Hardware (4.22)	0.62	0.79	0.71	1	1
IT Solutions (4.13)	0.55	0.72	0.64	1	1
Oil & Gas (3.75)	0.73	0.74	0.74	5	0
Healthcare (3.57)	0.62	0.79	0.71	4	4
Telecommunications (3.25)	0.57	0.63	0.65	3	0
Power & Water (3.00)	0.46	0.62	0.54	12	4
Construction (2.86)	0.56	0.64	0.60	0	0
Media & Entertainment (2.35)	0.50	0.92	0.71	7	3
Retail & Distribution (2.00)	0.77	0.94	0.86	3	2
Publishing (1.43)	0.71	0.43	0.57	10	2
Tourism & Leisure (0.66)	0.67	0.72	0.70	0	0
Overall Average	**0.61**	**0.72**	**0.67**	**6**	**2**
Process/Manufacture (5.25)	0.70	0.83	0.77	5	2
Project/Manufacture (4.44)	0.62	0.59	0.61	8	3
Project/Combined (3.58)	0.61	0.70	0.66	2	0
Process/Combined (3.27)	0.55	0.68	0.63	6	3
Process/Services (3.17)	0.56	0.75	0.66	11	5
Project/Services (1.51)	0.59	0.82	0.71	4	2
Overall Average	**0.61**	**0.72**	**0.67**	**6**	**2**

Table 7.7 was constructed by asking managers about their satisfaction levels with the tools and techniques they were using relative to the firm and functional level objectives that they were pursuing (see Tables 7.6 and 7.7 above). Respondents were asked to rank their satisfaction level on a scoring system ranging from +1 to –1, with 0 as a mid point demonstrating neither positive nor negative impact on the firm or the function. As the Table demonstrates in detail some industry sectors have a very high regard for the performance of the tools and techniques they are using both at the firm and the function level.

Thus Basic Chemicals reports a satisfaction level of 0.82 with the tools and techniques used for firm objectives, and 0.97 for those focused on improving the performance of the function. This gives this sector the highest satisfaction score in the whole study with a combined score overall of 0.90. The second highest score was recorded by the Retail & Distribution sector, with a performance satisfaction of 0.94 at the function level and 0.77 at the firm level, giving an average combined performance satisfaction score of 0.86. These two performance satisfaction scores are two of the three highest recorded in the study as whole. There was evidence of considerable satisfaction elsewhere amongst respondents, and particularly at the function impact level. Thus, on top of the high function performance satisfaction scores reported by the two sectors above, the Media & Entertainment sector recorded a score of 0.92 for satisfaction at the function level as well.

Beyond this most respondents were reasonably satisfied with the performance of their tools and techniques, reporting satisfaction scores in the 0.50 to 0.70 ranges consistently. There were, however, some industry sectors that were relatively less satisfied within this general appreciation of the benefits of implementing tools and techniques in this functional area. Thus, at the firm level Retail Financial Services only reported a performance satisfaction score of 0.35 and Power & Water scored only 0.46. At the function level the Publishing sector was least satisfied with a performance score of 0.43, most of the other sectors appeared, however, to be reasonably satisfied with the performance of the tools and techniques used for performance improvement at the functional level.

When considering the overall performance of operations and production tools and techniques it is interesting to note that the industry sector grouping that uses them the most often is also the one that has the highest combined performance satisfaction score. Thus, the *Process/Manufacturing* grouping uses operations and production tools and techniques more than any other grouping, with an average usage score of 5.25 and also reports the highest combined performance satisfaction score with 0.77 overall. This reinforces the argument developed earlier that, in this area, the need to focus continuously on operational improvement and to use tools and techniques regularly may pay dividends in achieving functional targets. It is interesting to note, however, that as with the strategy and marketing and sales functions, there is no necessary correlation between the frequency and scale of tool and technique use and performance satisfaction.

It is interesting, therefore, to note that the second highest performance score is recorded by the *Project/Services* grouping, which is by far the least frequent user of operations and production tools and techniques. One of the reasons for this may be that the Media & Entertainment industry sector reported, as one of its clear objectives, the desire to discover unique products and to reposition strategically rather than to just focus on operational improvement (see Table 7.6) and it was in the strategic impact on the firm that this function reported the highest performance satisfaction score (0.92). This perhaps indicates that, while the Media & Entertainment sector may not use function level tools and techniques as often as other industry sectors, when it does choose to use tools and techniques to assist strategic differentiation it is broadly satisfied with the outcome.

Table 7.8 adds a further level of detail to this discussion of the performance satisfaction levels of the industry sectors in operations and production by linking together the rank order usage of tools and techniques with the combined performance satisfaction impact scores by industry sector. What the Table demonstrates is that, when one disaggregates the data to the industry sector level, there is – as we saw in both the strategy and marketing and sales functions – little correlation between the use of tools and techniques. Thus, of the top five users of operations and production tools and techniques only one – Basic Chemicals – was in the top 5 rank order for performance satisfaction. Basic Chemicals was 4th in rank order of usage (4.86) and 1st in rank order for combined performance satisfaction (0.90). Furthermore, Retail Financial Services was 5th in usage (with an average score of 4.33) and 16th (and last) in performance satisfaction (with a combined score of 0.46). Transport Equipment was 2nd in usage (6.33 average uses) and 13th in the rank order for performance satisfaction (0.57).

At the other end of the scale Tourism & Leisure was the 16th (and last) in the rank order of users of tools and techniques (with an average usage score of 0.66) but 7th in the performance satisfaction rank order (0.70). Retail & Distribution was 14th in rank order for use (2.00) but 2nd in performance satisfaction (0.86). Media & Entertainment was 13th ranked in usage (2.35) but 4th in performance satisfaction (0.71). At the bottom end of the usage rank order league only Publishing, which was 15th in usage (1.43), was consistent in performance satisfaction, with 13th place and a score of 0.57.

Table 7.8 **Rank Order Comparisons for Usage and Impact**

Rank Order Usage Scores	Industry Sector	Rank Order Combined Impact Scores
1 (6.66)	Confectionery	7= (0.70)
2 (6.33)	Transport Equipment	13= (0.57)
3 (5.57)	Aerospace	9 (0.68)
4 (4.86)	Basic Chemicals	1 (0.90)
5 (4.33)	Retail Financial Services	16 (0.46)
6 (4.22)	Computer Hardware	4= (0.71)
7 (4.13)	It Solutions	11 (0.64)
8 (3.75)	Oil & Gas	3 (0.74)
9 (3.57)	Healthcare	4= (0.71)
10 (3.25)	Telecommunications	10 (0.65)
11 (3.00)	Power & Water	15 (0.54)
12 (2.86)	Construction	12 (0.60)
13 (2.35)	Media & Entertainment	4= (0.71)
14 (2.00)	Retail & Distribution	2 (0.86)
15 (1.43)	Publishing	13= (0.57)
16 (0.66)	Tourism & Leisure	7= (0.70)

Despite this it is still the case that the industry sector groupings and the industry sectors as a whole report very high levels of satisfaction with the well tried and tested tools and techniques that appear to be used. Nevertheless, while the operations and production function records a fairly high performance satisfaction level overall (none of the industry sectors falls below a 0.61 performance score), once again the data seems to indicate that there is no necessary correlation between the use of tools and techniques and performance satisfaction. As we argued earlier there may in fact be evidence that those who use tools and techniques most often tend to be somewhat dissatisfied compared with those who use them less frequently. This is because the more frequent users do not always achieve all of the gains expected, and this is normally because more frequent use tends to expose both the inadequacies of the tools and techniques used as well as the myriad of internal barriers that must be overcome when tools and techniques are introduced within a company. These topics are discussed in the next section.

The barriers to successful implementation of tools and techniques

It is interesting to note that when one considers the causes of failure in the successful implementation of operations and production tools and techniques that this function is, like strategy and marketing and sales, one that tends to blame the adequacy of the tools and techniques used slightly more than it does the internal barriers within the company. Thus, as Table 7.9 indicates, the operations and production function sees the failure of implementation to be 50% caused by tool inadequacy, with only 44% of failure caused by internal barriers. This compares with 58% for tool inadequacy in the strategy function (see Table 3.9) and 60% in marketing and sales (see Table 5.9). The procurement and supply function (see Table 9.9) tends to view internal barriers as slightly more important (50%) than tool and technique inadequacy (45%) overall.

When considering the data in Table 7.9 in more detail it is clear that virtually all of the industry sector groupings tend to view tool and technique inadequacy as relatively more important for the failure of implementation than internal barriers. The only major exception in this regard is in the *Process/Services* grouping where respondents reported scores of 25% for tool and technique inadequacy but 68% for internal barriers as the major cause of unsuccessful implementation. This is an interesting finding because this grouping includes both the Retail & Distribution and the Retail Financial Service sectors that are normally involved in extensive and complex operational delivery and transaction processes. It is hardly surprising that these industry sectors should report that, when trying to implement process and system improvement tools and techniques, they experience a very high incidence of internal barriers. This is because to improve complex operational delivery and logistic processes it normally requires complete or

Table 7.9 The Barriers to Effective Implementation in the Operations and Production Function

215

Industry	Causes Of Failure 100%			Types Of Barriers 100%						
	No Data (%)	Tool (%)	Barriers (%)	Culture	Wrong Performance Measure	Insufficient Resource	Senior Management	Disruptive Internal Reorganisation	Unrealistic Expectations	Other
Process/Manufacturing										
Basic Chemicals	5	66	29	58	0	0	0	25	0	17
Computer Hardware	2	50	48	31	0	19	23	12	4	11
Confectionery	23	34	43	74	10	16	0	0	0	0
Group Average	*10*	*50*	*40*	*54*	*3*	*12*	*8*	*12*	*2*	*9*
Process/Combined										
Healthcare	10	59	31	30	0	20	20	10	20	0
Power And Water	13	30	57	33	7	3	3	20	17	17
Telecoms	6	44	50	78	0	11	11	0	0	0
Group Average	*10*	*44*	*46*	*47*	*3*	*11*	*11*	*10*	*12*	*6*
Process/Services										
Financial Services	4	12	84	29	5	24	21	0	12	9
Retail And Distribution	9	39	52	33	8	8	33	0	0	18
Group Average	*7*	*25*	*68*	*31*	*6*	*16*	*27*	*0*	*6*	*14*
Project/Manufacturing										
Aerospace	14	39	47	26	0	0	4	22	17	31
Publishing	0	78	22	0	50	50	0	0	0	0
Transport Equipment	8	38	54	23	2	23	0	14	30	8
GroupAverage	*7*	*52*	*41*	*16*	*18*	*24*	*1*	*12*	*16*	*13*

Table 7.9 The Barriers to Effective Implementation in the Operations and Production Function – *continued*

Industry	Causes Of Failure 100%			Types Of Barriers 100%						
	No Data (%)	Tool (%)	Barriers (%)	Culture	Wrong Performance Measure	Insufficient Resource	Senior Management	Disruptive Internal Reorganisation	Unrealistic Expectations	Other
Project/Combined										
Construction	0	58	42	40	0	27	0	7	13	13
IT Solutions	7	62	31	11	22	22	11	0	33	1
Oil And Gas	2	61	37	29	0	0	0	29	0	43
Group Average	*3*	*61*	*36*	*27*	*7*	*16*	*4*	*12*	*15*	*19*
Project/Services										
Media & Entertainment	0	91	9	33	0	0	33	0	33	1
Tourism & Leisure	0	40	60	33	0	0	33	33	0	1
Group Average	*0*	*66*	*34*	*33*	*0*	*0*	*33*	*17*	*17*	*0*
Overall Average	6	50	44	35	6	14	12	11	11	11

partial redesign (as in the case say of moving to call and flow work design structures, or the creation of cross-docking and/or streamlined back-office transactional processing systems) or the need to implement complex information management systems (like ERP, MRP and product and management information systems) that require extensive restructuring of internal standard operating systems.

This problem of overcoming complex internal standard operating procedures of this kind is clearly significant in a number of industry sectors. This is indicated in the data by the fact that, while at the industry sector grouping level tools or technique inadequacy was primarily blamed for failure, at the industry sector level there were a number of respondents that reported internal barriers to be more significant than tool and technique inadequacy. Thus in the *Process/Manufacturing* grouping Confectionery reported internal barriers at 43% as a more significant cause of failure than tool or technique inadequacy (34%) – although this industry sector surprisingly had the highest recorded non availability of data (23%) to actually assess what the causes of failure were. In the *Process/Combined* grouping the Power & Water sector (with 57% versus 30%) and the Telecommunications sector (50% versus 44%) also tended to blame internal barriers more than tool or technique inadequacy. In the *Project/Manufacturing* grouping the Aerospace sectors reported 47% against 39% and the Transport Equipment sector reported 54% against 38% in favour of internal barriers. Finally, in the Tourism & Leisure sector in the *Project/Services* grouping the relative scores were 60% against 40% in favour of internal barriers.

When considering which internal barriers were more important than others in undermining successful implementation the results reported are similar in some but not in all respects to the findings from the other functions. Thus, the most significant barrier overall in operation and production is the culture of the organisation, which was reported by 35% of respondents to be a major obstacle. This problem – which encapsulates the current standard operating procedures within an organisation and its internal political processes and attitudes – is the single biggest barrier to successful implementation reported in all of the four functions analysed here (See Tables 3.9, 5.9, 7.9 and 9.9).

In the strategy and marketing and sales functions the second and third greatest barriers were insufficient resource and unrealistic expectations respectively. This is not quite the case for the operations and production function. In this area insufficient resource is the second major barrier (with a score of 14%), but after this the scoring is far more dispersed and across a wider number of barriers than those reported in strategy and marketing and sales. Thus, opposition from senior management (12%) is the third greatest barrier, closely followed by disruptive internal reorganisation (11%) and unrealistic expectations (11%). What these figures seem to indicate is that when compared with the strategy and marketing and sales functions the operations and production function (and this is also true for the procurement and supply function as we shall see in chapter 9), tends to face additional problems in implementation than these two more powerful functions within the firm.

In the strategy and marketing and sales functions it is clear that culture and insufficient resource and unrealistic expectations can hinder implementation, but for operations and production it is clear that on top of these problems are the additional ones associated with senior management preferences and their ability to continually reorganise the company with new initiatives. For the lower level operational functions like operations and production and procurement and supply there is, therefore, an additional burden of senior veto and change that creates barriers to successful implementation. For these functions there is often a need to 'push the ball (of change) up the hill', while for the strategy and marketing and sales functions there is more of an opportunity to 'push the ball down the hill'. These general internal problems appear to be endemic across the industry sector groupings and industry sectors, although Publishing (50%) and IT Solutions (22%) industry sectors both report the wrong performance measures as a significant barrier as well.

3.   Conclusions: The appropriateness of the use of tools and techniques in operations and production management

In this final section an attempt is made to assess to what extent the operations and production function can be seen to be using tools and techniques appropriately. This is always a difficult task to achieve because the issue of appropriateness is not always uncontested either by managers, academics or consultants. What can be said clearly, however, from the data presented here is that broadly speaking managers in the operations and production function appear to be the most satisfied with the performance of the tools and techniques that they use. The combined performance satisfaction scores in this area at 0.67 was the highest recorded in any of the four functions. There was also clear evidence that the managers in this function think carefully about their objectives and they have a very clear view about what is appropriate for their needs. The vast majority of respondents understand that their function must focus on operational effectiveness in order to deliver bottom-line process and workflow improvement to the business. This is indicated by the fact that fully 73% of the objectives reported by managers in this function were focused on operational effectiveness measures, with a wide range of functional improvement benefits being sought from cost reduction to increased communication and information flow.

If all of these findings demonstrate that the operations and production function is clearly well aligned in its role and responsibilities in the firm the function also suffers from a general problem seen in all of the other functions and that relates specifically to a failure to use tools and techniques as extensively as one might expect. As we saw, while the function uses the most tools and techniques by number (50), and records the second highest average use of tools and techniques (3.78 average uses), this is also the function that has the highest number of tools and techniques (73) to choose from. What is perhaps most surprising is that, given its responsibility for continuous improvement in process and system efficiency, so few companies appear to use many operations and production tools and techniques at all.

Most respondents from all industry sectors reported that they used only a few tools and techniques, and as we saw, almost 58% of total usage was reported by only the top ten tools and techniques found to be in use (see Figure 7.1). Once again this seems to indicate that, while there will always be instances when managers are duped into using tools and techniques that are not appropriate (this is indicated by the fact that 50% of failure was blamed on the inadequacy of the tools and techniques) there is also considerable evidence, not that managers are duped, but that they are highly sceptical about the use of formalised tools and techniques and/or do not have the time or resources to implement them within their businesses. This is as true in operations and production as it is in strategy and marketing and sales.

Given this general conclusion, that the users of tools and techniques use them sparingly but are broadly satisfied with those that they do use, the final issue to be addressed is whether there is any rational explanation for the pattern of tool and technique usage reported, or whether it is merely down to chance and/or inevitable statistical error based on the limited size of the survey sample. While there are always concerns in any quantitative study about these two problems the findings reported here and elsewhere in this study appear to be partially explained at least by reference to the degree of risk and uncertainty that companies have to manage in their business models. This was seen in the strategy and marketing and sales functions where the pattern of tool and technique use and performance appeared to have a reasonably high correlation with the degree of strategic risk that companies experienced.

If strategic risk is a significant problem that explains the incidence of tool and technique use in the strategy and marketing and sales functions it is arguably also a useful way of thinking about the pattern of use and performance in the operations and production function as well. In this area, however, it is argued that a slightly different categorisation is in order in terms of risk to that used in the strategy and marketing and sales functions. This is because for those managing operations and production the key performance indicators of success or failure are not overall strategic risks (although these are clearly of major importance) but rather the risks to the uptime and efficiency of the operational process and systems that have to be managed. Thus when categorising risks for the operations and production function it is not as important for managers to consider external operational threats at the customer and competitor level but rather to focus on three major factors that impinge directly on the risks to operational performance delivery.

The first of these three factors is the technical complexity of the operational processes and systems that must be managed. Some systems and processes require the application of high levels of technology, which is in a constant state of flux and innovation, than others. For example, a completed computer hardware system and a complex aerospace project will normally have much higher levels of technical complexity embedded within them than those faced by publishers of books and magazines, or by companies block booking hotel space in the Spanish islands. In these circumstances the risks to operations from technical complexity can be seen to be higher, with higher levels of uncertainty due to rapid innovation, for some industry sectors than for others.

The second factor is the level of financial sunk cost in the operational delivery and logistical processes that a product and/or service have to be managed through. Some industries have very high financial sunk costs, with extensive fixed dedicated investments in plant and machinery that others do not. These lower sunk cost industries normally have the option of outsourcing high levels of the risk to others, or they simply do not require high levels of sunk costs to operate at all. Thus, there is a major difference in this regard between a company operating in the Basic Chemicals, Oil & Gas and Power & Water industries when compared with companies operating in the Media & Entertainment, Publishing and Tourism & Leisure industry sectors.

The third factor is the regularity or frequency with which something has to be done transactionally and with what volume. Clearly some operational systems and processes are used on a 24 hour a day/7 days a week basis, these are normally referred to as process-based industries in the sense that these are industries in which the systems and processes that provide products and/or services are in continuous use. If the volume of demand and supply that is managed through the delivery processes and systems is high then these types of industries will have higher levels of operational risk and uncertainty to mange than those in which the company only enters the market infrequently and does not have to produce goods and/or services regularly. This is the difference between process-based industries operationally – like Confectionery, Basic Chemical, Retail Financial Services and Retail & Distribution Services – and primarily project-based industries – like Construction, Media & Entertainment and Tourism & Leisure.

If the three factors – technical complexity, sunk costs and volume /frequency – are combined together this provides a way of separating levels of operational risk in to high, medium and low categories. Thus, if an industry sector experiences a high level of technical complexity, with heavy financial sunk cost in dedicated infrastructure with regular and high volume transactions then it can be categorised as a *high operational risk* industry. In this category we locate the Aerospace, Basic Chemicals, Computer Hardware, Confectionery, IT Solutions, Retail Financial Services and Transport Equipment.

If companies do not have to manage high levels of technical complexity, with few financial sunk costs in dedicated infrastructure, and with low and/or infrequent levels of demand volume then we can categorise these as *low operational risk* industries. In this category we locate the Media & Entertainment, Publishing and Tourism & Leisure sectors. The *medium operational risk* category includes industries in which some of the high-risk factors occur, but not all. In this category we locate the Construction, Healthcare, Oil & Gas, Power & Water, Retail & Distribution and Tele-communications sectors. This (as can see by comparing Table 3.10. with Tables 5.10 and 7.10) provides a similar but yet slightly different categorisation of industry sectors for operational risk compared with those created by the strategic risk categorisation developed in the strategy and marketing and sales analyses.

As Table 7.10 demonstrates, however, while it may not include the exactly the same industry sectors in the high and medium risk categories as those found in the strategic risk categorisation, the operational risk categorisation does have the same industry sectors located in the low risk category and it does provide a way to explain the overall pattern and frequency of tool and technique usage for the operations and production function, and one that appears to be superior to the six fold categorisation by process/project and manufacturing/services and combined that informed much of the initial research in this survey. Thus the *high operational risk category* has the highest use score with 5.16 average usages, compared to the *medium operational* risk category with 3.07 average usages and the *low operational risk* category with only 1.48 average usages. This is a very similar pattern to that found in the strategy and marketing and sales functions were the high-risk categories consistently scored at the 4 to 5 average usage level.

The operational risk categorisation, like the strategic risk categorisation, shows a similar discontinuity between the level of use of tools and techniques and performance satisfaction scores. In the strategy and marketing and sales functions it was clear that the frequent use of tools and techniques did not always equate with the highest performance satisfaction scores. The same is true in the operations and production function, where the *medium operational risk* category recorded the highest combined performance satisfaction score (0.68). This is compared with both the *high* and *low operational risk* categories recording a combined satisfaction score of 0.66.

Table 7.10   The Use and Performance of Operations and Production Tools and Techniques in High, Medium and Low Risk Sectors

Type of Industry Sectors	Average Tool Usage	Performance Impact Scores		
		Firm	Function	Average Combined Score
High Operational Risk				
Aerospace	5.57	0.63	0.73	0.68
Basic Chemcials	4.86	0.82	0.97	0.90
Computer Hardware	4.22	0.62	0.79	0.71
Confectionery	6.66	0.66	0.74	0.70
IT Solutions	4.13	0.55	0.72	0.64
Retail Financial Services	4.33	0.35	0.56	0.46
Transport Equipment	6.33	0.51	0.62	0.57
Group Average	**5.16**	**0.59**	**0.73**	**0.66**
Medium Operational Risk				
Construction	2.86	0.56	0.64	0.60
Healthcare	3.57	0.62	0.79	0.71
Oil & Gas	3.75	0.73	0.74	0.74
Power & Water	3.00	0.46	0.62	0.54
Retail & Distribution	2.00	0.77	0.94	0.86
Telecommunications	3.25	0.57	0.63	0.65
Group Average	**3.07**	**0.62**	**0.73**	**0.68**
Low Operational Risk				
Media & Entertainment	2.35	0.50	0.92	0.71
Publishing	1.43	0.71	0.43	0.57
Tourism & Leisure	0.66	0.67	0.72	0.70
Group Average	**1.48**	**0.63**	**0.69**	**0.66**

These findings appear to support the view developed in the analysis of the strategy and marketing and sales functions that there is in fact an inverse relationship between high tool and technique use and performance satisfaction levels. It would appear that those who use tools and techniques the most are also those who are the most critical about them. This perhaps indicates the truth in the old saying that: 'familiarity breeds contempt'. On the other hand there is also clear evidence in the findings reported here that sometimes those that use them the least are the most satisfied. This appears to be the case for the Media & Entertainment and Tourism and Leisure sectors, which uses tools and techniques infrequently but still appear to have a very positive view of their performance when utilised.

This finding is perhaps the most appropriate one with which to conclude this discussion of the use and performance of tools and techniques in operations and production function. It is clear from the data reported here that in general managers do not use tools and techniques as extensively as they might, but that when they do use them in this function they are broadly satisfied with performance. Our view is that part of this relatively high performance satisfaction is clearly due to the fact that this function does not duplicate the efforts of others and has a clear focus on operational effectiveness and the tools and techniques that support this over-riding functional objective. The discussion of the procurement and supply function that follows reinforces this view since this function also tends to be heavily focused on function-specific tools and techniques, although its overall use of tools and techniques is not as positive as that recorded in the operations and production function.

References

Cox, A. et al. (2001), *The E-Business Report*, Helpston, UK: Earlsgate Press.

Crosby, P. B. (1979), *Quality is Free*, New York: McGraw Hill.

Dale, B. G. & Cooper, C. L. (1992), *Total Quality and Human Resources*, Oxford: Blackwell.

Deming, W. E. (1982), *Quality, Productivity and Competitive Position*, Cambridge, MA: Center of Advanced Engineering Study.

Deming, W. E. (1986), *Out of Crisis*, Cambridge, MA: MIT Center of Advanced Engineering Study.

Farmer, D. & van Amstel, R. P. (1991), *Effective Pipeline Management*, Aldershot: Gower.

Hammer, M. & Champy, J. (1993), *Re-engineering the Corporation*, New York: Free Press.

Taylor, F. (1911), *Scientific Management*, New York: Harper Brothers.

Womack J. P. & Jones, D. T. (1996), *Lean Thinking*, New York: Simon & Schuster.

Vollman, T. E. et al. (1992), *Manufacturing Planning and Control Systems*, Homewood, IL: Irwin.

Part IV

Procurement and Supply Management

8
Tools and Techniques for Procurement and Supply Management

The 65 tools and techniques below are not definitive but they do provide a comprehensive listing of some of the major tools and techniques regularly used by managers in procurement and supply, as well as some of the most recently developed by academics and consultants. When appropriate a reference source for further reading is provided. These tools and techniques provide a basis for comparison with the actual tools and techniques found to be in use by procurement and supply managers in the research survey. These findings are reported in chapter 9.

1. Activity Based Costing
See the reference in strategy tools and techniques (chapter 2).

2. Approved Supplier List
This is a company record of those suppliers that fall within its broad selection criteria, and hence, would be eligible to bid when work came up to tender. Past performance is obviously a key aspect in achieving 'approved' status.

3. Automatic Inventory Replenishment (AIR)
Primarily applied to multiple-use, low-value items in a manufacturing and engineering spares environment, this approach sees frequent stock replenishment via supplier visits to the storage location. A 'bag and bin system' establishes quantities (the stock bin contains two bags wherein the required quantity is stated), and subsequent to delivery, the buyer is invoiced electronically. Whilst this eradicates communication and negotiation costs, it does mean that a level of trust between the parties is imperative.

❖ Chadwick, T. and Rajagopal, S., *Strategic Supply Management* (1995).

4. Balanced Scorecard
See the reference in strategy tools and techniques (chapter 2).

5.   *Balanced Sourcing*

Moving beyond trust without reverting to an adversarial approach, this model (Figure 8.1) seeks to balance co-operative relationships with a commitment to competitive pricing:

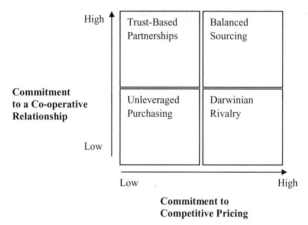

Figure 8.1   A Model of Balanced Sourcing
Source: *Balanced Sourcing, Co-operation, and Competition in Supplier Relationships*, Laseter, T. M., Copyright © 1998. This material is used by permission of John Wiley & Sons, Inc.

❖ Laseter, T. M., *Balanced Sourcing, Co-operation, and Competition in Supplier Relationships* (1998).

6.   *Benchmarking*

See the reference in strategy tools and techniques (chapter 2).

7.   *Cammish and Keough's Procurement Development Model*

Operating with the belief that a purchasing function must progress through four stages of transition, this model envisages procurement as supporting and strengthening the application of strategic activities. The stages are as follows:

1) *Serve the factory* – engaged in basic logistics and clerical transactions
2) *Lowest unit cost* – constitutes a strategic business unit, emphasising cost analysis and negotiation
3) *Co-ordinate purchasing* – centralised unit, utilising purchasing committees to co-ordinate between different business areas
4) *Strategic procurement* – central leadership provided by a cross-functional team with involvement in design specifications, and input into make-buy decisions

❖ Cammish, R. and Keough, M., 'A strategic role for purchasing', *McKinsey Quarterly* (1991).

8.   *Centralised Distribution Centres and Cross-Docking*

Increasingly 'pull' driven, deliveries by manufacturers tend to be routed to a central distribution point from which goods can be transferred to retailers. Optimal vehicle loading, route planning, and scheduling all receive substantial attention, since rapid, accurate response to customer demand is the primary aim. Integration of cross-docking can provide a dramatic reduction of handling and storage costs through the swift transfer of full-pallet loads.

❖ Chadwick, T. and Rajagopal, S., *Strategic Supply Management* (1995).

9.   *Competitive Advantage vs Strategic Vulnerability*

Quinn and Hilmer's model (Figure 8.2) provides a response to two fundamental questions:

1) What potential for competitive advantage does an activity possess?
2) To what extent would outsourcing that activity make the firm vulnerable in the case of market failure?

Market limitations, information asymmetries, and asset specificity are seen as conditioning strategic vulnerability, while competitive edge is dictated

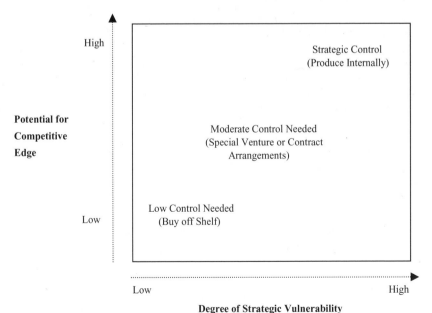

Figure 8.2   Competitive Advantage – Strategic Vulnerability Model
Source: Lonsdale, C., and Cox, A., *Outsourcing*. Copyright © 1998. Earlsgate Press.

by the development of core competencies. These are characterised in the following way:

- An amalgamation of skills and knowledge, rather than products or functions

A unique source of leverage in the value chain that enables firm domination.

- ❖ Quinn, J. B. and Hilmer, F. 'Strategic outsourcing', *Sloan Management Review* (1994).
- ❖ Lonsdale, C., and Cox, A., *Outsourcing* (1998).

10.   Contract Price Adjustment Formulae

Accounting for the risk of cost fluctuation over time, these formulae use data and indices published by governmental and professional bodies for specialist areas of industry. The process of establishing a formula must involve both buyers and suppliers.

- ❖ Chadwick, T. and Rajagopal, S., *Strategic Supply Management* (1995).

11.   Core Competence Thinking

See the reference in the strategy tools and techniques (chapter 2).

12.   De Toni and Tonchia

In analysing management by process and performance measurement, De Toni and Tonchia recognise three main organisational processes:

- New product development
- Manufacturing
- Logistics

Particularly relevant to the supply chain management function, their model for logistical performance measurement (Figure 8.3) assesses each process horizontally in terms of time, quality, and cost, and vertically at each phase of the process:

- ❖ De Toni, A. and Tonchia, S., 'Lean organisation: management by process and performance measurement', *International Journal of Operations and Production Management* (1996).

13.   EDI and CALS

Improving order-processing times by reducing the cycle from as long as fifteen days to only two or three, Electronic Data Interchange supports awareness and information exchange between buyers and sellers. Implementation

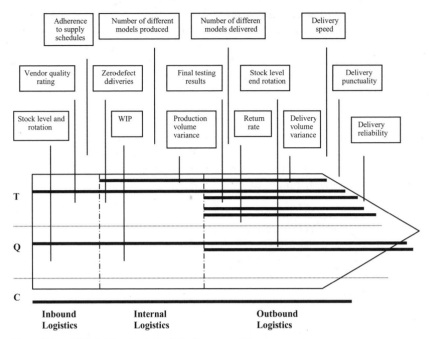

Figure 8.3 A Model for Logistical Performance Measurement
Source: De Toni, A. and Tonchia, S., 'Lean organisation: management by process and performance measurement', *International Journal of Operations and Production Management* (1996, Vol. 16, No. 2, p. 231).

not only facilitates JIT deliveries, but also enhances EPOS effectiveness. EDI is relevant to the following processes:

1) Information exchange between departments
2) Receipt of specifications and transferral to suppliers
3) Receipt and distribution of catalogue information
4) Issue of requests for quotation and tender
5) Issue and amendment of purchase orders and call-off demands
6) Receipt and monitoring of delivery schedules
7) Receipt and issue of invoices

CALS (Computer-aided Acquisition and Logistical Support) is the 'big brother' of EDI. Ensuring the effective flow of information between suppliers, it is particularly pertinent in the context of high-tech projects in which specifications require co-ordination between sub-contractors, or the same support documentation is required by all.

❖ Bungant, S. and Pinnington, A., 'EDI in Purchasing', *International Journal of Operations and Production Management*.
❖ Chadwick, T. and Rajagopal, S., *Strategic Supply Management* (1995).

14/15/16.   E-Business Applications
See the reference in strategy tools and techniques (chapter 2).

17.   ERP Systems
See the reference in operations and production tools and techniques (chapter 6).

18.   EOQ/EBQ
These techniques have been developed to support more accurate stock control in line with anticipated levels of supply and demand. Economic order quantity (EOQ) provides a measure for bought-in supplies, attempting to ensure replenishment as appropriate:

S = cost of raising a single order D = annual demand I = annual stockholding fraction V = value of one unit of stock

$$EOQ = \sqrt{\frac{2SD}{IV}}$$

For made-in items, the equivalent is economic batch quantity (EBQ). However, lack of communication with other parts of the chain, and negligible effort to understand changing conditions, constitute fundamental weaknesses.

❖ Chadwick, T. and Rajagopal, S., *Strategic Supply Management* (1995).
❖ Saunders, M., *Strategic Purchasing and Supply Chain Management* (1994).

19.   Failure Mode and Effects Analysis (FMEA)
Utilised at product and process design stage, FMEA is a quality-planning tool that identifies potential problems with manufacture or end use. Used in dialogue with suppliers to identify potential causes of failure, it enables the corrective action that can improve quality.

❖ Hutchins, G., *Purchasing Strategies for Total Quality* (1992).
❖ Saunders, M., *Strategic Purchasing and Supply Chain Management* (1994).

20.   First-Point Assessment (FPA)
Constituting a first filter for suppliers within the oil industry, FPA is an industry-wide initiative that has established standard performance criteria. Not only has it decreased search costs, but has also encouraged competition and self-auditing amongst suppliers, providing a feedback mechanism that highlights their faults.

21. *Generic Sourcing Strategies Matrix*

Probert's matrix (Figure 8.4) attempts to prioritise technology-sourcing decisions. Using the concept of key success factors (KSF), it categorises technologies as of high, medium, or low importance. It is crucial that those capable of affecting one or more KSF (quality, cost, flexibility, and delivery) be kept in-house. Hence, resources need to be dedicated to the top left box in particular.

- ❖ Probert, D., *Developing a Make or Buy Strategy for Manufacturing Business* (1997).
- ❖ Lonsdale, C. and Cox, A., *Outsourcing* (1997).

22. *ISO Technical Quality Standards*

See the reference in operations and production tools and techniques (chapter 6).

23. *Just-in-Time (JIT)*

See the reference in operations and production tools and techniques (chapter 6). Purchasing, stock control and production planning are all affected by JIT management. Its main impact in the sphere of procurement is to encourage close collaboration with suppliers, ensuring the delivery of correctly labelled and bar-coded goods to a given destination at the right time. The key is to provide a neat fit between delivery sequence and production schedule. In turn, this supports the overall aim of cutting inventory and storage costs, and generally eliminates waste from the system. Quality is also improved by corrective action following a more immediate identification of defects. Fundamental in supporting necessary communica-

Competitive Position		High	Medium	Low
	Strong	Invest. Maintain.	Consolidate. Keep pace.	Capability may open new market opportunities
	Neutral	Invest. Develop	Partnership	Stop. Outsource.
	Weak	Initiate R&D	Partnership	Stop sell/ licence design out

Importance to Business

Figure 8.4   The Generic Sourcing Strategies Matrix
Source: Lonsdale, C., and Cox, A., *Outsourcing*. Copyright © 1998. Earlsgate Press.

tion, both internal and external, is the electronic transfer of data. Integration of an MRP system is essential for the scheduling of accurate buy-list requirements, while a CIM (computer integrated manufacturing) system will not only provide internal flexibility, but will also enable the measurement of supplier performance with regards to delivery accuracy in terms of both time and quantity. Clearly, JIT encourages supply base rationalisation and partnering owing to the close co-ordination necessary for a successful system. Given the 'pull' nature of just-in-time, it is also beneficial if suppliers are located within a close proximity of their customers.

- ❖ Baily, P., *Purchasing Systems and Records* (1991).
- ❖ Hutchins, G., *Purchasing Strategies for Total Quality* (1992).

24.   *Key Performance Indicators (KPIs)*
See the reference in strategy tools and techniques (chapter 2).

25.   *Lean Supply*
This model is normally associated with close collaborative ways of working and involves extensive supplier development work, throughout the supply chain to focus on process improvement and the eradication of all unnecessary waste and inefficiency (known as 'muda'). Its extension into the extended supply chain is based on notions of partnership sourcing and the development of extend transparency.

- ❖ Lamming, R., Partnership Sourcing (1993).

26.   *Life Cycle Costing*
One of the key techniques used to enable a buyer to understand the true costs of ownership of its product or services is to focus on the total cost of ownership rather than the purchase price of a product or service. Life cycle costing takes account of the transaction costs of internal sourcing plus the initial purchase price and the life cycle costs for use and disposal. Sometimes also referred to as the total cost of ownership. Also referred to as 'womb to tomb', or total cost of ownership, this involves accounting for the true cost of any material or service both before and after its delivery date. It demands assessment of the following:

1) *Pre-acquisition costs* – involve investigation, specification, design, budget allocation, and preparation for receipt
2) *Acquisition costs* – involve purchase price (including delivery, insurance and taxes), installation, commissioning, and training
3) *Operating costs* – involve labour, materials, consumables, and energy supply
4) *Maintenance costs* – involve specialist labour, specialist tooling, spare and replacement parts, and the question of reduced output with age

5) *Down-time costs* – involve lost profits, and extra costs as a result of overtime and sub-contracting charges
6) *Disposal costs* – involve safe disposal by re-sale (including any ongoing liabilities), cost of removal for sale or scrap, and re-instatement of land or buildings for alternative use

❖ Chadwick, T. and Rajagopal, S., *Strategic Supply Management* (1995).

27. Management Information Systems (MIS)

All procurement managers need up to date information and many organisations are data rich but information management poor. To assist managers in the making of timely decisions about supplier selection, leverage and the management of post-contractual performance and fulfilment there is a need to develop complex MIS to allow for the effective management of a multitude of suppliers. There are many different types of MIS available in the market, ranging from data cleansing and warehousing systems to supply chain optimisation systems.

28. Matching Organisation to Innovation

Chesbrough and Teece define systemic innovations as those that can only be developed in conjunction with related innovations, whereas autonomous innovations can be pursued in isolation. Such a distinction is necessary in developing appropriate organisational design (Figure 8.5). The danger with systemic innovation is that it requires greater collaboration with players outside the company – outsourcing processes concerned with its development, a company runs the risk of losing control (as happened to IBM when it outsourced fundamental technology to Microsoft and Intel). The opposite of 'vertical integration', the idea of 'going virtual' sees

	Type of Innovation: Autonomous	Type of Innovation: Systemic
Exist outside	Go virtual	Ally with caution
Must be created	Ally or bring in-house	Bring in-house

Figure 8.5 Matching Organisation to Innovation
Source: Reprinted by permission of *Harvard Business Review* from 'Organizing for Innovation: When is Vertical Virtuous?' by Chesbrough, H. and Teece, D. (1996), p. 76.

practically everything outsourced, and thus, the principal activity of the company is co-ordination.

❖ Chesbrough, H. and Teece, D. 'When is virtual virtuous?' *Harvard Business Review* (1996).

29.   *MRP System*
See the reference in operations and production tools and techniques (chapter 6).

30.   *Negotiation Process*
Some companies provide a structured negotiation process for their buyers in order to ensure that all of the necessary pre-work has been done during the request for proposal and information prior to the negotiation of contractual terms and conditions. In this way the buyer is aware of the key questions that need to be asked in the face to face meeting, where standard behavioural conditioning techniques may be adopted.

31.   *Network Sourcing*
This approach was originally developed, like lean thinking, in Japanese business practice and involves the creation of an extended networks of inter-linked suppliers within a supply chain, all of whom are focused on delivering innovation in products and services, either in the form of functional or cost reduction improvements. The practice normally involves the creation of extended long-term supplier associations focused on passing value improvements throughout the supply chain to the customer.

❖ Hines, P., *Creating World Class Suppliers* (1994).

32.   *Open Book Agreements*
This procedure refers to a process by which the buyer insists that the supplier provides open accounts so that the buyer can judge the real costs of operations and the profit margins being made by the supplier for the delivery of a particular product and/or service.

33.   *Outsourcing Procedure*
To assist companies in the make-buy decision it is normally necessary for companies to have a framework by which they can understand the opportunity costs and risks of insourcing or outsourcing activities. A formalised process will normally assess the current internal costs of ownership against the external costs of ownership. More advanced models may well try to understand deskilling, the loss of critical assets and post-contractual lock-in and moral hazard over time if activities are outsourced.

❖ Lonsdale, C. and Cox, A., *Outsourcing* (1998).

34. Pareto Analysis

In most companies 80% of the spend is in the hands of 20% of the suppliers, while 20% of the total spend is in the hands of 80% of the suppliers. Procurement professionals often use this technique of understanding where the high value spend is and differentiating it from the low value spend (which may account for most of the volume activity) in order to focus their limited resources on strategically important suppliers rather than focusing on low value non-strategic suppliers.

35. Partnership Sourcing Model

Based on a 'win-win' pretext, the partnership model has the following characteristics:

1) High frequency of both formal and informal communication
2) Co-operative attitudes
3) A trusting relationship
4) Problem-solving, 'win-win' negotiating techniques, and emphasis on managing total cost
5) Long-term business agreements
6) Open sharing of information by multi-functional teams
7) Vendor certification and defect prevention approaches

❖ Saunders, M., *Strategic Purchasing and Supply Chain Management* (1994).

36. Pipeline Mapping

This tool provides a beginning to the process of ascertaining where improvement may be possible within complex supply chains. A pipeline map is constructed to show the time taken by, and between, each process, thus highlighting points of potential action. The *'length'* of a pipeline is the sum of its horizontal lines (average time spent in the major processes *between* stockholding points). Its *'volume'* is the sum of both horizontal and vertical lines (average time spent waiting *at* stockholding points). The overall objective is to reduce both vertical and horizontal lines, with a view to eliminating some of the vertical lines altogether by introducing a 'pull system' of production. Identifying added value and cumulative inventory costs are integral components of this process, as is flexibility analysis. It is crucial to maintain flexibility until the last possible moment in order to respond appropriately to 'pull' signals.

❖ Scott, C. and Westbrook, R., 'New strategic tools for supply chain management', *International Journal of Physical Distribution and Logistics Management* (1991).

37.   *Price Indexing (PI)*
Aiming to keep the procurement function in touch with market forces on a daily basis, this tool sees users subscribe to a central database that provides a comparison of real prices with the highest, lowest, and market average. Some also offer information on annual usage, and quantities purchased. In addition, the PI Price Management Service provides details on a broad range of sectors – the health service, higher education, and financial services.

❖ Chadwick, T. and Rajagopal, S., *Strategic Supply Management* (1995).

38.   *Project Management Techniques*
In one-off purchasing situations, especially for highly complex and high value projects, organisations have to develop skills for the design and specification and delivery of the project – often in circumstances of high levels of uncertainty and risk. As a result structured project management tools and techniques have been developed to assist in the effective management of these problems. These normally involve commercial and scheduling methodologies.

❖ Lock, D., *Project Management* (2000).

39.   *Purchasing Cards*
Usually applied in the case of low-value, low-risk purchases, these cards constitute a credit card system with authorised users. Improving efficiency and smoothing the supply chain, the immediacy of this method reduces transaction costs, and furthermore, tends to support the rationalisation of suppliers.

40.   *Purchasing Consortium*
Strategic alliance within a 'purchasing club' increases the bargaining power of the organisations involved, and hence, often results in substantial cost savings.

41.   *Purchasing Portfolio Matrix*
Kraljic's model (Figure 8.6) aims to identify the extent to which a product constitutes a strategic component of the company's competitive advantage. Leverage can be gained thereafter by directing greater analytical resources towards items of strategic importance.

The focus in *purchasing management* is non-critical items for which the key performance criterion is functional efficiency. In *materials management*, leverage items come to the forefront, with emphasis shifting to cost/price and materials flow. Bottleneck items are the main consideration in *sourcing management*, and performance measures centre on cost management and reliable short-term sourcing. *Supply management* focuses on strategic items, and long-term availability becomes the most important factor.

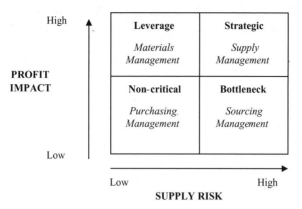

Figure 8.6 The Purchasing Portfolio Matrix
Source: Reprinted by permission of *Harvard Business Review* from 'Purchasing must become supply management' by Kraljic, P. (1983).
Copyright © 1983 by the Harvard Business School Publishing Corporation; all rights reserved.

Kraljic provides a thorough classification of the requirements for different purchasing materials (Figure 8.7).

❖ Kraljic, P., 'Purchasing must become supply management', *Harvard Business Review* (1983).

42. Quality Management Techniques
See the reference in operations and production tools and techniques (chapter 6) and the reference below to the EFQM (European Foundation for Quality Management) Excellence Model.

Similar to the balanced scorecard framework, this model (Figure 8.8) employs a detailed set of scoring criteria to determine how a company identifies process, shows leadership, sets policy, allocates resources, etc. It thus highlights areas for improvement.

The procurement function is integrated in the following ways:

1) **Leadership:**
   Involvement in the development of mission, vision, and values at a senior level enhances procurement's contribution to the whole organisation, and ensures co-operative relations with customers, suppliers, and stakeholders.
2) **Policy and Strategy:**
   Early involvement in policy development avoids the evolution of conflicting practices. Constant assessment of the procurement function's contribution via monitoring and measuring activities identifies those processes that are fundamental to strategy delivery.
3) **People:**
   Professional development and flexibility of resources are fundamental. Teams and individuals are encouraged to work with suppliers, customers, and other functional areas of the organisation, towards

Procurement focus	Main tasks	Required Information	Decision level
Strategic items	Accurate demand forecasting Detailed market research Development of long-term supply relationships Make-buy decisions Contract staggering Risk analysis Contingency planning Logistics, inventory, and vendor control	Highly detailed market data Long-term supply and demand trend information Good competitive intelligence Industry cost curves	Top level (vice president, purchasing)
Bottleneck items	Volume insurance (at cost premium if necessary) Control of vendors Security of inventories Back-up plans	Medium-term supply/demand forecast Very good market data Inventory costs Maintenance plans	High level (department heads)
Leverage items	Exploitation of full purchasing power Vendor selection Product substitution Targeted pricing strategies/negotiations Contract/spot purchasing mix Order volume optimisation	Good market data Short-to-medium-term demand planning Accurate vendor data Price/transport rate forecasts	Medium level (chief buyer)
Non-critical items	Product standardisation Order volume monitoring/optimisation Efficient processing Inventory optimisation	Good market overview Short-term demand forecast Economic order quantity inventory levels	Low level (buyers)

Figure 8.7   Classification of Purchasing Material Requirements
Source: Reprinted by permission of *Harvard Business Review* from 'Purchasing must become supply management' by Kraljic, P. (1983).

mutual benefit, compensated in line with quality and performance objectives.

4) **External Relationships and Internal Resources:**
The ability to create, maintain, and exploit collaborative relationships is assessed. Restrictions on resources, both tangible and intangible, are identified to enable effective management.

5) **Processes:**
Flexibility is essential in satisfying end users, auditors, the finance division, suppliers, and staff. Innovation is encouraged whole-heartedly.

6) **Customer Results:**
It is necessary to judge the satisfaction of both the immediate customer, and those along the whole chain of distribution.

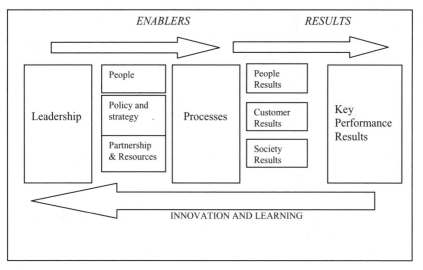

Figure 8.8   The EFQM Excellence Model
Source: Copyright © 1999–2003 EFQM

7) People Results:
   All individuals involved in procurement activities must be asked for their perception of the function's achievements.
8) Society Results:
   Society's perception of procurement activities with regards to quality of life, the environment, and the preservation of global resources, needs to be assessed.
9) Key Performance Results:
Results achieved, trend analysis, and benchmarking illustrate whether or not the needs and expectations of an organisation and its stakeholders have been effectively served by procurement activities.

❖ H. M. Treasury, *A Guide to Using EFQM Excellence Model in Procurement* (1999).

43.   QV Methodology
This Quo Vectius methodology was developed by Robertson Cox consulting practice to enable practitioners to understand how to align business strategy and operational practice with effective external resource management in supply chains and markets. The methodology (See Figure 8.9) is not fully published but it operationalises in detail the power positioning and relationship management approach.

❖ Cox, A. et al., *Business Relationships for Competitive Advantage* (2004).
❖ Andrew Cox et al., *Power Regimes* (2000).

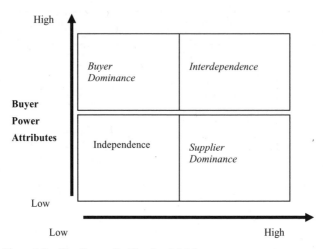

Figure 8.9   The Power Positioning Matrix

❖ Andrew Cox et al., *Supply Chains, Markets and Power* (2002).
❖ Andrew Cox et al., *Supply Chain Management: A Guide to Best Practice* (2003).
❖ Andrew Cox et al., *Business Relationships for Competitive Advantage* (2004).

44.   Relationship Assessment Programmes (RAP)

The RAP model was developed as an alternative to traditional vendor assessment methods. Its principal notion is that both parties involved in a supply contract should work together to 'improve its performance and value adding/waste reduction potential'. Given that collaboration can't be imposed, both parties must have specific 'Influencers' and 'Enablers' in place. A relationship assessment programme basically operates on the basis of the following three observations:

• Organisations in a dyadic relationship frequently don't understand clearly what is actually going on between them.
• Actors in a dyadic relationship frequently don't understand what's expected of them.
• Organisations have no structured way of clarifying these two issues.
  Having identified benefits and mismatches in a relationship, and clarified the ideal, appropriate resources can subsequently be allocated. It is now linked with the transparency concept (see below).

❖ Lamming, R. et al., *Beyond Vendor Assessment: Relationship Assessment Programmes* (1996).

45.   Risk Analysis Tools

Most procurement professionals are involved in managing complex trade-offs between opportunity and cost, but they also have to develop tools to allow them to understand the risks and uncertainties that they may experience in the future. This has led to the development of risk management tools and techniques such as purchase price forecasting analysis (PPFA).

❖ Hughes, J. et al., *Transform your Supply Chain* (1998).

46. *Robert Beck and Brian Long's Maturity Classification*
An attempt to demonstrate the changing phases of purchasing and supply management, this model postulates the following stages of development, with key guidance on how to reach the end state goal of excellence:

1) *Passive* – no strategic direction, reactive to problems and other functions
2) *Independent* – strategic focus, but divorced from firm's competitive strategy
3) *Supportive* – careful selection of suppliers to strengthen firm's competitive position
4) *Integrative* – full integration of purchasing strategy with other functions

❖ Saunders, M., *Strategic Purchasing and Supply Chain Management* (1994).

47. *Russell Syson's Developmental Model*
This model enables firms to position themselves in improving their purchasing department through the following categories:

1) *Clerical* – routine, monitoring function, with the main focus on administrative efficiency
2) *Commercial* – adversarial treatment of suppliers results in cost advantages and savings
3) *Strategic* – purchasing function provides competitive advantage, focusing on supply chain logistics and procurement engineering teams

Assessing the firm's current position, it is possible to establish whether or not momentum for change exists, and to determine the degree of acceleration required in order to progress.

❖ Chadwick, T. and Rajagopal, S., *Strategic Supply Management* (1995).
❖ Saunders, M., *Strategic Purchasing and Supply Chain Management* (1994).

48. *Service Level Agreement*
This is a standardised contractual agreement between buyer and supplier by which the latter is required to achieve a certain level of performance in their provision of a service or product. This may be assessed in terms of the fulfilment of measurable criteria, or may involve a more informal appraisal. Failure to satisfy agreed standards might result in monetary penalties or even wholesale withdrawal of business.

49.   Six Sigma

This methodology was developed initially within Motorola to develop and enhance process improvement and efficiency. The technique involves an extensive structured process with tollgates between different stages to focus on process optimisation. Training is provided by specialist consulting firms to develop the competence of staff as process optimisation experts – known as 'black belts'.

50.   Stages of Excellence Framework

Developed by A. T. Kearney, this framework (Figure 8.10) enables a purchasing function to determine its current position, and to assess its potential for future development.

❖   Kohn, L. F., 'Global sourcing: broadening your supply horizons', *Business Forum* (1993).

What to Aim For				
Sourcing Criteria	**1** **Undeveloped**	**2** **Emerging**	**3** **Leading**	**4** **World Class**
Supplier Relationship **Type of Supplier** **Number of Suppliers** **Supplier Training** **Documentation**	No specific Personally known Vast number None Informal document	Preferred supplier Well reputed Some reduction Ad -hoc information Manual files	Certified supplier Leading companies Limited number Limited support Partially on EDP	Partnerships Word-class suppliers Few key suppliers Programmed support Fully on EDP
Contract Length **Terms an d Conditions** **Contract Clauses**	Order related Just prices None	Annual frames Price and quality Price improvements	Some long -term Price, quality, and service Fixed future price	Mainly long-term Total costs Multiple formula
Geographical Scope **Number of Sources** **per item**	Mainly local areas Multiple sources	Mainly domestic Multiple and dual	Continental Dual and single	World-wide Mostly single
Supplier Marketing **Supplier Selection**	Hearsay/ reference Know from past	Public registers Competitive bidding	Some act ive search Occasional assessment	Systematic search Full assessment
Supplier Evaluation	None	Subjective ratings	Some metrics	Systematic ratings
Design involvement of **suppliers** **Standardisation**	None Very limited	Informal Casually	Formal, some parts Production parts	Formal, all key parts All/sub -assemblies
Quality Control **Inventory Level**	100% Excess inventory	Fixed statistical Controlled reserves	Skip lot inspections Targeted inventory	Self -certification Supplier -owned stocks
Cost Reductions	Below infla tion rates	Some price reductions	Target prices	Total cost targets

Figure 8.10   The Stages of Excellence Framework
Source: Adapted from: Kohn, L. F., 'Global sourcing: broadening your supply horizons', *Business Forum* (1993).

51. Statistical Process Control (SPC)

Rather than allowing wholesale manufacture of a flawed product, SPC aims to identify and correct defects at an early stage. Subscribing to the theory that 'if the supplier's process is running satisfactorily and is capable of meeting specifications, the products coming out of the process conform', this method reassures customers that their supplier is engaged in processes of quality monitoring and control. Capable of application to all the processes involved in a product value-chain (conception, marketing, production and selling), SPC operates on the basis of the following fundamental principles:

1) Quality is conformance to specifications
2) Processes and products vary
3) Variation in processes and products can be measured
4) Normal variation follows a bell-shaped curve
5) Abnormal variation distorts the bell shape
6) Causes of variation can be isolated and identified

Employment of SPC can result in several benefits:

- Objective and measurable feedback on supplier quality performance
- Improvement of product flow
- Imperative of quality control by the supplier
- Elimination of sorting and incoming inspection
- Improvement of product quality
- Reduction of need to accept off-standard parts
- Reduction of costs
- Reduction of scrap and re-working

Much like JIT and TQM, statistical process control requires such in-depth collaboration with suppliers that it tends to precipitate single sourcing.

❖ Hutchins, G., *Purchasing Strategies for Total Quality* (1992).

52. Supplier Appraisal Techniques

Less formalised than vendor rating, these techniques nevertheless provide a means both for supplier selection and the assessment of subsequent performance. By application of informal criteria of appraisal, it can be determined whether a supplier meets the requisite standards. The process normally includes requests for information, quotations and proposals before an appraisal is made.

53. Supplier Development Programmes

When a long-term supplier contract is necessary it may also be appropriate to develop a long-term collaborative relationship. This might involve a strategic alliance or joint development agreement. Prior to establishing a supplier development programme, however, it is necessary to undertake an assessment of both parties to determine their compatibility. Once instituted, a programme will demand joint improvement work to improve value for money through the aggregation of supplier and buyer expertise, and definition of mutually shared objectives. This approach will also normally include such lean principles as process improvement mapping, and JIT, as well as the development of suppliers to undertake supplier managed inventory activities and, eventually supply chain management work in their own supply chains. It will also normally require extensive use of performance measurement and management tools and techniques.

❖ Cox, A. et al., *Supply Chain Management: A Guide to Best Practice* (2003).

54. Supplier Rationalisation
This procedure refers to the process by which buyers analyse their supply base and understand where the value and volume of activity occurs. This is often undertaken using Pareto techniques. The basic idea is to concentrate supplier development activities on the high value suppliers who manage most of the monetary value of the spend for the organisation. For the low value suppliers the normal aim is to drastically reduce the number of suppliers and transactions involved.

55. Sourcing Methodology
Classically procurement professionals have relied on a structured approach to sourcing that involves a number of key phases. The standard methodology involves the development of a robust design and specification process, followed by an RFX process (requests for information, proposals and quotation). This stage is then normally followed by a detailed supplier selection process based on structured competition and quotation analysis and detailed supplier negotiation, with contract award and post-contractual performance management at the end. This approach when formalised normally involves a systematic approach to category management. In which individual categories of spend are managed according to underlying leverage opportunities within them using a standard sourcing methodology, which often includes strategic source planning techniques. See also the QV Methodology reference above.

❖ Cox A et al., *Supply Chain Management: A Guide to Best Practice* (2003).
❖ Hughes, J. et al., *Transform Your Supply Chain* (1998).

56. Supplier Managed Inventory (SMI)

SMI is different from consignment stocking in that it can be initiated by the supplier (see also supplier development above). The following options are all open to consideration in its management of goods:

1) Third-party distribution organised by the purchaser, utilising the third party's assets
2) Third-party distribution utilising vehicles and equipment owned by the purchaser
3) Third-party distribution utilising vehicles and equipment leased by the purchaser
4) Third-party distribution organised by the supplier
5) Distribution managed by the supplier using their own assets
6) Distribution managed by the purchaser using their own assets

Decision-making on this front rests on the following criteria:

• The respective power of the purchaser and supplier
• The power acquired by a third-party in the process
• The ease of switching third-party distributors
• The size and frequency of the required deliveries
• The total cost of each item

❖ Chadwick, T. and Rajagopal, S., *Strategic Supply Management* (1995).

57. Supply Chain Management

See the reference in Operations and Production Tools and Techniques (chapter 6).

58. Synchronised Production

This approach involves supplier production of items at a rate that matches the purchaser's production. It requires enormous co-operative efforts from both parties:

1) Investment in 'flexible' manufacturing equipment
2) Re-design of business processes around a 'pull' system
3) Variable-quality, fixed production
4) Off-line set-ups of tooling, and the achievement of improved process reliability
5) Review of the design tolerances with impact on running speed and reject-rate
6) Improvement of material/component availability for the manufacturing process

7) Institution of manufacturing improvement teams dedicated to process analysis, opportunity identification, and project management of the required process improvements

❖ Chadwick, T. and Rajagopal, S., *Strategic Supply Management* (1995).

59.   Target Based Costing
In achieving lean supply conditions, both buyer and supplier are encouraged to collaborate in identifying opportunities for cost reduction. Embedded in TQ and JIT philosophies, this approach focuses on long-term agreements as the basis for identifying improvement areas. Primary aims are to ensure that appropriate product value is delivered to the customer, that required volume is maintained, and that margin contribution is not eroded.

❖ Hughes, J., Ralf, M. and Michels, B., *Transform your Supply Chain* (1998).
❖ Shank, J. K. and Fisher, J., 'Target costing as a strategic tool', *Sloan Management Review* (1999).

60.   Transparency
An approach to sourcing that involves the buyer and supplier mutually adopting open and transparent approaches to relationship management. The aim is to move beyond the opaque transparency associated with traditional open-book costing models, which still provide scope for opportunism, in favour of true transparency over strategies, operational practices and financial data for mutual benefit.

❖ Lamming, R et al., 'Transparency in supply relationships: concept and practice', *Journal of Supply Chain Management* (2001).

61.   Value Analysis
Around 1950, Lawrence Miles of GE described this technique as 'an organised creative approach which has for its purpose the efficient identification of unnecessary cost – cost which contributes neither quality, nor use, nor life, nor appearance, nor customer features'. It involves the following three steps:

1) Identify and list the major cost elements
2) Arrange in descending order
3) Examine each principal cost driver with questions

❖ Chadwick, T. and Rajagopal, S., *Strategic Supply Management* (1995).

62. Value Engineering

This is a process by which, prior to manufacturing, attempts are made by crodsds0-functional teams from the business to develop products or services with higher functional value or lower costs of production and supply for the same functional value, or both. This normally occurs at the design and specification process stage for new product and service development.

❖ Mudge, A. E., *Value Engineering: A Systematic Approach* (1971).

63. Value Stream Management

This refers to a process by which the value stream between consumer and raw materials is systematically mapped and then managed on the basis of waste reduction and optimisation tools and techniques. Similar in many ways to the lean manufacturing and production models used within the operations and production function but extended beyond the focal firm into the supply chain.

❖ Hines, P. et al., *Value Stream Management* (2000).

64. Vendor Rating

In its simplest form, vendor assessment involves a rating scheme across a range of performance criteria. Though often based on objective and subjective criteria the process is normally improved when cross-functional personnel participate, and the speed of analysis is a definite advantage. Information can subsequently be shared with suppliers in order to prompt performance monitoring. A more sophisticated computerised form can also prove of substantial benefit to both customer and supplier.

❖ Chadwick, T. and Rajagopal, S., *Strategic Supply Management* (1995).

65. Vulnerability Analysis

This form of analysis (Figure 8.11) recognises that make-buy decisions should be taken in view of potential future vulnerability:

❖ Hughes, J. et al., *Transform your Supply Chain* (1998).

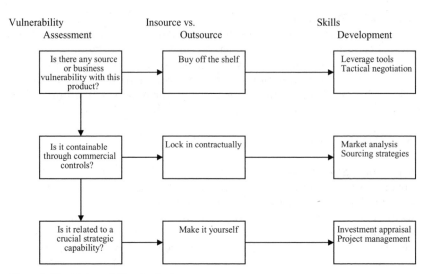

Figure 8.11   Vulnerability Analysis
Source: Hughes, J., Ralf, M. and Michels, B., *Transform your Supply Chain* (1998) International Thompson Business Press, London.

9
The Use of Procurement and Supply Management Tools and Techniques

In recent years there has been a marked increase in the attention given to the issue of operational efficiency. All of these tools seek to obtain more from a firm's inputs by driving down its cost base and, consequently, achieving higher levels of profitability. This growing preoccupation with operational efficiency can be dated to the competitive challenge mounted by Japanese companies in the 1970s and 1980s. For a while Japanese firms in some industrial sectors were so far ahead of their Anglo-Saxon and Continental European counterparts that they were able to simultaneously offer customers lower prices and superior products. The source of Japanese competitiveness in this period cannot be traced to a single source. However, one feature of Japanese management practice that does stand out then, and now, is the emphasis that it has traditionally placed on external resource management. The Japanese appear, when compared with other cultures, to have placed procurement and supply management issues at the core of their business model.

For a number of reasons Japanese firms have historically been far less vertically integrated than their Western counterparts. Instead of undertaking all of the design and manufacture of their products internally Japanese firms preferred instead to look to their extensive networks of contractors and sub-contractors for much of their production. By American and West European standards relationships between the firm and its suppliers have traditionally been close and long lasting. However, there is a conditional element to these associations. Since the pursuit of operational effectiveness sits at the heart of the Japanese model, the major Japanese firms have normally looked to their suppliers to take the lead in delivering the required cost reductions and improvements in functionality of supply inputs (Nishiguchi, 1994).

The impact of the Japanese model on the shape of some Western businesses and on Western business thought was dramatic. Industries threatened with severe competition initially pursued protectionism. Eventually, however, some Western academics began to urge the wholesale adoption of

Japanese production and contracting methods. Distilling what they took to be the essentials of Japanese practice academics developed what they have collectively described as the lean manufacturing, lean enterprise and lean supply models (Lamming 1993; Hines, 1994; Womack & Jones, 1996).

Although, there are some obvious differences between these authors all agree on the same basic internal and external resource management essentials. First, the lean philosophy requires the firm to concentrate on its core competencies (Hamel & Prahalad, 1990). Two, it requires the firm to outsource all non-essential processes and activities. Three, it requires the firm to consolidate all supply inputs into categories of spend. Four, it requires the firm to concentrate internal resources on a limited number of long-term collaborative relationships with preferred suppliers. Five, it requires the firm to enhance operational effectiveness through proactive supply chain management and development. Some champions of lean thinking have argued that this model has an almost universal applicability and partly, as a consequence, lean (sometimes also termed alliancing or partnering) thinking has become the dominant philosophical approach to best practice in procurement and supply management in recent years.

Furthermore, it has had the effect of raising the status of the function in the minds of business managers more generally. Prior to development of the lean paradigm procurement and supply had been seen as the Cinderella function. Many businesses regarded it essentially as a clerical function concerned with transactional and tactical order placement, fulfilment, and inventory control and invoice reconciliation. It was not regard as of central importance to the competitiveness of the firm. Consequently, even today, in many companies the procurement and supply function retains this junior tactical status. Furthermore, even though many companies now employ 'supply chain managers' these individuals still often lack the internal influence and/or resources to implement plans as ambitious as those advocated by the proponents of lean thinking.

Notwithstanding this fact, procurement and supply is clearly an emerging function. As it has emerged, the stranglehold that lean philosophy once enjoyed over the discipline has started to weaken and this has led to an explosion of alternative perspectives, not least the power and leverage perspective, and the management tools to support them (Cox et al., 2000, 2001, 2002, 2003, 2004a & 2004b). The major issues are, therefore, how significant this upsurge in interest has been and how effectively have the tools it has produced performed. In theory procurement and supply management should constitute a fertile ground for such initiatives. Since it is a process-oriented function it should also respond well to standardised solutions to frequently encountered problems.

This chapter focuses, first, on the general use of tools and techniques in the procurement and supply area and then assess the objectives behind implementation, and concludes with an analysis of their overall performance, with a discussion of the major barriers experienced in implementation. The analysis is undertaken in general but also by individual and grouped industry sectors.

1. The general use of tools and techniques in procurement and supply

The discussion that follows analyses the general functional use of procurement and supply tools and techniques in total, and across the 7 business activities outlined earlier in chapter 1. The analysis then focuses on the use of tools in general within the 16 industry sectors and the 6 industry sector groupings also outlined in chapter 1.

The use of tools and techniques in general

Table 9.1 shows that only 42 individual tools and techniques were discovered to be in use in the 122 surveyed companies (see Appendix E), but there were 456 incidences in which tools and techniques were in use. This indicates that the procurement and supply function appears to use tools and techniques relatively less than most other functions and that companies appear to be using many of the same tools. Table 9.1 below shows that 63% of all usage were accounted for by the top ten tools and techniques, and that almost 87% of all tool and technique use is accounted for by just twenty applications. What also stands out is that, despite the considerable debate within the profession – especially amongst academics and consultants – about what constitutes best practice, the tools and techniques that are actually used by managers are fairly traditional. There is only limited evidence of the adoption of the more recently advanced best practice tools associated with lean (0.22% of total recorded uses), power (0.44%) and balanced sourcing (no uses) approaches.

As Table 9.1 also indicates certain tools and techniques are in far more regular use within companies across all of the 16 industrial sectors surveyed than others. Thus, vendor rating systems stand as the key tool and technique being used, with the highest number of incidences (49) and accounting for over 10% of all usage in this function. This is unsurprising at one level because all companies have to rate the relative standing of potential suppliers, before selecting them. What is perhaps more surprising is the fact that only 49 of the 122 companies surveyed were actually using vendor rating tools. This means that close to 60% of companies appear not to be formally rating their potential suppliers before selecting them! This confirms the general concern (expressed elsewhere in this volume) that, while there is considerable evidence of tool and techniques being used, what is often surprising is the lack of a formalised and structured process within companies around the basic activities that have to be managed on a fairly regular basis.

Table 9.1   The Total Use of Procurement and Supply Tools and Techniques (42 Tools with 456 Tool Usages in Total Recorded)

Tool	Incidence	%	Tool	Incidence	%
Vendor Rating	49	10.75	Benchmarking	5	1.10
Purchasing Portfolio Matrix	40	8.77	Quality Mgmt Techniques	5	1.10
ERP Systems	39	8.55	Value Stream Management	5	1.10
Supplier Development	30	6.58	First Point Assessment	4	0.88
Service Level Agreements	27	5.92	Balanced Scorecard	3	0.66
Core Competence Thinking	24	5.25	E-Business Seller Side Software	3	0.66
Purchasing Cards	24	5.25	EDI	3	0.66
Key Performance Indicators	20	4.39	ISO Technical Standards	3	0.66
E-Business Buyer-Side Software	18	3.94	Purchasing Consortium	3	0.66
Management Information System	18	3.94	Supplier Managed Inventory	3	0.66
Supplier Appraisal	16	3.51	Supplier Rationalisation	3	0.66
E-Business Internal Applications	14	3.07	Life Cycle Costing	2	0.44
Approved Supplier List	13	2.85	Project Management	2	0.44
Supplier Sourcing Methodology	13	2.85	Qv Methodology	2	0.44
Pareto Analysis	11	2.41	Supply Chain Management	2	0.44
Risk Analysis Tools	10	2.19	Lean Supply	1	0.22
MRP System	9	1.97	Open Book Agreements	1	0.22
Activity Based Costing	8	1.75	Relationship Asses. Programme	1	0.22
Negotiating Procedure	7	1.54	Six Sigma	1	0.22
JIT	6	1.32	Target Based Costing	1	0.22
Outsourcing Procedure	6	1.32	Value Engineering	1	0.22

That said, most of the tools and techniques in use (apart from those linked with the pervasive impact of the Internet) appear to be those that focus on the traditional concerns of the procurement and supply function. Thus, it is nor surprising to discover that the list of most frequently used and cited tools and techniques includes: vendor rating (10.75%); the purchasing portfolio matrix (8.77%); supplier development (6.58%) service level agreements (5.92%); purchasing cards (5.25%); KPIs (4.39%); supplier appraisal (3.51%); approved supplier lists (2.85%); supplier sourcing methodologies (2.85%); Pareto analysis (2.41%); risk analysis (2.19%); negotiation procedures 91.54%); and, outsourcing procedures (1.32%). More surprising is the fact that so few companies were using these standard and traditional tools very much at all. For example, only 27 respondents (22% of the sample surveyed) appear to be using service level agreements, only 24 (20% of those surveyed) were using purchasing cards and only 16 (13%) were using supplier appraisal techniques.

When one analyses the more esoteric and recently developed tools and techniques associated with lean, power and balanced sourcing approaches it is clear that managers do not appear to be using these approaches very much at all. Indeed, even the fairly well established best practice approach known as category management (referred to here under the concept of supplier sourcing methodology) recorded only 13 uses (2.85% of usages and 11% of users). The more advanced approaches to lean sourcing were also under-represented. Value stream management had only 5 uses (1.10% of usages and 4% of users) and relationship assessment programmes had only 1 use (0.22% of usages). Set against this there was a high incidence of supplier development activity with 30 uses cited (this accounts for 6.58% of usages and 25% of users). This activity also recorded the development of lean approaches to sourcing associated with alliancing and partnering strategies, although not all respondents believed they were engaged in lean approaches when undertaking supplier development work.

Set against this apparent resistance to change is the obvious success of Internet and IT based applications in recent years. The table demonstrates clearly that there has been a growing reliance on these types of tools and techniques: ERP systems were the third most cited application with 39 uses (8.55% of total usages), closely followed by a range of E-Business buyer-side software applications and management information systems each accounting for 18 uses, with 3.94% of usages. E-Business seller-side applications were less in prominence with only 3 uses (0.66% of usages). The growth in IT and Internet tools and techniques is clearly apparent everywhere in business and the procurement and supply function is no different in this respect. Interestingly enough – and somewhat surprising given that it is a tool that was developed for strategy thinking – is the high recorded use of core competence thinking, with 24 uses (5.25% of total recorded usages, by

20% of respondents). This appears to be due to two phenomena. First, the growth in popularity of outsourcing has recently questioned vertically integrated business models, and this appears to have extended the role of procurement and supply and forced managers in the function to use core/non-core ideas as part of outsourcing risk management. Second, core competence thinking has been a pervasive 'fad' in recent years and one that procurement and supply managers appear not to be immune from, anymore than other functions.

Table 9.2 demonstrates, however, that while managers may be gullible to some extent, in that they do sometimes tend to follow the latest fashionable ideas, they do not appear willing to buy any tool and technique that is offered to them. The table demonstrates that there are a number of tools and techniques – 23 in total (or 35% of all of those specified in the literature search) – that were not discovered to be in use within the 122 surveyed companies. When arguing that these tools and techniques were not in use we mean that there was either no recognition by respondents of what these tools or techniques were, or that they had no formalised and structured process that required them to use the ideas or processes linked to the tools and techniques specified regularly.

Table 9.2   **The 23 Procurement and Supply Tools and Techniques Not Found in Use**

Automatic Inventory Replenishment (AIR)
Balanced Sourcing
Cammish And Keough's Procurement Development Model
Centralised Distribution Centres and Cross-Docking
Competitive Advantage Vs Strategic Vulnerability
Contract Price Adjustment Formulae
De Toni and Tonchia Model
EOQ/EBQ
Failure Mode and Effects Analysis (Fmea)
Generic Sourcing Strategies Matrix
Matching Organisation to Innovation
Network Sourcing
Partnership Sourcing Model
Pipeline Mapping
Price Indexing (PI)
Robert Beck and Brian Long's Maturity Classification
Russell Syson's Developmental Model
Stages of Excellence Framework
Statistical Process Control (SPC)
Synchronised Production
Transparency
Value Analysis
Vulnerability Analysis

The use of tools and techniques by business activity

Having analysed the general use of tools and techniques in procurement and supply it is now possible to analyse for which business activities within the function these tools and techniques are being used most. The survey findings in this regard are presented in Table 9.3.

The total business activity usage scores were calculated by linking the key tools and techniques reported with the 7 major business activities outlined for the procurement and supply function in chapter 1 (the totals do not sum to 100% because some tools have multiple applications across a range of business activities). As is clear from Table 9.3 the findings demonstrate that it is in the transactional process and fulfilment aspects of the procurement and supply role that most tools and techniques are being utilised. Thus, the most popular tools and techniques were clearly those that focused on performance measurement (28.75% of total usages). This is closely followed by *process enhancement* (27.62%) and *IT and Internet applications* (22.79%). While tools and techniques for a more strategic purpose are clearly in use these were less utilised than those of a more transactional nature. Thus, *supplier selection and negotiation* activities account for only 22.60% of total activity usage and the more sophisticated and strategic approaches focused on *supplier development* activities account for only 19.11% of total business activity usage, with *segmentation of spend* somewhat lower at 11.62% and the most strategically critically important sourcing activity – *make/buy* – at a mere 9.20% of total usage. These findings appear to confirm the lack of strategic focus within the procurement and supply function and its continuing focus on operational, transactional and tactical activities.

The use of tools and techniques by industry sector and by industry sector groupings

When it comes to considering the use of procurement and supply tools and techniques by industry sector it is clear that some sectors tend to use them more than others, and there are grouping differences as well. Thus, as Table 9.4 demonstrates, the Oil & Gas industry, with an average score of 6 tools and techniques in use per firm surveyed (calculated by dividing the number of tools and techniques found in use in the industry by the number of firms interviewed) scored considerably higher than any other sector. The nearest competitors were the Power & Water sector with an average score of 5.44 tools per firm surveyed, followed by Healthcare (4.90), Basic Chemicals (4.55), Retail Financial Services (4.50) and Construction (4.33). In the middle rank of tool and technique industrial usage was IT Solutions (3.90), Confectionery (3.82), Computer Hardware (3.70), Transport Equipment (3.60) and Aerospace (2.83). Beneath these were the low usage sectors, these include in rank order: Media & Entertainment (2.00), Telecommunications

Table 9.3   The Use of Procurement and Supply Tools and Techniques by
Business Activity

(The total % figures do not sum to 100% because some tools and techniques can be
used for more than one business activity)

Rank Order of Tools and Techniques by Business Activities Score	Tools and Techniques	% of Total Usage Recorded	Total Business Activity Usage
1 Performance Measurement	Vendor Rating System	10.75	28.75%
	Service Level Agreement	5.92	
	KPIs	4.39	
	Activity Based Costing	1.75	
	JIT	1.32	
	Benchmarking	1.10	
	Quality Management Techniques	1.10	
	Balanced Scorecard	0.66	
	ISO-Technical Quality Standards	0.66	
	Project Management	0.44	
	QV Methodology	0.44	
	Target Costing	0.22	
2 Process Enhancement	ERP	8.55	27.62%
	Purchasing Cards	5.25	
	MIS	3.94	
	MRP	1.97	
	Activity Based Costing	1.75	
	JIT	1.32	
	Quality Management Techniques	1.10	
	Value Stream Management	1.10	
	Balanced Scorecard	0.66	
	EDI	0.66	
	Supplier Managed Inventory	0.66	
	QV Methodology	0.44	
	Six Sigma	0.22	
3 IT and Internet Applications	ERP	8.55	22.79%
	E-Business Buyer-Side Software	3.94	
	MIS	3.94	
	E-Business-Internal Applications	3.07	
	MRP	1.97	
	EDI	0.66	
	E-Business Supplier-Side Software	0.66	
4 Supplier Selection and Negotiation	Vendor Rating System	10.75	22.60%
	Supplier Appraisal System	3.51	
	Approved Supplier-List	2.85	
	Supplier Sourcing Methodology	2.85	
	Negotiation Procedures	1.54	
	Supplier Rationalisation	0.66	
	QV Methodology	0.44	

Table 9.3   The Use of Procurement and Supply Tools and Techniques by
Business Activity – *continued*

(The total % figures do not sum to 100% because some tools and techniques can be
used for more than one business activity)

Rank Order of Tools and Techniques by Business Activities Score	Tools and Techniques	% of Total Usage Recorded	Total Business Activity Usage
6 Supplier Development	Supplier Development Programme	6.58	19.11%
	KPIs	4.39	
	JIT	1.32	
	Quality Management Techniques	1.10	
	Value Stream Management	1.10	
	First Point Assessment	0.88	
	ISO-Technical Quality Standards	0.66	
	Purchasing Consortium	0.66	
	Life Cycle Costing	0.44	
	QV Methodology	0.44	
	Supply Chain Management	0.44	
	Lean Supply	0.22	
	Open Book Agreement	0.22	
	Relationship Assessment Programme	0.22	
	Target Costing	0.22	
	Value Engineering	0.22	
7 Segmentation of Spend	Purchasing Portfolio Matrix	8.77	11.62%
	Pareto Analysis	2.41	
	QV Methodology	0.44	
8 Make/Buy Decision	Core Competence Thinking	5.25	9.20%
	Risk Analysis	2.19	
	Outsourcing Procedure	1.32	
	QV Methodology	0.44	

(1.40), Tourism and Leisure (1.50), Retail & Distribution (1.33) and, finally,
Publishing (1.00).

When disaggregating by the 6 core groupings of industrial sectors
(Figure 9.1) there were some broad differences between process and project
based, as well as between manufacturing, combined manufacturing and
services and services, industries. In general terms firms in the 8 process
based industries analysed appeared to use tools and techniques in this area
more frequently and extensively (3.62 average usages) than those firms
from the 8 project industries (2.92 average uses). Despite this process based
industries did not provide for the most extensive use of tools and techniques. Interestingly, it is the *Project/Combined* group of industrial sectors

Table 9.4   The Rank Order Use of Procurement and Supply Tools and
Techniques by Industry Sector

Industry	Total Tool Usages	No. of Firms	Average
Oil & Gas	60	10	6.00
Power & Water	49	9	5.44
Healthcare	44	9	4.90
Basic Chemicals	50	11	4.55
Retail Financial Services	18	4	4.50
Construction	26	6	4.33
IT Solutions	39	10	3.90
Confectionery	42	11	3.82
Computer Hardware	37	10	3.70
Transport Equipment	34	10	3.40
Aerospace	17	6	2.83
Media & Entertainment	10	6	1.66
Telecommunications	16	10	1.60
Tourism & Leisure	9	6	1.50
Retail & Distribution	4	3	1.33
Publishing	1	1	1.00
Overall Average	456	122	3.74

(Construction, IT Solutions and Oil & Gas) that scored the highest average usage rate (4.74), followed by *Process/Manufacturing* (Basic Chemicals, Computer Hardware and Confectionery) with 4.02, and then by the *Process/Combined* (Healthcare, Power & Water and Telecommunications) grouping with 3.91. The *Project/Manufacturing* grouping (Aerospace, Publishing and Transport Equipment) scoring 2.48 average uses and *Process/Services* (Retail & Distribution and Retail Financial Services) with 2.92 made up the middle rank of groupings. It is perhaps no surprise that the *Project/Services* group (Media & Entertainment and Tourism and Leisure) with an average score of 1.55 usages was the least likely to use tools and techniques.

The reason for the superior take up of tools and techniques by the *Project/Combined* group appears to be a function of the highly dynamic market environment in these industrial sectors (Construction, IT Solutions and Oil & Gas), in which firms often are engaged in high value projects, with a constant need to develop new supply offerings under conditions of extensive operational and financial risk. In such circumstances the need for standard routines systems and processes (and therefore supporting tools and techniques) will be of highest value. Similarly, the process based industries (*Process/Manufacturing* and *Process/Combined*) manufacturing products and services through standardised and routinised systems and processes, with high levels of capital invested as a sunk cost, are also likely to value the use of such tools and techniques. On the other hand, the services

TYPE OF OPERATIONAL DELIVERY

	PROCESS/ MANUFACTURING	PROCESS/ MANUFACTURING & SERVICES	PROCESS/ SERVICES	
	Group Average Usage 4.02	*Group Average Usage 3.91*	*Group Average Usage 2.92*	
PROCESS	Basic Chemicals (4.55) Computer Hardware (3.70) Confectionery (3.82)	Healthcare (4.90) Power & Water (5.44) Telecommunications (1.40)	Retail & Distribution (1.33) Retail Financial Services (4.50)	*Total Process Average Usage:* **3.62**
	PROJECT/ MANUFACTURING	PROJECT/ MANUFACTURING & SERVICES	PROJECT/ SERVICES	
	Group Average Usage 2.48	*Group Average Usage 4.74*	*Group Average Usage 1.55*	
PROJECT	Aerospace (2.83) Publishing (1.00) Transport Equipment (3.60)	Construction (4.33) IT Solutions (3.90) Oil & Gas (6.00)	Media & Entertainment (1.66) Tourism & Leisure (1.50)	*Total Project Average Usage:* **3.27**
	Total Manufacturing Average Usage 3.25	*Total Combined Average Usage 4.33*	*Total Service Average Usage 2.24*	
	MANUFACTURING	COMBINED MANUFACTURING & SERVICES	SERVICES	

TYPE OF GOODS AND/OR SERVICES

Figure 9.1 The Use of Procurement Supply Tools and Techniques by Industry Groups

industries scored the lowest overall for tool and technique usage (only 2.24 usages on average, compared with 3.25 for manufacturing and 4.33 for combined industries).

The reason for this is obviously a function of the difficulty of standardising service offerings, which tends to vitiate attempts within organisations to use routinised systems and processes. There is also another – and perhaps more important reason – service based industries tend to be more labour intensive and more vertically integrated than manufacturing firms. This means that the share of total corporate spend on external rather than internal resources is often lower in services-based firms and industries than in manufacturing, and this reduces the role and significance of procurement and supply in the business and undermines the case for the extensive use of management tools and techniques. There is also normally less sunk cost in invested capital infrastructure that must be financed and sustained in services industries. Whatever the cause, it is clear that usage rates are much lower in the service based industry groupings. *Project/Services* industries (Media & Entertainment and Tourism and Leisure) scored the lowest group average usage score (1.55).

2.   The performance of the tools and techniques used in procurement and supply

Having analysed the use of tools and techniques in some detail it is now possible to focus on the performance of the tools and techniques that were adopted. This section focuses on the objectives behind the use of tools and techniques and the impact of these on both the firm and the function. This is followed by an analysis of the impact of tools and techniques by industrial sector and industrial sector groupings. Finally, there is a discussion of the major barriers to effective implementation.

The corporate and functional objectives for implementing tools and techniques

Table 9.5 provides an overview of the general objectives behind the use of tools and techniques by the managers surveyed. The Table summarises the respondents overall views about why any particular tools or technique was used by making an initial broad distinction between *strategic* (defined as a choice from the development of uniquely differentiated products, cost leadership advantages or to assist with competitive market repositioning for the firm as a whole) and *operational* (all other functional process and transactional improvement) objectives.

As the table demonstrates, in terms of offering the organisation a competitive advantage, the gains that managers expect to obtain from using tools and techniques in the area of procurement and supply are limited. The survey evidence suggests that 80% of all tools and techniques are used

Group	Industry	Strategic Objectives			
		Unique Products %	Cost Advantage %	Repositioning %	Operational Effectiveness %
Process/Manufacturing Group	Basic Chemicals	0	3	0	97
	Computer Hardware	1	0	0	98
	Confectionery	0	9	0	91
	Group Average	*1*	*4*	*0*	*95*
Process/Combined Group	Healthcare	0	18	5	77
	Power And Water	0	0	0	100
	Telecommunications	8	18	4	70
	Group Average	*3*	*12*	*3*	*82*
Process/Services Group	Retail And Distribution	0	0	0	100
	Retail Financial Services	4	0	0	96
	Group Average	*2*	*0*	*0*	*98*
Project/Manufacturing Group	Aerospace	3	17	0	72
	Publishing	0	0	8	100
	Transport Equipment	5	18	3	74
	Group Average	*3*	*12*	*3*	*82*
Project/Combined Group	Construction	3	27	0	70
	It Solutions	0	2	5	93
	Oil & Gas	0	35	4	61
	Group Average	*1*	*22*	*3*	*75*
Project/Services Group	Media And Entertainment	8	40	0	52
	Tourism & Leisure	12	36	0	52
	Group Average	*10*	*38*	*0*	*52*
Overall Average (%)		2	16	2	80

to deliver improvements in operational effectiveness. Only 20% of the managers using them believed that what they were doing would contribute meaningfully to the firm's general business strategy. These findings are consistent with those reported in the operations and production function, which also demonstrated a clear understanding of the need to focus on operational effectiveness objectives (see Table 7.5).

What is also apparent is that of the 20% who thought they were making a strategic contribution, 16% believed that it would be made in cost leadership. Only 4% of managers believed that the use of procurement and supply tools could assist the organisation to develop innovative products or services, or to reposition itself in new markets strategically. This is despite the fact that the growing trend towards outsourcing means that an increasing proportion of a firm's offerings to its own customers now depends on the performance of suppliers operating outside of the boundary of the organisation. These findings are interesting also because they are the opposite of those reported by the operations and production function, which felt that if it was involved at all in assisting the firm strategically it would tend to be through differentiation by discovering or developing unique products and/or services (16% of firm level objectives). This clearly shows the influence of internally imposed cost reduction KPI targets on procurement and supply functional thinking and performance.

While this broadly describes the overall picture there are some significant differences when one looks at the question of strategic intent from an industry perspective. By analysing the six industry sector groupings it is clear that the preoccupation with operational effectiveness was overwhelming amongst the *Process/Services* (98%), *Process/Manufacturing* (95%) and *Process/Combined* (82%) and *Project/Manufacturing* (82%) industries. Of the ten industries covered within these four groupings, only four deviated from this overall trend: Healthcare (77%), Transport Equipment (74%), Aerospace (72%) and Telecommunications (70%). But even in these cases the focus on operational effectiveness objectives was still paramount because the strategic benefits expected were also focused almost exclusively on providing cost leadership advantages – Healthcare (18%), Transport Equipment (18%), Aerospace (17%) and Telecommunications (18%). What is also interesting is that managers in Power & Water, Retail & Distribution and Publishing did not believe that procurement and supply tools and techniques can provide any strategic advantages to the firm.

It is interesting to note, however, that in the *Project/Combined* and *Project/Services* groupings managers did believe that procurement and supply tools could provide them with a strategic competitive advantage, but once again this was primarily focused on cost leadership considerations rather than differentiation or market repositioning. This trend was most evident for Construction (27%) and Oil & Gas (35%) in the *Process/Combined* and for Media & Entertainment (40%) and Tourism & Leisure

(36%) in the *Project/Services* groupings. Interestingly it was the later two industry sectors (with 8% and 12% respectively) that felt that procurement and supply tools and techniques could most assist corporate strategy by finding unique products and services for differentiation. IT Solutions stands out in these groups of industries as the one that is more like the rest in that it did not believe that it could provide any real strategic advantage for the firm through the use of procurement and supply tools and techniques. The somewhat unique position of Media & Entertainment and Tourism & Leisure in the survey is perhaps a function of the fact that, in the project environment, having access to scarce external talent or venues may provide a strategic lever that is denied procurement and supply managers in other industries.

Notwithstanding this privileged position for firms in Media & Entertainment and Tourism & Leisure the findings overall reinforce the view that procurement and supply sees itself as a primarily tactical and operationally focused function. This is particularly true in all types of process-based industries and also in project-based manufacturing industries. Even when managers in these industries believed that they could provide some strategic advantages for the firm these tend to be focused on cost leadership rather than differentiation and market repositioning goals. What is perhaps interesting was that in only four of these industries – Healthcare (18%), Telecommunications (18%), Transport Equipment (18%) and Aerospace (17%) – did managers believe that they could have any significant strategic role through cost leadership. The reason for this somewhat depressing conclusion may well be because price competition in many of the process industries is often extreme. This downward pressure on prices may have already squeezed costs to such an extent that any strategic benefits (even of a cost kind) have largely been exhausted. By contrast, many of the project-based industries are notorious for their time inefficiency and price overruns. The Construction, IT Solutions and Aerospace industries are all cases in point, as is Media and Entertainment. Consequently, any firm that is able to streamline its internal processes efficiently and manage its supply base effectively in the project environment may have a competitive advantage over its rivals.

If procurement and supply tools and techniques do not provide much scope for strategic influence within firms it is still important to understand what the functional objectives are for introducing them operationally in the first place. Table 9.6 provides findings about this issue. Survey respondents were asked to explain the primary purpose for which they used tools and techniques based on whether they used them to improve: the functional performance of their departments; their departmental costs of operations; to improve communication and information flow management; to provide a more flexible and responsive service to others in the business; to improve staff skill sets; and, to increase departmental

Table 9.6 The Functional Objectives for Introducing Procurement and Supply Tools and Techniques (%)

Industry	Functionality	Cost	Communication	Information	Flexibility	Skill Sets	Number Employed	Other	No Data
Process/Manufacturing									
Basic Chemicals	1	19	20	24	4	3	2	26	1
Computer Hardware	0	6	36	39	1	4	0	14	0
Confectionery	0	28	29	31	1	11	0	0	0
Group Average	*0*	*18*	*28*	*31*	*2*	*6*	*1*	*13*	*0*
Process/Combined									
Healthcare	24	38	12	20	1	3	0	2	0
Power & Water	36	34	5	13	9	0	1	2	0
Telecommunications	37	10	6	33	12	0	2	0	0
Group Average	*32*	*28*	*8*	*22*	*7*	*1*	*1*	*1*	*0*
Process/Services									
Retail & Distribution	44	44	0	11	0	0	1	0	0
Retail Financial Services	29	33	4	5	16	0	13	0	0
Group Average	*36*	*39*	*2*	*8*	*8*	*0*	*7*	*0*	*0*
Project/Manufacturing									
Aerospace	20	28	11	35	4	0	0	2	0
Publishing	33	33	0	33	0	0	0	0	0
Transport Equipment	23	34	12	26	1	3	0	0	0
Group Average	*25*	*32*	*8*	*31*	*2*	*1*	*0*	*1*	*0*

Table 9.6 The Functional Objectives for Introducing Procurement and Supply Tools and Techniques (%) – *continued*

Industry	Functionality	Cost	Communication	Information	Flexibility	Skill Sets	Number Employed	Other	No Data
Project/Combined									
Construction	33	15	16	18	5	2	5	7	0
IT Solutions	0	9	22	30	1	9	1	29	0
Oil And Gas	32	14	15	25	6	4	2	1	0
Group Average	*22*	*13*	*18*	*24*	*4*	*5*	*2*	*12*	*0*
Project/Services									
Media & Entertainment	41	11	7	30	0	9	0	0	2
Tourism & Leisure	35	16	23	13	10	0	3	0	0
Group Average	*38*	*14*	*15*	*21*	*5*	*5*	*1*	*0*	*1*
Overall Average	25	24	14	22	4	4	2	5	0

headcount. The findings show that the primary functional objective for the use of procurement and supply tools and techniques appears to be three-fold. First, it was to facilitate the production, exchange and dissemination of information. Second, it was to improve the functional performance of service level delivery to other clients in the business. Third, it was to achieve departmental cost reduction targets.

These conclusions are supported by the fact that 36% of total respondents were introducing tools and techniques to facilitate communication (14%) and information production and exchange (22%). This objective was particularly marked in *Process/Manufacturing* (59%), *Project/Combined* (42%) and *Project/Manufacturing* (39%) industries. It was least significant in the *Process/Services* (10%) industries. The overall score of 25% for this objective indicates the significance of the achievement of improved functional service level delivery. It was of major significance in all the firms and industries surveyed except *Process/Manufacturing*. The achievement of departmental cost reduction targets was also an equally significant objective across virtually all firms and industry sectors. Thus, although cost reduction was the most significant objective in the *Process/Services* industries (39%), it was also significant in *Project/Manufacturing* (32%), *Process/Combined* (28%), with an average figure overall of 25%.

Finally, as we found in the other three functions surveyed, there was only limited interest in the use of tools and techniques to improve the skill sets of procurement and supply staff (4%). This is depressing given that many of the tools and techniques being used are an attempt to encourage 'best practice' through the use of structured and routinised approaches that force managers to ask the right questions and collect the information to allow them to make better decisions. This indicates either that managers do not understand the epistemological rationale for tools and techniques, or they do, but focus on more immediate objectives that they must meet in the short-term.

The impact of tools and techniques by industry sector and industry sector grouping

In this section the performance or impact of the tools and techniques being used is analysed. Managers were asked to rate the performance of the tools and techniques they used on a scale from high-positive impact on either the firm or the function (+1) to high-negative impact on either the firm or the function (–1), zero recorded a neutral impact of neither good nor bad. Finally, data was collected when the respondent had no real information about performance one-way or the other. In this way it was possible to assess whether or not managers were using tools without any clear idea about performance outcomes. Once again the data is provided by individual and by grouped industrial sectors.

In general, most managers felt that procurement and supply tools and techniques had a positive impact upon both the performance of the firm and the function. This is indicated by the overall positive combined score for the impact of tools and techniques on the performance of both the firm and the function at 0.63. This overall positive impact is even more marked for the function (0.70) than it is for the firm (0.54). When disaggregating the data at the industry group level it is clear that there was no clear correlation between the scale and frequency of tool and technique usage and performance, either at the firm or the functional level.

As Table 9.7 indicates, the industry groupings most commonly using tools and techniques were not those recording the highest positive impact scores. The highest positive combined score was for the *Process/Services* group (0.85). This group also had the highest firm impact score (0.90) and the second highest functional impact score (0.79). Interestingly, those groupings that had the highest rank order usage scores also had reasonably

Table 9.7 The Use and Impact of Procurement and Supply Tools and Techniques by Industry Sector and Groupings

Rank Order of Most Usages by Industry Sector	Performance Score			No Data %	
	Firm	Function	Average Combined Score	Firm	Function
Oil & Gas (6.0)	0.67	0.84	0.76	12	8
Power & Water (5.44)	0.67	0.76	0.72	49	34
Healthcare (4.90)	0.54	0.66	0.60	22	5
Basic Chemicals (4.55)	0.47	0.73	0.60	11	6
Retail Financial Services (4.50)	0.80	0.83	0.82	35	13
Construction (4.33)	0.43	0.59	0.51	22	7
IT Solutions (3.90)	0.54	0.75	0.65	10	0
Confectionery (3.82)	0.67	0.90	0.79	0	0
Computer Hardware (3.70)	0.57	0.77	0.67	0	0
Transport Equipment (3.40)	0.59	0.71	0.65	17	4
Aerospace (2.83)	0.39	0.54	0.47	0	0
Media & Entertainment (1.66)	−0.17	0.50	0.33	85	25
Telecommunications (1.60)	0.48	0.50	0.49	17	13
Tourism & Leisure (1.50)	0.67	0.69	0.68	0	0
Retail & Distribution (1.33)	1.00	0.75	0.88	80	20
Publishing (1.00)	0.25	0.75	0.50	50	50
Overall Average	**0.54**	**0.70**	**0.63**	**26**	**12**
Project/Combined (4.74)	0.55	0.73	0.64	15	5
Process/Manufact (4.02)	0.57	0.80	0.69	11	6
Process/Combined (3.91)	0.56	0.64	0.60	29	17
Process/Services (2.92)	0.90	0.79	0.85	43	13
Project/Manufact (2.48)	0.41	0.67	0.54	22	18
Project/Services (1.55)	0.25	0.60	0.43	38	17
Overall Average	**0.54**	**0.70**	**0.63**	**26**	**12**

positive firm and function and combined scores. *Project/Combined* (with the highest group usage score) had a combined impact score of 0.64. *Process/Manufacturing* (the second highest group user of tools and techniques) has a combined impact score of 0.69, with the third highest group user, *Process/Combined*, with a combined impact score of 0.60. Even those groups not heavily involved in tools and technique usage had a broadly positive view about the impact of tools and techniques. *Project/Manufacturing*, which only scores 2.48 usages on average, had a very positive combined impact score of 0.54 and even *Project/Services* (with an average usage score of only 1.55) recorded a positive combined impact score of 0.43.

In general, managers appear to be positive about the use of tools and techniques, although as Table 9.8 indicates there are some interesting industry sector differences in the relationship between performance and usage. Industry sectors most using tools and techniques, although reasonably positive about their impact on performance, were not as positive as some of those who do not use tools very often. Thus, the industrial sector that was the leading user of tools and techniques, Oil & Gas (6.0 usages), ranked only 4th in the positive impact rankings (with a score of 0.76). Similarly, Power & Water, the second heaviest user (with 5.44) was only 5th (with 0.72) in the positive impact rankings. Interestingly the industry sector that recorded the highest combined impact score was Retail & Distribution (with 0.88) even though it ranked 15th in the usage rankings (with only an average of 1.33 usages). Relatedly, the Tourism & Leisure sector scored 14th in the usage rankings (1.55 average uses), but 6th (0.68) in the impact satisfaction rankings.

Table 9.8 Rank Order Comparisons for Usage and Impact

Rank Order Usage Scores	Industry Sector	Rank Order Combined Impact Scores
1 (6.00)	Oil & Gas	4 (0.76)
2 (5.44)	Power & Water	5 (0.72)
3 (4.90)	Healthcare	10 = (0.60)
4 (4.55)	Basic Chemicals	10 = (0.60)
5 (4.50)	Retail Financial Services	2 (0.82)
6 (4.33)	Construction	12 (0.51)
7 (3.90)	IT Solutions	8 = (0.65)
8 (3.82)	Confectionery	3 (0.79)
9 (3.70)	Computer Hardware	7 (0.67)
10 (3.40)	Transport Equipment	8 = (0.65)
11 (2.83)	Aerospace	15 (0.47)
12 (1.66)	Media & Entertainment	16 (0.33)
13 (1.60)	Telecommunications	14 (0.49)
14 (1.50)	Tourism & Leisure	6 (0.68)
15 (1.33)	Retail & Distribution	1 (0.88)
16 (1.00)	Publishing	13 (0.50)

These figures may indicate that there is no necessary correlation between tools and technique usage and performance satisfaction. It may well be that some industry sectors are more discerning in their use of tools and techniques and are, therefore, highly satisfied with those that they do use. On the other hand, it may be that sectors that feel compelled to use a wide variety of tools and techniques may do so in haste and may not always receive the benefits they expect as a result. Since managers often claim that they do not always have the time to properly implement initiatives due to constant demand for innovation as a result of the modern pressure for short-term results, it may well be that it is the ability to use tools consistently and appropriately that is more important than how many are used.

Despite the very positive view of practitioners about the tools and techniques that they use it is clear that their performance is most marked in the functional improvement area (with an overall score of 0.70) rather than on the strategic objectives of the firm overall (an overall score of 0.54). This once again reinforces the essentially transactional and tactical nature of the procurement and supply function in most companies. There is, however, one further worrying point that can be gleaned from the data embedded in Table 9.7 and this relates to the level of no data recorded during the survey. While managers, subjectively, are reasonably happy with the impact on firm and functional performance of the tools and techniques they use, there is considerable evidence that managers have opinions about the performance of tools even though they often lack robust and objective information about their impact in the business. Thus, at the firm level, in 26% of all cases, managers lacked robust and rigorous data to measure the performance of the tools and techniques they were using. This is less problematic at the functional level, where the no data score was only 12%, but these findings overall raise concerns about the ability of managers to objectively (rather than subjectively) assess the impact of the tools and techniques they use.

The barriers to successful implementation of tools and techniques

Having recognised that the subjective view of managers is almost wholly positive about the tools and techniques that are used (only the Media & Entertainment sector reported a negative view of the impact of tools and techniques on firm, if not functional, performance), it is interesting to analyse the factors that most impact detrimentally on implementation. Interestingly, as Table 9.9 demonstrates, managers across all industry sectors and firms believed that failures of implementation were nearly always as much due to the lack of adequacy of the tools and techniques themselves (45% of causes) as they were due to internal obstacles within the firm (50% of causes). This seems counter-intuitive, given that managers are generally positive about the tools and techniques that they use, and can only be explained by the fact that, while managers are generally happy

Table 9.9 The Barriers to Effective Implementation in the Procurement and Supply Function

Industry	Causes Of Failure 100%			Types Of Barriers 100%						
	No Data (%)	Tool (%)	Barriers (%)	Culture	Wrong Performance Measure	Insufficient Resource	Senior Management	Disruptive Internal Reorganisation	Unrealistic Expectations	Other
Process/Manufacturing										
Basic Chemicals	3	64	33	13	0	0	0	21	25	42
Computer Hardware	0	59	41	25	10	5	0	30	0	30
Confectionery	18	27	55	80	3	3	0	10	3	0
Group Average	*7*	*50*	*43*	*40*	*4*	*3*	*0*	*20*	*8*	*25*
Process/Combined										
Healthcare	18	46	37	19	0	19	14	24	14	10
Power And Water	24	49	27	19	6	13	0	0	13	50
Telecoms	0	88	13	0	0	0	0	0	33	67
Group Average	*14*	*61*	*26*	*13*	*2*	*10*	*5*	*8*	*20*	*42*
Process/Services										
Financial Services	0	32	68	6	0	71	6	6	6	5
Retail And Distribution	0	25	75	50	17	0	33	0	0	0
Group Average	*0*	*29*	*72*	*28*	*9*	*35*	*20*	*3*	*3*	*2*
Project/Manufacturing										
Aerospace	5	18	78	16	10	16	6	13	29	10
Publishing	0	33	67	50	0	50	0	0	0	0
Transport Equipment	13	42	44	26	0	13	13	4	39	4
Group Average	*6*	*31*	*63*	*31*	*3*	*26*	*6*	*6*	*23*	*5*

Table 9.9   The Barriers to Effective Implementation in the Procurement and Supply Function – *continued*

Industry	Causes Of Failure 100%			Types Of Barriers 100%						
	No Data (%)	Tool (%)	Barriers (%)	Culture	Wrong Performance Measure	Insufficient Resource	Senior Management	Disruptive Internal Reorganisation	Unrealistic Expectations	Other
Project/Combined										
Construction	0	56	44	56	19	0	6	0	19	0
IT Solutions	3	40	57	25	0	17	8	11	0	39
Oil And Gas	0	76	24	11	11	61	0	11	0	6
Group Average	*1*	*57*	*42*	*31*	*10*	*26*	*5*	*7*	*6*	*15*
Project/Services										
Media & Entertainment	0	41	59	6	0	41	41	6	6	0
Tourism & Leisure	0	29	71	33	0	0	0	25	25	17
Group Average	*0*	*35*	*65*	*19*	*0*	*21*	*21*	*15*	*15*	*9*
Overall Average	5	45	50	27	5	19	8	10	13	18

with tools and techniques, there is a widespread feeling that they could be improved.

Table 9.9 outlines the findings from a series of questions focused on the extent to which tool and technique inadequacy or internal barriers where responsible for failures of implementation. At the group level only the *Process/Combined* (with 61%) and the *Project/Combined* (with 57%) groups blamed tool inadequacy more than internal barriers for failures of implementation. All of the other groupings tended to blame internal barriers rather than tool and technique inadequacy as the primary cause of failure. At the industry sector level there was a wider differentiation. Those most blaming tool and technique inadequacy included: Telecommunications (88%), Oil & Gas (76%), Basic Chemicals (64%) and Computer Hardware (59%). Those most blaming internal barriers included: Aerospace (78%), Retail & Distribution (75%), Tourism & Leisure (71%), Retail Financial Services (68%), Publishing (67%), IT Solutions (57%) and Confectionery (55%).

When assessing in general which internal barriers most often hinder the successful implementation of tools and techniques the survey findings show that cultural factors (27% of overall causes) associated with internal resistance to change was the single biggest obstacle to implementation, closely followed by insufficient internal resources (19%), unrealistic expectations (13%) and other disruptive internal reorganisations (10%). These findings were fairly consistent across all industry groupings and industry sectors. Virtually all of the industry groupings reported internal cultural resistance as the single biggest obstacle to implementation. Only the *Process/Combined* group, with unrealistic expectations scoring higher (20%) than cultural factors (13%), stands out. These findings are consistent across all of the four functions surveyed.

At the specific industry sector level there are wider differences but cultural factors against internal change was the major factor for most respondents. Certain sectors did report other factors as more important than cultural resistance to change, but in virtually all cases cultural opposition is normally the second biggest obstacle. The Oil & Gas (with insufficient resource at 61%) the Aerospace (29% for unrealistic expectations), the Retail Financial Services (71% for insufficient resource), the Transport Equipment (35% for unrealistic expectations), the Basic Chemicals (25% for unrealistic expectations) the Telecommunications (with 33% for unrealistic expectations), the Healthcare (24% for disruptive reorganisation) and the Computer Hardware (30% for disruptive reorganisation) sectors all had a somewhat different rank ordering of barriers.

The data appears to support the view that while there are a wide range of potential internal barriers to implementation for tools and techniques, and that any implementation strategy must focus on the unique problems within particular organisations, all implementation strategies are in fact change management programmes and must be treated as such. Procurement and supply managers often overlook this. Managers sometimes have a functional enthusiasm for new tools and techniques that sometimes runs ahead of their ability to convince the rest of the business internally to change their behaviour to accommodate the new approach.

3. Conclusions: the appropriateness of the use of tools and techniques for procurement and supply management

It is clear that procurement and supply managers use tools and techniques to varying degrees in particular industry sectors and groups, and with different levels of impact on corporate and functional performance. The first broad conclusion that one can make, however, is that managers in this area rarely appear to be the gullible dupes of self-interested academics and consultants as some have claimed. The reason for this conclusion is because managers tend to use fairly well tried and tested tools and techniques and appear to innovate only very gradually, remaining fairly sceptical about the early adoption of newly developed approaches. Furthermore, the evidence here demonstrates that procurement and supply managers are fairly objective about their lack of a strategic role in their businesses – irrespective of the industry sectors they work in. Most managers believe that they should be using standard and routinised tools and techniques primarily to assist the firm and function with operational improvement. This demonstrates an attachment to realism and pragmatism rather than flights of fancy and an overweening attachment to the latest fads.

There is also considerable evidence that managers are, by and large, positive about the use of tools and techniques. Despite this it is clear that there are some significant issues that need to be addressed by the practitioner community. Perhaps the most important is the overall lack of use of tools and techniques in many companies, even when structured tools and techniques do exist to support the regular and standard processes that have to be managed by all practitioners in procurement and supply. It is surprising that, with 65 tools and techniques discovered in the literature, only 42 of them were being used at all and, of these, ten tools alone account for 63% of total usage. Furthermore, even amongst those tools and techniques most commonly used there was considerable evidence of non-use amongst respondents. The top three tools and techniques in use were only being used by around a third of the companies surveyed – vendor rating (40%), purchasing portfolio matrix (33%) and ERP systems (32%). This lack of usage overall is a major concern and demonstrates that, rather than managers using too many tools and techniques, they may not be using some basic tools and techniques as frequently as they should.

The second major concern from this survey is the clear lack of robust and objective performance measurement and management data to support the subjective views by managers about the utility of tools and techniques. Without such data it is extremely difficult to assess the performance of particular tools and techniques and ascertain whether or not, objectively, managers are using *the right tools for the job*. Subjectively there is evidence that procurement and supply managers believe that they are using the right tools but the objective evidence is still limited to be able to fully substantiate this view. The third most important finding is that the use of tools and techniques nearly always necessitates a fundamental change management approach in companies. This is because the attempt to codify any internal way of working is almost always bound to challenge existing internal standard operating procedures and the internal power structures of individuals and departments within any business. This implies that any implementation strategy must focus on change management if it is to be successful.

The final topic to be addressed relates to the issue of appropriateness, and why it is that the use of procurement and supply tool and techniques was more apparent in some sectors than others. As Figure 9.1 shows tool and technique use was in general much more evident in the *Project/Combined* (4.74 average uses per firm surveyed), *Process/Manufacturing* (4.02) and *Process/Combined* (3.91) industry groupings, when compared with *Process/Services* (2.92), *Project/Manufacturing* (2.48) and *Project/Services* (1.55). One explanation for this could be that the managers in the first three groupings of industries are just more influenced by scientific management principles and/or that the managers in the sectors least using them are either unaware of tools and techniques or are aware of them but do not accept scientific management principles. They may also be sceptical about the unsolicited blandishments of academics and consultants.

While each of these explanations might be relevant on closer reflection there could be very sound practical reasons why some industry sectors do see a need to use tools and techniques extensively and others do not. In other words, whether or not managers are using the right tools and techniques for particular procurement and supply tasks and activities, there could be perfectly rational explanations for why it is appropriate for managers to use more tools and techniques in some industry sectors than others.

Some of the most user intensive industry sectors were in process-based industries. In this category are included the Basic Chemicals, the Computer Hardware, the Confectionery and the Power & Water industry sectors. For all of these industries it is clear that the standard operating model for the delivery of goods and/or services requires the management of complex routinised systems and processes, through heavily capital intensive sunk cost infrastructure, with relatively high levels of operational and financial risk. Also, in recent years, many of these industries have experienced very high levels of competition and/or regulation and, most importantly of all in the context of the discussion of the use of tools and techniques by the procurement and supply function, a major shift from vertical integration to the outsourcing of production to external suppliers – such that for many manufacturing companies today 80% of the total costs of sales are spent on external supply. In these circumstances the need for standardised tools and techniques that allow managers to focus on even slight improvements in external operational and financial efficiency and effectiveness are likely to be at a premium. Furthermore, there may be high switching costs for process-based industries that have to rely on capital-intensive dedicated investments by supplies to ensure certainty of supply under conditions of regular souring need. This may, in part, explain the higher levels of tool and technique use in these types of industry sector.

There are of course some project-based industry sectors – Construction and Oil & Gas – that also are heavily outsourced for the delivery of their basic goods and services. In the case of the upstream Oil & Gas industry the degree of outsourcing of operations and production can be as high as 85% of the costs of sales. This figure is normally equally as high for firms in the Construction sector, where there is a heavy premium placed on turnkey solutions in which the a large share of any project risk is undertaken by firms with a highly outsourced operational delivery process. It is clear, therefore, that even in the project environment there are very high levels of operational and, in particular, financial risk. Major energy and construction projects nearly always require practitioners to manage high levels of risk and uncertainty, often involving major projects that require extensive financial investment over very many years before a profit can be made. Furthermore, the level of environmental uncertainty about future markets and operating conditions with external suppliers is often far greater than for those working in process-based industries. Given this, it is fairly obvious why managers in these industry sectors often use procurement and supply tools and techniques more than those in other industry sectors.

In general terms, then, it would appear that firms in some industry sectors have to find ways of minimising the very high levels of external resource management risks to which they are exposed, both operationally and financially. While these cannot always be fully understood or mitigated it is likely that companies in such an environment will tend to use a wide range of tools and techniques to manage external environmental complexity and uncertainty. Given this it could be that the extensive use of tools and techniques in procurement and supply can be explained by the extremely high levels of external operational and financial risk, under conditions of uncertainty, experienced in firms and industries. Such industries, which include Basic Chemicals, Computer Hardware, Construction, Confectionery, Oil & Gas and Power & Water, can be characterised as *High Sourcing Risk* sectors.

In this light, through rational scientific insight or pragmatic common sense, managers in these industries clearly do appear to be operating appropriately. This is because, given the external risks to be managed, they appear to understand that they ought to be using tools extensively and more than others. Given this it is fairly obvious why it is that tool and technique usage is so low relatively in some other industry sectors. In the Media & Entertainment, Publishing and Tourism & Leisure sectors, while there may be high levels of environmental and market uncertainty, there is proportionately far less operational and financial complexity, uncertainty and risk to be managed with external suppliers when compared with other types of industry. This is because in these types of industry firms are often heavily insourced for the personnel to deliver the services they provide, and rely on external sources of supply much less than those in industries outsourcing a substantial share of the delivery of their product and/or service to the customer.

Even in circumstances when the external source of supply (a headline star or celebrity) is the major attraction the risk to the firm is normally limited to a one-off, or one-off series of events, rather than the product or service offering as a whole. In other words, in these industries, while having the right external supplier may assist the corporate strategy (a fact attested to by the relatively high score (48%) for strategic objectives in using tools and techniques recorded in the Media & Entertainment sector in Table 9.5) its failure is unlikely to destroy the business as a whole, This, plus the lack of need for routinised and standardised approaches, due to the constant need to be innovative about supply offerings, reduces the need by managers to have standardised tools and techniques for external resource management. This is also because there are relatively low switching costs for buyers in these industries in relatively highly contested supply markets.

The Media & Entertainment, Publishing and Tourism & Leisure sectors can therefore be characterised as *Low Sourcing Risk* industries, which are not likely to use tools and techniques for procurement and supply extensively. The Publishing industry sector falls into this category since the publishing of individual books in particular is relatively low risk on an individual project basis, and the supply market for printing and book production is also highly contested with very low switching costs for buyers when they search for alternative suppliers.

The remaining industries – Aerospace, Healthcare, IT Solutions, Retail & Distribution, Retail Financial Services, Telecommunications and Transport Equipment – can be characterised as experiencing *Medium Sourcing Risk*. This may be somewhat arbitrary but it is clear that the *Project/Manufacturing* sectors (Aerospace and Transport Equipment) do not have the same levels of regular and routinised process requirements of some industries, nor are they normally as heavily outsourced as the more process-based manufacturing companies, and they may not be as heavily locked into suppliers and have, therefore, have lower switching costs on a project by project basis. The

Process/Combined industries (Healthcare and Telecommunications) also do not normally outsource their core operating activities as extensively as the higher sourcing risk categories and consequently are less exposed to external sourcing uncertainty.

The *Process/Services* industries (Retail & Distribution and Retail Financial Services) are also managing less technically complex and risky operational processes and often, especially in the case of Retail Financial Services, have their own back office insourced staff managing many of their complex transactional operational processes. This may, of course, be changing as more and more companies in this sector recognise the opportunity to out-source back office transactional service functions to lower cost third world supply markets, and this may partly explain the relatively high tool and technique usage (4.50 average uses) reported in this particular industry in the survey. This outsourcing trend may eventually push the Retail Financial Services sector into the high risk souring category in the future. The Retail & Distribution sector, while quite heavily dependent for the logistical delivery of its products on external suppliers, is arguably at much lower risk than other industries externally because of the relatively low switching costs that prevail when searching for logistics services providers in what remains a highly contested sourcing market. Finally, IT Solutions are often managed by companies with a heavy reliance on insourced staff and this exposes them to much less external resource management risk and uncertainty.

Given this threefold distinction it is interesting to see if there is a close correlation or not with the use of tools and their performance. Table 9.10 provides indicative summary data to test these correlations based on the survey responses reported here.

The findings in Table 9.10 reinforce the conclusions above since they show that *Low Sourcing Risk* industry sectors do not normally use procure-ment and supply tools and techniques extensively (1.39 usages), and have the lowest performance impact scores for both the firm (0.25) and the func-tion (0.65), across the three risk categories. These findings reinforce the general conclusion throughout this study that Media & Entertainment, Publishing and Transport & Leisure tend to use tools and techniques very infrequently and are not as satisfied with their utility as the other functions in this study. Indeed in the procurement and supply area the firm level sat-isfaction levels were very low and, in one case, tool use was actually regarded as detrimental to the success of the firm.

Interestingly, the *High Sourcing Risk* category had the heaviest use of tools and techniques (4.64) – as one might expect – and the highest combined and function level performance scores (0.77 and 0.68 respectively), indicat-ing clearly that in the procurement and supply function at least there is a strong correlation between tool and technique use and performance satis-faction, especially at the function, if not the firm, level. The *Medium Sourcing Risk* category had the second highest average usage score (3.21)

Table 9.10   The Use and Performance of Procurement and Supply Tools and Techniques in High, Medium and Low Risk Sectors

Type of Industry Sectors	Average Tool Usage	Indicators of Use and Performance		
		Performance Impact Scores		
		Firm	Function	Average Combined Score
High Sourcing Risk				
Basic Chemicals	4.55	0.47	0.73	0.60
Computer Hardware	3.70	0.57	0.77	0.67
Confectionery	3.82	0.67	0.90	0.79
Construction	4.33	0.43	0.59	0.51
Oil & Gas	6.00	0.67	0.84	0.76
Power & Water	5.44	0.67	0.76	0.72
Group Average	**4.64**	**0.58**	**0.77**	**0.68**
Medium Sourcing Risk				
Aerospace	2.83	0.39	0.54	0.47
Healthcare	4.90	0.54	0.66	0.60
IT Solutions	3.90	0.54	0.75	0.65
Retail & Distribution	1.33	1.00	0.75	0.88
Retail Financial Services	4.50	0.80	0.83	0.82
Telecommunications	1.40	0.48	0.50	0.49
Transport Equipment	3.60	0.59	0.71	0.65
Group Average	**3.21**	**0.62**	**0.68**	**0.65**
Low Sourcing Risk				
Media & Entertainment	1.66	−0.17	0.50	0.17
Publishing	1.00	0.25	0.75	0.50
Tourism & Leisure	1.50	0.67	0.69	0.68
Group Average	**1.39**	**0.25**	**0.65**	**0.45**

and the second highest performance impact score for the function (0.68), but the highest impact score for the firm (0.62).

These findings can perhaps be explained by reference to the fact that in the industries that have high external risks the extensive historical use of procurement and supply tools and techniques reinforces performance satisfaction since it mitigates the risks that have to be managed and ensures the fulfilment of functional level objectives. The industries with the highest risks appear, therefore, to be using tools and techniques more extensively and with higher satisfaction levels than the medium risk industries, where the lower risks reduce the need for such an extensive use of tools and techniques.

This adds further support to the view that there must be rational explanations for why there is a significant difference in tool and technique usage and performance across industry sectors, and that managers appear to be behaving rationally when this occurs. In this sense it seems clear that, while significant gaps in competence exist, with many firms not using tools and techniques at all or in a fairly derisory way, managers that do use them appear to so do in ways that appear to be rational relative to the industry sectors they operate within. Procurement and supply managers may not be always using *the right tools for the job* in all circumstances (this is because they often lack the objective data to know one way or the other) but at least there appears to be a logical correlation in the procurement and supply function between tool and technique usage and the external risks that have to be managed. The key problem to be overcome in this area would appear, therefore, not to be opportunistic advisers but a lack of use of even the most basic tools and techniques by the managers in the majority of the firms surveyed.

References

Cox, A. et al. (2000), *Power Regimes,* Helpston, UK: Earlsgate Press.

Cox, A. et al. (2001), 'The Power Perspective in Procurement and Supply Management', *The Journal of Supply Chain Management*, Vol. 376, No. 4, Spring.

Cox, A. et al. (2002), *Supply Chains, Markets and Power*, London: Routledge.

Cox, A. et al. (2003), *Supply Chain Management: A Guide to Best Practice*, London: Financial Times/Prentice Hall.

Cox, A. et al. (2004a), *Business Relationships for Competitive Advantage*, Basingstoke & New York: Palgrave Macmillan.

Cox, A. et al. (2004b), 'Power Regimes and Supply Chain Management', *Supply Chain Management: An International Journal*, October.

Hamel, G. & Prahalad, C. K. (1990), 'The core competence of the corporation', *Harvard Business Review* (May–June), pp. 79–91.

Hines, P. (1994), *Creating World Class Suppliers*, London: Pitman.

Lamming, R. (1993), *Beyond Partnership: Strategies for Innovation and Lean Supply*, New Jersey: Prentice Hall.

Nishiguchi, T. (1994), *Strategic Industrial Sourcing: The Japanese Advantage*, Oxford: Oxford University Press.

Womack, J. & Jones, D. (1996), *Lean Thinking*, New York: Simon Schuster.

Conclusions

10
A Curate's Egg: On the Use and Performance of Management Tools and Techniques

The survey work reported here was predicated on the assumption that there has been only very limited systematic analysis of the use and performance of management tools and techniques. Furthermore there is anecdotal evidence that managers are often dissatisfied with the tools and techniques that they use. Finally, some writers contend that managers often feel they are taken advantage of by academics and consultants (and publishers) selling them the latest fashionable ideas. The research reported here does not support this general conclusion.

While it is clear that not all managers are a completely satisfied with the tools and techniques that they use it is clear that most managers are reasonably satisfied with the performance of those that they do use. Furthermore, when managers use tools and techniques there appear to be rational explanations for the different patterns of use found across the four functions. This is based on a correlation between the types of risks and uncertainties that have to be managed within each of the four functions analysed, which appear to be more marked in some industries than others. This finding supports the view that, while managers may not always use *the right tools for the job*, they do understand that there are environmental circumstances within some industries that impel them to use tools and techniques more than in others. Tool and technique usage does not, therefore, appear to be driven only by fads or by chance.

Despite this fairly positive finding it is clear that in general the news, for those who believe in the use of tools and techniques as the basis for the development of a scientific approach to business management, is not good. The evidence from the survey is that the use of management tools and techniques is much like the famous *curate's egg* – it is good in parts, but very bad elsewhere. This is because, while there is some evidence of managers understanding that there are appropriate tools and techniques to use in particular industry sectors and functions, the overwhelming evidence is that most firms do not use very many tools and techniques at all, and that when they do use them most managers tend to rely on a very small number of those that are fairly well tried and tested. This finding is true in all four of the functions analysed and not confined to any one of them.

This leads us to conclude that, while there is evidence that some managers understand what the right tools and techniques are, there is even more evidence to support the claim that managers and the companies that they work for are often *flying blind*. What this means is that most business management appears not to be conducted on the basis of the continued rational and structured assessment of specific functional problems, but is much more based upon pragmatism and applied common sense. Managers in the survey reported here do not appear to use tools and techniques very often to assess their circumstances, or to manage them. This can only mean that they operate on the basis of standard operating procedures that may, or may not, allow them to understand whether they are tackling the key strategic and operational problems facing the firm.

In this sense the dilemma for companies may not be the one that Christensen & Rayner (2003) remarked upon in the quote with which we opened this volume (see chapter 1). There the two authors likened the management problem to one in which managers were offered a prescription for their illness of the basis that, since the prescribed medicine had worked pretty well for some other patients, it might work just as well for them. Our research seems to indicate that a rather better analogy is that of airline pilots who know roughly where they want to go, but who have no navigation equipment to allow him to know where they are currently, or where they are actually going. This is not because the navigation equipment does not exist but because either they or the airline they work for thinks that good pilots are borne and do not need navigation equipment, or, if they do think it is necessary, the company they work for does not have the resources currently to buy it, or will only install it once it is clear that it has worked for another pilot in a different plane going to a different location – by which time of course the airline's own plane may well have crash landed on a different continent than the one that was intended.

This is what saying that companies and managers are *flying blind* means: managers do not use tools and techniques in any of the four functions analysed very often at all. This major problem, which is discussed in general terms below, is then followed by an analysis of the good parts of the metaphorical curate's egg of management tool and technique usage. The chapter concludes with a discussion of some other bad parts of the curate's egg.

1.   The really bad part of the egg: flying blind and the non-use of management tools and techniques

The findings in Table 10.1 reinforce this finding about *flying blind* dramatically. As the Table demonstrates, while 483 interviews were conducted in

Table 10.1   The Average Tool and Technique Usage by Function and in Total

Function	The Number of Firms Surveyed	Total Tool and Technique Uses Reported	Average Corporate Tool and Technique Usage
Strategy	131	478	3.65
Marketing and Sales	116	465	4.01
Operations and Production	114	431	3.78
Procurement and Supply	122	456	3.74
Total	*483*	*1830*	*3.8*

the 237 companies participating in the study, the overall tool and technique usage across all respondents and in all of the four functions was only 3.80 per company surveyed. Amongst the four functions surveyed the marketing and sales function reported the highest incidence of total tool and technique usage with a score of 4.01, with the operations and production and procurement and supply functions (with 3.78 and 3.74 average total usages respectively) close behind. The strategy function was last and well below the average with 3.65 total usages. This is perhaps due to the fact that companies do not constantly refresh their strategies but they do have to constantly monitor their ability to attract and retain customers and manage operational delivery.

What is perhaps more surprising is the fact that even when tools and techniques are available and well known within a function they still do not appear to be used extensively across all firms or in all industry sectors. As Table 10.2 demonstrates there was a very high incidence of non-usage for all of the top tools and techniques found to be in use in each of the functions surveyed. In the strategy function, where the top ten tools and techniques account for 68.06% of the total usage reported, even the most generically useful applications had relatively few users amongst our survey sample. Thus, seven of the top ten applications reported between 80% and 89% non-usage, with even the three most popular tools and techniques reporting between 61% and 24% non-usage.

The findings were similar for all of the other three functions. The top ten applications in the procurement and supply function reported an overall usage coverage of 63.34%, with the bottom five of these reporting over 80% non-usage and the top five reporting between 60% and 78% non-usage. The operations and production function, with a top ten usage total of 57.78%, reported between 65% and 84% non-usage for all of the top ten tools and techniques in use. Finally, the strategy function, with an overall top ten total coverage of 56.91% total usages, reported the top five tools and techniques with between 63% and 80% non-usage, and the next best

Table 10.2 The Total Usages and the Percentage of Industry Users and Non-Users of the Top Ten Tools and Techniques by Function

Rank	Operations & Production Tool & Techniques	% of Total Usages	% of Users	% of Non-Users	Rank	Marketing & Sales Tools & Techniques	% of Total Usages	% of Users	% of Non-Users
1	Market Research	10.04	37	63	1	Pricing Models	18.81	76	24
2	Benchmarking	7.53	28	72	2	Market Research	11.98	48	52
3	Core Competence Thinking	6.90	25	75	3	Consumer Profiling	9.63	39	61
4	Swot Analysis	6.70	24	76	4	Swot Analysis	4.93	20	80
5	Discounted Cash Flow	5.44	20	80	5	E-Business Seller-Side Software	4.71	19	81
6	Scenario Planning	4.60	17	83	6	Benchmarking	4.28	17	83
7	Balanced Scorecard	4.39	16	84	7	Competitor Analysis	4.07	16	84
8	Competitor Analysis	3.98	14	86	8	Relationship Marketing	4.07	16	84
9	Key Performance Indicators	3.77	13	87	9	Brand Management	2.79	11	89
10	E-Business Seller-Side Software	3.56	13	87	10	Focus Groups	2.79	11	89
Total	Top Ten Total % Usages	56.91			Total	Top Ten Total % Usages	68.06		

Table 10.2 The Total Usages and the Percentage of Industry Users and Non-Users of the Top Ten Tools and Techniques by Function – *continued*

Rank	Operations & Production Tool & Techniques	% of Total Usages	% of Users	% of Non-Users	Rank	Marketing & Sales Tools & Techniques	% of Total Usages	% of Users	% of Non-Users
1	Quality Management Techniques	9.28	35	65	1	Vendor Rating	10.75	40	60
2	Project Management Techniques	7.20	27	73	2	Purchasing Portfolio Matrix	8.77	33	67
3	ISO – Quality Standards	6.50	25	75	3	ERP Systems	8.55	32	68
4	Business Process Re-Engineering	5.57	21	79	4	Supplier Development	6.58	25	75
5	Continuous Improvement (Kaizen)	5.57	21	79	5	Service Level Agreements	5.92	22	78
6	JIT (Lean)	4.87	18	82	6	Core Competence Thinking	5.25	20	80
7	Key Performance Indicators	4.87	18	82	7	Purchasing Cards	5.25	20	80
8	MRP Systems	4.87	18	82	8	Key Performance Indicators	4.39	16	84
9	Process Mapping	4.64	17	83	9	E-Business Buyer-Side Software	3.94	15	85
10	ERP Systems	4.41	16	84	10	Management Information Systems	3.94	15	85
Total	*Top Ten Total % Usages*	*57.78*			*Total*	*Top Ten Total % Usages*	*63.34*		

Overall Average Total % Usages = 61.52 Across All 4 Functions

five scoring between 83% and 87% non-usage. Clearly, if these findings can be generalised across companies as a whole most managers do not use tools and techniques extensively.

That said it is not the case, however, that all managers eschew the use of tools and techniques. This is because some managers within each function do use tools and techniques much more regularly than others. Those that are most often used are presented in Table 10.2. As the Table indicates, if one takes the top ten tools and techniques found to be in use in each of the four functions surveyed, these account for 61.52% of total usages across the four functions as a whole. This means that just 31 tools and techniques (because 9 of the tools and techniques are used in common across the four functions) account for close to 62% of all usage. The problem with this is of course that managers are using tried and tested tools and techniques but do not appear, as we saw, to be using very many other tools and techniques extensively at all. This reinforces the view that most of the time managers and their firms are flying blind more than they are being duped by 'snake-oil salesmen' into using tools and techniques that are of limited value.

It is clear, therefore, that two broad conclusions can be drawn. The first is that by and large most companies do not use tools and techniques very often at all. Second, when they do they tend to rely heavily on only a few well-tried and tested applications. Beyond this a third broad conclusion can be drawn. In each of the four functions analysed there is evidence that the overall pattern of usage is related to both the business activities within the function and the levels of risk and uncertainty that each industry sector has to manage.

These broad conclusions are explained in summary in what follows. The first section analyses the use of tools and techniques by business activities and shows that each function tends to use tools and techniques appropriately to focus on the key roles and responsibilities it has to discharge. In this sense the study shows that when managers do use tools and techniques they do appear to understand *the right tools for the job* to some extent. There is, however, some concern in the findings that the strategy and marketing and sales functions may be involved in duplicating effort by using the same tools and techniques extensively for the same tasks.

This is followed by a discussion of how one might explain the overall pattern of tool and technique use across industry sectors in each of the functions. This discussion shows that there appears to be relatively rational reasons based on function and industry specific risk profiles to explain the heavier use of tools and techniques in some industry sectors than others. Finally, a summary is made of the overall findings in relation to the performance of tools and techniques. The evidence shows that managers are broadly satisfied with performance when they use tools and techniques, even though they sometimes lack objective evidence to validate their subjective opinions.

2.   A good part of the egg: the right tools for the appropriate business activities

The survey analysed the extent to which each for the four functions used particular tools and techniques to achieve particular functionally relevant business activities. The reason for doing this was to ascertain which business activities were most likely to have tools and techniques in place and also to understand where each function placed its greatest effort in this respect. What the survey findings demonstrate quite clearly is that most of the functions do seem to understand appropriateness, although there was some concern about a potential duplication of effort between the strategy and marketing and sales functions. This concern was specifically related to the duplication of tool and technique use in the business activity associated with *market and environmental analysis* and focused around the use of tools and techniques such as: market research; business stream analysis; consumer profiling; scenario planning; benchmarking; SWOT analysis; Porter's Five Forces; PEST analysis; technology watch; and, value chain analysis. There was also a concern that both functions were also duplicating effort in the business activity associated with *product and competence development*, especially related to such tools and techniques as: core competence thinking; benchmarking; competitor analysis; gap analysis; knowledge management; and, decision gates.

Despite these concerns, in general the functions appear to have an appropriate emphasis on the key business activities given their functional roles and responsibilities. This in itself is an indication that when managers choose to use tools and techniques they do appear to have an understanding of what the jobs are that need to be done, and also know which tools and techniques are best suited to assist in that process. Thus, as Table 10.3 shows, each of the four functions tends to focus its tools and techniques usage in the areas that one might expect, given their primary roles and responsibilities. The table provides a break down of the percentage of tool and technique usage that has been ascribed to a particular business activity. The totals do not sum to 100% because a particular tool or technique's share of usage could be used for more than one business activity. The totals provide, however, an indicative guide to which of the business activities in each function were most supported by the tool and technique use that was reported.

As the table reveals in the strategy function the most prevalent tool and technique usage occurs in the two primary business activities associated with *market and environmental analysis* (46.06%) and *product and competence development* (40.62%). These are clearly the two primary roles and responsibilities of the strategy function in any firm. Following this the function places somewhat less emphasis on the *resource allocation* (24.08%), *performance management* (18.63%) and *financial management* (16.74%) business

Table 10.3   Rank Order Usage by Business Activity and by Function

Rank	Strategy Function	Total Reported % Usage	Rank	Marketing & Sales Function	Total Reported % Usage
1	Market and Environmental Analysis	46.06	1	Market and Environmental Analysis	49.21
2	Product and Competence Development	40.62	2	Product and Competence Development	33.72
3	Resource Allocation	24.05	3	Pricing	29.34
4	Performance Management	18.63	4	Promotion and Relationship Management	26.65
5	Financial Management	16.74			
6	Make/Buy	7.52	5	Performance Management	13.14
7	It and Internet Solutions	5.86	6	It and Internet Solutions	6.44

Rank	Operations & Production Function	Total Reported % Usage	Rank	Procurement & Supply Function	Total Reported % Usage
1	Planning, Design and Work Organisation	67.75	1	Performance Management	28.75
2	Process and Systems Improvement	52.20	2	Process Enhancement	27.62
3	Performance Management	44.54	3	It and Internet Solutions	22.79
4	Product and Competence Development	29.92	4	Supplier Selection and Negotiation	22.60
5	It and Internet Solutions	16.48	5	Supplier Development	19.11
			6	Segmentation of Spend	11.62
			7	Make/Buy	9.20

activities. The least effort is focused on business activities associated with *make/buy* (somewhat surprisingly given the recent prominence of outsourcing and core/non-core competence thinking) and *IT and Internet solutions*. In the marketing and sales function *market and environmental analysis* (49.21%) and *product and competence development* (33.72%) are also both prominent, as one might expect, as are the *pricing* (29.34%) and the *promotion and relationship management* (26.65%) business activities. These are clearly key activities for this function. The more operationally focused business activities associated with *performance management* (13.14%) and *IT and Internet solutions* (6.44%) figure much less prominently.

If these first two functions are primarily focused on strategic challenges the remaining two functions in this study are much more focused on operational effectiveness business activities. The operations and production function appears to place a tremendous emphasis on tools and techniques to support the *planning, design and work organisation* (67.75%), *process and system improvement* (52.20%) and *performance management* (44.54%) business activities. *Product and competence development* (29.92%) activities also figure reasonably prominently, as do *IT and Internet solutions* (16.48%). There is little doubt, therefore, that this function understands that its primary role and responsibility is not for strategy but for operational delivery and improvement.

The same can be said for the procurement and supply function which places the greatest emphasis on those operational effectiveness business activities associated with *performance management* (28.75%), *process enhancement* (27.62), *IT and Internet solutions* (22.79%). The function also puts considerable effort into its key functional role and responsibility associated with *supplier selection and negotiation* (22.60%), *supplier development* (19.11%) and *segmentation of spend* (11.62%) activities. The function clearly understands that it must deliver external resources efficiently and effectively at the operational level. This is borne out by the fact that it devotes least effort to the more strategic *make/buy* (9.20%) business activities.

All of this demonstrates that, not only do the four functions appear to understand what their roles and responsibilities are, but they also focus their efforts on the use of tools and techniques to fulfil their primary corporate missions. It is interesting, however, to reflect beyond this on the uses to which tools and techniques are put across the four functions collectively. This is achieved in Table 10.4, which merges the duplicated business activities across the four functions and provides a rank order listing of tool and technique use across all of the functions.

Table 10.4 demonstrates that the most popular business activity for the use of tools and techniques is *performance management* (105.06%), closely followed by *product and competence development* (104.26%) and *market and environmental analysis* (95.27%). All three of these activities are undertaken by two or more of the functions, which explains the greater emphasis on these activities. After these three major business activities come *process and system enhancement* (79.82%), *planning, design and work organisation* (67.75%) and *IT and Internet solutions* (51.57%). Of these only one is not undertaken by more than one function. The remaining business activities – *pricing* (29.34%), *promotion and relationship management* (26.65%), *resource allocation* (24.05%), *supplier selection and negotiation* (22.60%), *supplier development* (19.11%), *financial management* (16.74%) and *segmentation of spend* (11.62%) – tend to be undertaken by only one of the functions. The only exception is the *make/buy*

Table 10.4   **Total Rank Order Usage by Business Activities**

Rank	Business Activity	Total Reported % Usage	Functions Involved
1	Performance Management	105.06	Strategy, Marketing & Sales, Operations & Production, Procurement & Supply
2	Product and Competence Development	104.26	Strategy, Marketing & Sales, Operations & Production
3	Market and Environmental Analysis	95.27	Strategy, Marketing & Sales
4	Process and System Improvement	79.82	Operations & Production, Procurement & Supply
5	Planning, Design & Work Organisation	67.75	Operation & Production
6	It and Internet Solutions	51.57	Strategy, Marketing & Sales, Operations & Production, Procurement & Supply
7	Pricing	29.34	Marketing & Sales
8	Promotion and Relationship Management	26.65	Marketing & Sales
9	Resource Allocation	24.05	Strategy
10	Supplier Selection and Negotiation	22.6	Procurement & Supply
11	Supplier Development	19.11	Procurement & Supply
12	Financial Management	16.74	Strategy
13	Make/Buy	16.72	Strategy, Procurement & Supply
14	Segmentation of Spend	11.62	Procurement & Supply

(16.72%) business activity which is undertaken by both the strategy and the procurement and supply functions.

The findings here seem to confirm that there is some duplication of effort across functions, but also that *performance management, product and competence development, process and system improvement* and *external environmental analysis* (of markets, competitors and suppliers) are the primary business activities for which tools and techniques are being used within companies as a whole. This seems to support the view that, when managers use tools and techniques, they appear to understand by and large what are *the right tools for the job*. This is clearly a good part of the metaphorical curate's egg of tool and technique use.

3.   Another good part of the egg: linking risk and uncertainty with the pattern of tool and technique use

The survey was originally structured to allow the research team to ascertain whether there were any clear patterns of tool and technique usage related to the types of function and/or the types of industry sectors being analysed. The study attempted to provide a broad coverage of different types of industries across the four selected functions. To achieve this 16 industry sectors were chosen and segmented into six broad industry sector groupings – *Process/Manufacturing* (Basic Chemicals, Computer Hardware, Confectionery), *Process/Combined Manufacturing and Services* (Healthcare, Power & Water, Telecommunications), *Process/ Services* (Retail & Distribution), *Project/Manufacturing* (Aerospace, Publishing, Transport Equipment), *Project/Combined Manufacturing and Services* (Construction, IT Solutions, Oil & Gas) and *Project/Services* (Media & Entertainment, Tourism and Leisure).

The reason for this was because it was felt, initially, that process-based industries would tend to have higher tool and technique usage requirements than project-based industries, and that manufacturing industries would also tend to have more need than service base industries, with combined industries somewhere in between. The rationale here was that manufacturing and process-based industries would tend to need more routinised and standardised approaches to business that would favour tool and technique usage across all four functions. On the other hand it was hypothesised that project-based and services related industries, with a more ad-hoc and less routinised approach to business, would use tools and techniques much less across all of the four functions.

The overall findings from the survey demonstrate that while there was some mileage in this segmentation approach it does not fully explain the pattern of tool and technique usage across all industries or functions. This is demonstrated in Table 10.5 and Table 10.6, which show the overall pattern of tool and technique use by industry sector and by function, and by industry sector grouping and by function.

Table 10.5 demonstrates that across all four functions some industry sectors use tools and techniques much more regularly than others. Thus relatively heavy users of tools and techniques (those reporting usage rates significantly higher than the overall study average usage rate of 3.80) include: Basic Chemicals (5.67 average uses across all four functions analysed); Power & Water (5.56); Transport Equipment (5.49); Aerospace (5.38); Confectionery (5.12); and, Oil & Gas (4.23). Medium users (those scoring just above or below the overall average score) include: Retail Financial Services (4.09); Healthcare (3.99); Computer Hardware (3.81); IT Solutions (3.24); Retail & Distribution (2.74); and, Construction (2.72). Finally there are relatively low users (those significantly below the

Table 10.5 The Total Use of Tools and Techniques by Industry Sector and by Function

	Industry Sector	Strategy Function	Marketing & Sales Function	Operations & Production Function	Procurement & Supply Function	Sector Average Usage
1	Aerospace	7.10	6.00	5.57	2.83	5.38
2	Basic Chemicals	7.50	5.75	4.86	4.55	5.67
3	Computer Hardware	3.22	4.09	4.22	3.70	3.81
4	Confectionery	4.36	5.63	6.66	3.82	5.12
5	Construction	1.67	2.00	2.86	4.33	2.72
6	Healthcare	3.50	4.00	3.57	4.90	3.99
7	IT Solutions	1.44	3.50	4.13	3.90	3.24
8	Media & Entertainment	1.33	1.50	2.35	1.66	1.71
9	Oil & Gas	5.56	1.60	3.75	6.00	4.23
10	Power & Water	6.14	7.67	3.00	5.44	5.56
11	Publishing	1.63	4.17	1.43	1.00	2.06
12	Retail & Distribution	2.63	5.00	2.00	1.33	2.74
13	Retail & Financial Services	3.40	4.14	4.33	4.50	4.09
14	Telecommunications	1.50	1.11	3.25	1.60	1.87
15	Tourism & Leisure	1.38	1.88	0.66	1.50	1.36
16	Transport Equipment	6.38	5.86	6.33	3.40	5.49
	Total Sector Average	3.65	4.01	3.78	3.74	3.80

average) including: Publishing (2.06); Telecommunications (1.87); Media & Entertainment (1.71); and, Tourism & Leisure (1.36).

These findings offer partial support for the original hypotheses that manufacturing and process-based industries would have the highest use of tools and techniques. This is because there are a number of *Process/Manufacturing* industries (Basic Chemicals and Confectionery) amongst the heavier users overall. The problem is that Computer Hardware from the same grouping falls into the medium user category. Similarly, although the Power & Water sector from the *Process/Combined* group is in the heavy user category the two other industries from this grouping are in the medium user (Healthcare) and the low user (Telecommunications) categories. Furthermore, those in the heavier user category are not only from project-based industries but also from combined and service industry sectors as well. Thus the Aerospace and Transport Equipment industries from the *Project/Manufacturing* grouping are in the heavy user category, but so also is Oil & Gas from the *Project/Combined* grouping.

The only clear confirmation of the original hypotheses appears to be in the case of the low user category, where the two *Project/Services* industry sectors (Media & Entertainment and Tourism and Leisure) are located. Despite this even within this low usage category are also located Publishing from the *Project/Manufacturing* grouping and Telecommunications from the *Process/Combined* grouping. The findings, therefore, appear to offer only partial confirmation of the original hypotheses. This is reinforced if we assess the results reported in Table 10.6 at the overall industry sector grouping level.

The findings in Table 10.6 demonstrate that there is some partial support for the original hypotheses in the sense that the highest average incidence of tool and technique usage across all of the four functions surveyed is in the *Process/Manufacturing* grouping (4.87 average uses across all four functions surveyed) and the lowest is in the *Project/Services* grouping (1.53). This does provide positive support for the original hypotheses but the problem is that the findings do not really provide a way of explaining the heavy usage in the *Project/Manufacturing* grouping (4.33).

In order to try to explain these anomalies in the data it was decided to disaggregate the data on the basis of the levels of risk and uncertainty that managers had to face in managing their business roles and responsibilities within particular functions. The basic rationale for doing this was that managers in particular functions have to weigh different types of risk and uncertainty and that, what might constitute a high risk function for one industry (finding competent suppliers in the Oil & Gas industry), might not be as significant in another (finding competent suppliers in the Publishing industry). Given this the data presented in Table 10.7 segments usage on the basis of the levels of perceived risk (high, medium or low) experienced by each function when managing particular functional

Table 10.6 The Total Use of Tools and Techniques by Industry Sector Grouping and by Function

	Industry Sector Grouping	Strategy Function	Marketing & Sales Function	Operations & Production Function	Procurement & Supply Function	Grouping Average Usage
1	Process/Manufacturing	5.03	5.16	5.25	4.02	4.87
2	Process/Combined	3.71	4.26	3.27	3.91	3.79
3	Process/Services	3.02	4.57	3.17	2.92	3.42
4	Project/Manufacturing	5.04	5.34	4.44	2.48	4.33
5	Project/Combined	2.89	2.37	3.58	4.74	3.40
6	Project/Services	1.36	1.69	1.51	1.55	1.53

Table 10.7   The Relationship Between Risk and Tool and Technique Usage by Function and in Total

Type of Industry Specific Risk	Strategy Function	Marketing & Sales Function	Operations & Production Function	Procurement & Supply Function	Overall Functional Average Usage
High	5.51	4.80	5.16	4.64	5.03
Medium	2.64	3.79	3.07	3.21	3.18
Low	1.45	2.52	1.48	1.39	1.71

business activities and discharging corporate roles and responsibilities within specific industries.

Thus, a high risk industry for the strategy function is one in which there are heavy financial sunk costs for the firm in technically complex operational delivery processes, where the market is highly contested or regulated with relatively low profit margins. In such industries the consequences for the firm of not having a well-developed strategy can mean failure (low profits) and/or market exit. On the other hand there are relatively lower risk industries in which to do business, where the failure of a particular product or service strategy (say for the publication of a book or the booking of a headline act) would not constitute a threat to the overall survival of the firm.

Given this broad approach, which is explained in greater detail in the analytical chapters in this volume (see chapters 3, 5, 7 and 9 respectively), Table 10.7 demonstrates that there appears to be a very strong link between the overall use of tools and techniques and the levels of risk and uncertainty that must be managed by particular functions in specific industries.

As the findings demonstrate across all of the four functions there is a very strong correlation between the level of risk to a function's ability to meet its functional objectives for the firm within a particular industry sector and the overall level of tool and technique use. Thus, when there is a clear perception that a particular business activity must be undertaken within an industry to mitigate risks to the key roles and responsibilities of the function, then there is a much higher incidence of usage (high risk industries score 5.03 average uses). On the other hand, when the business activities are perceived within an industry sector to be of medium risk to both the firm and the function then usage declines (3.18 average uses), and when it is perceived to be of low risk to the survival and effective operation of the firm it is at its lowest (1.71 average uses).

This is indicated clearly both overall and by function in the data presented in Table 10.7. The strategy function has the highest recorded average use of tools and techniques (5.51) in those industry sectors where not managing the strategic function well is a high risk to corporate survival. Industries in this category include: Aerospace, Basic Chemicals, Confectionery, Oil & Gas, Power & Water, Telecommunications and Transport Equipment. Where the industry risks are lower then tool and technique usage is also much lower. In medium strategic risk industries (like Computer Hardware, Construction, Healthcare, IT Solutions, Retail & Distribution and Retail Financial Services) the average usage rate was 2.64. For the industries in the low strategic risk category (which includes industries such as Media & Entertainment, Publishing and Tourism and Leisure) the average usage score was only 1.45. The same strategic risk profiles exist for industries covered by the marketing and sales function, where the same industries appear in the high usage (4.80), medium usage (3.79) and low usage (2.52) categories.

When analysing the operations and production and procurement and supply functions it is clear that we are not discussing the same functional roles and responsibilities as those within the strategy and marketing and sales functions. In these two functions the major role and responsibility is to deliver strategic direction. In the operations and production and procurement and supply functions the role and responsibility is to deliver operational effectiveness and efficiency in the management of internal and external sourcing and delivery of goods and/or services. Given this the sixteen industry sectors are categorised differently in terms of high, medium and low risks for operational and sourcing performance when compared with the strategy and marketing and sales functions.

Despite this (the exact segmentation is explained in more detail in chapters 7 and 9) it is still clear that there is a significant link between high operational risk (for the operations and production function) and high sourcing risk (for the procurement and supply function) and the levels of use of tools and techniques. Thus, in the operations and production function, those industries categorised as having high risks of operational failure if the function does not manage operational performance continuously, reported an average tool and technique usage rate of 5.16, compared with those categorised as medium risk (3.07 average uses) and those as low risk (1.48). Similarly in the procurement and supply function those industries categorised as being exposed to high levels of external sourcing risk were those reporting the highest usage rates for tool and technique use (4.64). The medium risk industries recorded 3.18 and the low risk industries scored only 1.71 average uses.

All of this seems to demonstrate that, depending on the levels of risk to the function, there is a strong link with tool and technique use. This provides an explanation for why firms operating in both process-based and project-based industries, as well as in manufacturing and combined manufacturing and services and services industry sectors, can sometimes report relatively heavy usage rates. Clearly, firms in some industry sectors are exposed to more risk (whether strategic, operational or sourcing) than others, and this goes some way to explain the overall pattern of tool and technique usage. Indeed in this study this appears to be a much better indicator of tool and technique use than whether a company is process or project-based, or in a manufacturing or services or combined industry sector.

Thus project industries (of whatever type) that are exposed to high levels of strategic, operational or sourcing risk can be expected to be just as likely to see the need for tools and techniques to help manage and mitigate these risks as a firm operating in a process-based manufacturing industry sector. Of course, the findings show that it is often the process-based manufacturing industries that are most exposed to these types of risks. The data also shows that, when these types of risk are high, it does not matter which industry sector a firm is operating in, they are just as likely to use tools and techniques as readily. Obviously firms operating in lower risk industry sectors – like Media & Entertainment, Publishing and Tourism and Leisure – are much more likely to record lower usage rates. This is because they do not experience the same levels of strategic, operational or sourcing risks as the other firms and industry sectors.

This indicates that there are rational explanations for the overall patterns of tool and technique use. These findings confirm the view that some parts of the metaphorical curate's egg of management tool and technique use are good. This means that tool and technique usage, when it occurs at all, may be based on solid foundations and not just on chance or the latest fashions. As we shall see when one considers the overall objectives behind the use of tools and techniques and their performance there is also evidence that managers are, by and large, reasonably satisfied with what they achieve.

4.   The final good part of the egg: the objectives and performance of tools and techniques

When analysing the reasons why managers use tools and techniques it is clear that the strategy and marketing and sales functions are focused primarily on strategic objectives, while the operations and production and procurement and supply functions are focused overwhelmingly on operational effectiveness criteria.

Table 10. 8 shows that overall operational effectiveness considerations (61%) are relatively more important than strategic ones (49%). Despite this both the strategy and the marketing and sales functions tend to put a greater emphasis on strategic objectives. The strategy function reports 56% of its objectives as strategic and the marketing and sales function reports 52%. It is the operations and production and procurement and supply functions that demonstrate the most positive focus on operational effectiveness considerations, reporting 73% and 80% in favour of operational considerations respectively. Once again this seems to indicate that there is

Table 10.8 The Overall Objectives for Using Tools and Techniques by Firm and Function

Function	Firm Level					
	Strategic Objectives			Operational Effectiveness	Functionality	Cost
	Unique Products	Cost Leadership	Repositioning			
Strategy	27	9	20	44	24	11
Marketing &Sales	23	8	21	48	22	7
Operations & Production	16	7	4	73	27	12
Production & Supply	2	16	2	80	25	24
Average Total	*17*	*10*	*12*	*61*	*25*	*13*

	Functional Level						
	Communication	Information	Flexibility	Skill Sets	Number Employed	Other	No Data
Strategy	16	31	3	7	1	5	2
Marketing &Sales	20	34	5	3	0	7	2
Operations & Production	19	20	6	7	1	7	1
Production & Supply	14	22	4	4	2	5	0
Average Total	*17*	*27*	*5*	*5*	*1*	*6*	*1*

a clear alignment of the objectives behind tools and techniques use and the roles and responsibilities of the four functions that have been analysed. In this sense there is further evidence to support the view that managers using tools and techniques may broadly understand what are *the right tools for the job.*

There is also clear evidence at the functional level that managers understand the need to improve their own functional performance (25% of overall functional objectives), to improve communication internally (17%) and to access and provide more information for decision-making (27%). Despite this there is also some concern with the overall goals of managers in using tools and techniques. The functional level findings show that few managers have the desire to improve the skill sets of their staff when they introduce tools and techniques. This is something of a surprise because one of the major reasons for creating tools and techniques is to force managers to ask the basic questions and to collect and analyse the basic data that is required to make informed decisions about key issues and problems. By doing this, the intention of those who create tools and techniques is, normally, to turn raw data into useful management information to improve decision-making within the organisation. This must, ultimately, be an attempt to improve the skill sets and competence of internal staff.

It would appear, however, and this point is supported anecdotally by many years of experience of consulting work in companies, that too many managers adopt tools and techniques as a quick fix and do not understand that they must be used continuously for there to be an significant benefit for organisational competence development. In these circumstances the fact that only 5% of the functional objectives behind the use of tools and techniques is to improve the skill sets of the staff is a disappointing finding (a piece of the metaphorical curate's egg that is clearly bad). Similar conclusions can be made about the performance of tools and techniques. Overall managers appear to be reasonably satisfied with the tools and techniques they use. This fact is borne out by the findings reported in Table 10.9 that shows that managers score the performance of tools and techniques positively.

Table 10.9 Overall Performance Scores by Function and in Total

Function	Performance Scores			No Data %		
	Firm	Function	Combined	Firm	Function	Combined
Strategy	0.63	0.69	0.66	30	16	23
Marketing & Sales	0.59	0.63	0.61	9	4	7
Production	0.61	0.72	0.67	6	2	4
Procurement & Supply	0.54	0.70	0.63	26	12	19
Average Total	*0.59*	*0.69*	*0.64*	*18*	*8*	*13*

The combined satisfaction score for all of the four functions was 0.64 out of a possible 1.00 perfect score. This indicates most managers are positive about the tools and techniques they use. Overall there is more satisfaction with functional level (0.69) rather than firm performance (0.59). This is to be expected as the ability of managers and their firms to impact on strategic constraints is arguably more difficult than to overcome internal impediments in the way of functional improvement. Not surprisingly the procurement and supply function, which arguably has the least direct impact on the strategic direction of the firm of all of the functions surveyed here, had the least satisfaction with the impact of tools and techniques at the strategic level (0.54). The operation and production function was the most satisfied with the performance of tools and techniques applied to functional level objectives (0.67). This is to be expected from the function that has the single biggest impact on the operational delivery processes of the firm.

If these are all positives that show that managers are not simple-minded dupes who are the playthings of unscrupulous academics and consultants selling the latest fads there are some indicators that cause concern. What is perhaps most worrying in the findings presented here is the fact that some functions (strategy and procurement and supply in particular) appear not to have a high level of data with which to assess the performance of the tools and techniques that are used. This is worrying because there is little point in using tools and techniques if there is no way of measuring their performance. Despite this the evidence seems to indicate a fairly positive view by managers of the tools and techniques that they use.

5.   The final parts of the egg: future research needs in understanding the use and performance of management tools and techniques

The general conclusions above are fairly positive in the sense that the managers who use tools and techniques appear to have rational reasons for introducing them, and the pattern of use across functions is broadly explicable in terms of the levels of risk that have to be managed in specific industry sectors. That said a note of caution is in order. The overwhelming evidence in this study is that most firms and their managers do not use tools and techniques very much at all. Furthermore, when they do use them they normally only use the same ones as everyone else and those that are tried and tested. In this sense it would appear that managers are inherently conservative.

This is the bad part of the metaphorical curate's egg. The evidence from the survey supports a general conclusion the authors have developed after many years of teaching MBA students and undertaking consultancy. This conclusion is that most managers get by on a wing and a prayer – which is another way of saying that most companies are *flying blind* when it comes to understanding the key problems that face them and how to manage them properly. Most management practice appears to be based on experience and applied commonsense (even though Mark Twain explained a long time ago in the novel Huckleberry Finn that sense is not common).

Despite this companies survive and prosper, or at least some of them do some of the time. It can be argued, however, that this is not good enough and that what is really needed is not survival but an understanding of which tools or techniques, if utilised, are the most appropriate to achieve improvements in performance. It is here that this study draws a major blank. It is one thing to argue that managers using tools and techniques are broadly positive about the experience, and that there appear to be rational reasons for the overall pattern of tool and technique use, but this is not the same as saying that there is a clear correlation between tool and technique use and corporate performance improvement. In fact, despite the positive views of managers in the survey, it is difficult to fully accept this conclusion at face value. The reason for this is because managers do not have always have objective performance data with which to measure the success or failure of particular tools and techniques. When pressed managers insist they have such data but are rarely able to provide it for the omniscient observer to analyse.

This being the case there is something bad in the curate's egg and that is that the data does not in any way show a definite correlation between the use of tools and techniques and objective performance improvement rather than subjective performance satisfaction. Indeed the data in the survey actually shows that there is an inverse relationship between heavy use and performance satisfaction. This may be because tools and techniques are used most often in circumstances where there are risks that cannot always be resolved satisfactorily. Given this it may be that the regular use of tools and techniques that are only partially successful is likely to result in managers being less satisfied than those who do not use as many, or who do so in circumstances of lower risk, where performance outcomes may be easier to achieve. This explanation cannot, however, hide the fact that there is only limited evidence amongst the managers surveyed of a robust and rigorous approach to performance measurement and management of the tools and techniques being used.

If this is one of the major problems with the current use of tools and techniques the second major difficulty is associated with the bad workman and his tools syndrome. Table 10.10 provides comparative data across the functions about the barriers to successful implementation of tools and techniques. The table demonstrates that when managers implement tools and techniques there is a broad tendency for them to blame failure on the tools and techniques more than the internal barriers to implementation within the firm.

Table 10.10 Barriers to Effective Implementation by Function and in Total

Function	Causes of Failure (%)						Internal Barriers (%)			Other
	Tool	Barriers	No Data	Culture	Wrong Performance Measure	Insufficient Resource	Senior Management	Disruptive Internal Reorganisation	Unrealistic Expectations	
Strategy	58	32	10	24	9	30	5	5	14	3
Marketing & Sales	60	33	7	25	1	33	6	8	21	6
Production	50	44	6	35	6	14	12	11	11	11
Procurement & Supply	45	50	5	27	5	19	8	10	13	18
Average Total	*53*	*40*	*7*	*28*	*5*	*25*	*8*	*9*	*15*	*10*

The table shows that on average 53% of respondents blame the inadequacy of the tool or technique for failures of implementation and lay the blame on internal barriers only 40% of the time. The authors were sceptical about this claim by managers when its was reported because, having worked closely with companies implementing management tools and techniques, this finding may well be an excuse by managers. All too often managers blame the tool or technique if it does not lead to an immediate benefit or if, after initial benefits, the tool does not lead to continuous improvement without additional effort or resource. The problem with this viewpoint is that managers often fail to understand the change management requirements necessary within an organisation to successfully implement tools and techniques effectively once the academic or consultants have left the company, and the initial enthusiasm dissipates as everyone returns to business as usual.

Once again it is clear that it is much easier for managers to blame the tool or technique than the inability of the firm to focus consistently on the implementation of what is required. This is also because sometimes the tools and techniques being adopted require managers to do far more than they normally would when they make decisions and, because managers are under time and resource pressures, they cannot find the time or resource to do what is necessary. In these circumstances it is much easier to blame the tool or technique than to deal with the internal issues.

That said it is clear that when managers focus on the causes of failure internally the findings point to a major change management problem for companies and their managers. As Table 10.10 demonstrates the two greatest obstacles to successful implementation in most companies are the existing culture (political structures, mindset and standard operating procedures) and the lack of sufficient resource to implement the new tools and techniques effectively. These two barriers respectively accounted for 28% and 25% of the reasons for failure overall, and these findings are consistent across all of the four functions analysed. Beyond this problem, and linked to the discussion above, it is clear that a third major obstacle is unrealistic expectations on the part of managers about what could be achieved with the time and resources available (15% of barriers).

Clearly, these findings show that a significant proportion of the failure of implementation must be caused by a failure to understand what effort is required to implement tools or techniques in the firm or function. This, plus the fact that managers do not seem to understand that they should be using tools and techniques to improve the skill sets of their staff, appear to be the remaining bad parts of the metaphorical curate's egg of management tool and technique use and performance. Overall, of course, the major problem is that management tools and techniques are simply not used extensively at all.

It will be interesting, if others decide to analyse this broad area in the future, to understand to what extent the findings reported here are consistent across the industry sectors that have not be analysed and across the other corporate functions not covered here. If, however, the findings reported here go some way to correcting the view that the managers who use tools and techniques are gullible fools then they will have served their purpose. The fact that most firms and managers appear to be *flying blind* or *flying by intuition* does not mean that those managers who do decide to use tools and techniques are unable to understand when a quack is prescribing snake oil. There is clear evidence, therefore, that when managers use tools and techniques they do so based on at least some understanding of what are *the right tools for the job*. The major problem is that so few of them using them at all in the functions and industry sectors covered in this study.

References

Christensen, C. & Raynor, M. (2003), 'Why Hard-Nosed Executives Should Care About Management Theory', *Harvard Business Review*, September.

Appendices

Appendix A: An Alphabetical Listing of the 123 Individual Management Tools and Techniques Found in Use in the 237 Companies Surveyed

4Ps Analysis
Activity-Based Costing
Agile
Approved Supplier List
Audience Share Research
Balanced Scorecard
Batch Production
BCG Competitive Advantage Matrix
Benchmarking
Best Practice Club Initiative
Brainstorming
Brand Equity Analysis
Brand Management
Business Excellence Model
Business Operating Model
Business Process Re-engineering
Business Stream Analysis
Capability Maturity Model
Capture Planning
Cell Layout and Product Flow Analysis (PFA)
Change Management
Cognitive Mapping
Competency Achievement Analysis
Competency Model
Competitive Advantage Mapping
Competitive Position-Market Attractiveness Matrix
Competitor Analysis
Consumer Profiling
Contact Management System
Continuous Improvement/ Kaizen
Continuous Production
Core Competence Thinking
Cost-Benefit Analysis
Decision Gates
Design for Manufacture
Design to Cost
Direct Marketing
Discounted Cash Flow Analysis
E-Business – Buy-Side Software

E-Business – Internal Software
E-Business – Sell-Side Software
Economic Profit Measures
Economic Value Added
EDI
ERP System
Failure Rate Analysis
First Point Assessment
Five 'S' Strategy Analysis
Focus Groups
Gap Analysis
Growth Share Matrix
Hazard Analysis
ISO Quality Standards
Just-in-Time
Key Account Management
Key Performance Indicators
Knowledge Management
Lean Supply
Life-Cycle Costing
Maintenance Techniques
Management Information System
Manpower Planning
Market Research
Marketing Information System
MRP System
Negotiation Procedures
New Product Development Process
Open Book Agreements
Outsourcing Procedure
Pareto Analysis
Partnership Sourcing
Payback Analysis
PEST Analysis
Plan-o-Grams
Porter's Five Forces
Portfolio Analysis
Price Elasticity
Pricing Models
Problem-Solving Techniques
Process Layout

Process Mapping
Product Development Process
Product Market Diversification Matrix
Production Information Systems
Project Life Cycle Management
Project Management Techniques
Project Teams
Purchasing Cards
Purchasing Consortium
Purchasing Portfolio Matrix
Quality Management Techniques
QV Methodology
Relationship Assessment Programme
Relationship Marketing
Resource Agreement Model
Reverse Engineering
Risk Analysis Tools
Scenario Planning
Scheduling Tools
Service Level Agreements
Six Sigma
SMART Targets

Sponsorship
Statistical Process Control
Stock Control System
Succession Planning
Supplier Appraisal
Supplier Development Programme
Supplier Managed Inventory
Supplier Rationalisation
Supplier Sourcing Methodology
Supply Chain Management
SWOT Analysis
Synergy Analysis
Target Based Costing
Technology Watch
Value Based Management
Value Chain Analysis
Value Engineering
Value Stream Management
Variance Analysis
Vendor Rating
Virtual University

Appendix B: The 131 Companies Surveyed in Strategic Management by Industry Sector

Aerospace (10 Companies)	Aeropia BAE Systems Computing Devices Dunlop Aviation Gkn Westland Mckechnie PMES Rolls-Royce TRW Umeco
Basic Chemicals (6 Companies)	Akcros Chemicals BASF Plc Crosfield Chemicals EKA Chemicals ICI Chlor Chemicals Solvay Interox
Computer Hardware (9 Companies)	Compaq Fujitsu Siemens Computers Lexmark Psion Sharp Electronics Synnex Technologies Tatung Tulip Xyratex
Confectionary (8 Companies)	Britvic Cadburys Coca-Cola Enterprises Ltd Geest Golden Wonder Sela Sweets Thorntons Trebor Basset
Construction (6 Companies)	Amec Anglo Holt Bovis Homes Carillion Faithful and Gould How Group

Financial Services (10 Companies)	Alliance and Leicester Bradford and Bingley Britannia Building Society Cheltenham and Gloucester Churchill Insurance Endsleigh Insurance Nationwide Norwich Union Virgin Direct Woolwich
Healthcare (8 Companies)	Advanced Medical Solutions Biocompatibles Biofocus Evotec OAI Intercare Profile Therapeutics Quadrant Healthcare Sr Pharma
IT Solutions (9 Companies)	Action CSC Docent EDS Electron Economy Kalamazoo Computer Group Logic Peoplesoft Unisys
Media and Entertainment (9 Companies)	Anglia Television BBC BRMB Carlton Central Channel 4 Galaxy FM Heart FM Sky Wildtrack Television
Oil and Gas (9 Companies)	Agip UK BG Plc BP Centrica Edecco Lasmo Rigblast Salamis Shell

Power and Water Utilities (7 Companies)	Calor Gas Dynegy Innogy International Power npower Vivendi Water Partnership Yorkshire Water
Publishing (8 Companies)	Birmingham Post and Mail Heinneman Secondary John Wiley and Sons Oxford University Press Pearson Pearson Education REPP Sage Publications
Retail and Distribution (8 Companies)	Allied Carpets Amtrak C Butt Ltd Courts Next Plc Somerfield Tesco Whsmith
Telecommunications (8 Companies)	Advent Communications BCH Comdev Crown Castle European Antennas Hughes Motorola GSM Voice
Tourism and Leisure (8 Companies)	Airtours plc Britannnic Travel Ltd First Choice Travel Ltd Keyline Continental Lancaster Landmark Hotel Group Ltd Queens Moat Houses Shearings Holidays Ltd Travel by Appointment
Transport Equipment (8 Companies)	Dennis Eagle Ldv Mayflower Vehicle Systems Pendennis Shipyard Reynard Motorsport Unipart West Coast Traincare Whale Tankers

Appendix C: The 116 Companies Surveyed in Marketing and Sales Management by Industry Sector

Aerospace (7 Companies)	Aeropia BAE Systems Britax International Dowty Aerospace Dunlop Aviation Linread Northbridge Rolls Royce
Basic Chemicals (8 Companies)	AKCROS Chemicals BASF plc CIBA Chemicals Houghton plc ICI Chlor Chemicals Nalco-Exxon Energy Chemicals Rhodia Solvay Interox
Computer Hardware (11 Companies)	Compaq Dell Fujitsu Siemens Computers Hewlett Packard Mitac Psion Sharp Electronics Sun Microsystems Tatung Tulip Xyratex
Confectionary (8 Companies)	Britvic Cadburys Coca-Cola Enterprises Ltd Geest Nestle Red Bull Thorntons Trebor-Bassett
Construction (3 Companies)	Balfour Beatty Faithful and Gould Tilbury Douglas
Financial Services (7 Companies)	Barclays Mercantile Bradford and Bingley Cheltenham and Gloucester Hill House Hammond Nationwide Virgin Direct Woolwich

Healthcare (8 Companies)	Advanced Medical Solutions
	Biocompatibles
	Biofocus
	Goldshield
	Hypoguard
	Profile Therapeutics
	Smith and Nephew
	Sr Pharma
IT Solutions (8 Companies)	Action
	Docent
	EDS
	Electron Economy
	Kalamazoo Computer Group
	Logica
	Peoplesoft
	Unisys
Media and Entertainment (8 Companies)	BRMB Radio
	Carlton Central
	Carlton Television
	Channel 5
	Heart FM
	Phoenix Television
	Scottish Media Group
	Sony Music (S2)
Oil and Gas (5 Companies)	Agip UK
	Enterprise Oil
	Rigblast
	Salamis
	Shell
Power and Water Utilities (6 Companies)	British Energy
	British Gas
	Calor Gas
	Dynegy
	npower
	United Utilities
Publishing (6 Companies)	Birmingham Post and Mail
	Heinneman Secondary
	IPC Media
	Sage Publications
	Taylor and Francis
	Yorkshire Post

Retail and Distribution (7 Companies)	Allied Carpets Amtrak Britannia Music Courts Next plc Somerfield Statesman
Telecommunications (9 Companies)	Advent Communications BCH Comdev Crown Castle European Antennas Hughes Motorola Motorola Gsm Voice
Tourism and Leisure (8 Companies)	First Choice Travel Limited Going Places Leisure Travel Ltd Hilton Group Plc Holiday Autos International Ltd JAC Travel Regent Inn plc St. Giles Hotel Ltd Travel by Appointment
Transport Equipment (7 Companies)	Adtranz Dennis Eagle LDV Pendennis Shipyard Schmidtz Cargobull West Coast Traincare Whale Tankers

Appendix D: The 114 Companies Surveyed in Production and Operations Management by Industry Sector

Aerospace (7 Companies)	BAE Systems C J Fox and Sons Computing Devices Dowty Aerospace Dunlop Aviation GK Westland Rolls Royce
Basic Chemicals (7 Companies)	AKCROS Chemicals BASF plc CIBA Chemicals Crosfield Chemicals ICI Chlor Chemicals Nalco-Exxon Energy Chemicals Rhodia
Computer Hardware (9 Companies)	Apple Integrated Device Technology Lexmark Psion Sharp Electronics Synnex Information Technologies Tatung Tulip Xyratex
Confectionary (6 Companies)	Allied Domecq Britvic Cadburys Geest Paynes Trebor-Bassett
Construction (7 Companies)	Anglo-Holt Balfour Beatty Bovis Homes Carillion Crosby Homes Drake And Scull Tilbury Douglas
Financial Services (6 Companies)	Bradford and Bingley Cheltenham and Gloucester Churchill Insurance Endsleigh Insurance Nationwide Norwich Union

Healthcare (7 Companies)	Advanced Medical Solutions Biofocus Deltex Medical Hypoguard Martindale Nycomed Amersham Quadrant Healthcare
IT Solutions (8 Companies)	Action Cisco Systems CSC Docent EDS Electron Economy Kalamazoo Computer Group Logica
Media and Entertainment (3 Companies)	BBC Resources UCI Warner Bros. Cinemas
Oil and Gas (8 Companies)	Agip UK BP Edecco Enterprise Oil Intrepid Lasmo Salamis Weir Pumps
Power and Water Utilities (10 Companies)	British Energy British Gas Calor Gas Corby Power Station GPU Power Innogy London Electricity Magnox Electric Plc United Utilities Vivendi Water Partnership
Publishing (7 Companies)	Birmingham Post and Mail Butterworth Heinneman Cambridge University Press John Wiley and Sons Pearson Education Taylor and Francis Yorkshire Post

Retail and Distribution (6 Companies)	Allied Carpets Autologic plc Britannia Music C Butt Ltd Courts Tradeteam
Telecommunications (8 Companies)	Advent Communications BCH Canon Comdev European Antennas Hughes Infonet Motorola
Tourism and Leisure (6 Companies)	Blue Harbour Ltd Britannic Travel Ltd JAC Travel Queens Moat Houses Shearings Holidays Ltd Sta Travel
Transport Equipment (9 Companies)	Dennis Eagle LDV Mayflower Vehicle Systmes Reynard Motorsport Schmidtz Cargo Bull Unipart West Coast Traincare Whale Tankers Wrightbus

Appendix E: The 122 Companies Surveyed in Procurement and Supply Management by Industry Sector

Aerospace: 6 Companies	Aeropia BAE Systems C J Fox And Sons Martin-Baker Mckechnie Rolls-Royce
Basic Chemicals (11 Companies)	Air Products plc AKCROS Chemicals BOC BP Chemicals CIBA Chemicals Houghton Plc ICI Chlor Chemicals Nalco-Exxon Energy Chemicals Rohm and Haas Solvay Interox Unichem Ltd
Computer Hardware: 10 Companies	Apple IBM Integrated Device Technology Lexmark Psion Sharp Electronics Synnex Information Technologies Tatung Tulip Xyratex
Confectionary (11 Companies)	Allied Domecq Bernard Matthews Britvic Cadburys Fox's Biscuits Geest Golden Wonder Lindt Chocolates Nestle Paynes Trebor-Bassett
Construction (6 Companies)	Alfred Mcalpine Homes Balfour Beatty Bovis Homes Carillion Drake and Scull Tilbury Douglas

Financial Services (4 Companies)	Barclays Bradford And Bingley Churchill Insurance Woolwich
Healthcare (9 Companies)	Acambis Advanced Medical Solutions Astrazeneca Deltex Medical GlaxoSmithKline Hypoguard Martindale Nycomed Amersham Quadrant Healthcare
It Solutions (10 Companies)	Action Bull Information Systems Cisco Systems CSC EDS ICL Kalamazoo Computer Group Logica Perot Systems Unisys
Media and Entertainment (6 Companies)	Carlton Central Rank Group Sky Telewest Communications UCI Warner Bros. Home Cinemas
Oil and Gas (10 Companies)	Agip UK Amerada Hess BG plc BP Centrica Global Marine Lasmo Ranger Salamis Shell

Power and Water Utilities (9 Companies)	GPU Power Innogy International Power London Electricity Magnox Electric plc Northern Electric and Gas plc Severn Trent Water Yorkshire Electricity and Gas Yorkshire Water
Publishing (1 Company)	Ipc Media
Retail and Distribution (3 Companies)	Allied Carpets C Butt Ltd Tibbet and Britten
Telecommunications (10 Companies)	Advent Communications BCH Canon Comdev European Antennas Hughes Motorola Motorola GTSS Orange Voice
Tourism and Leisure (6 Companies)	Compass Group plc Going Places Leisure Travel Ltd Lancaster Landmark Hotel Group Ltd Scottish Courage Ltd Sunsail Ltd Travelbag plc
Transport Equipment (10 Companies)	Dennis Eagle LDV Mayflower Vehicle Systems Pendennis Shipyard Reynard Motorsport Schmidtz Cargobull Unipart West Coast Traincare Whale Tankers Wrightbus

Index

MRP systems   178–9, 236
  usage rate   195
multi-dimensional scaling   120
multivariate analysis   120

Nakajima, Seiichi   178
neatness (*seiton*)   42
negotiation process   236
  usage rate   255
net present value (NPV)   40–1
network analysis   179–80
network sourcing   236
new product development process   39,
    104, *105*, 180
Newton, Isaac   7

observation   104
Ohno, Taiichi   173
oil and gas industry   *14–5*
  marketing and sales tools and
      techniques
    performance of   142
    use of   133, 152, 154
  operations and production tools and
      techniques use   207
  procurement and supply tools and
      techniques
    performance of   270
    use of   257, 264, 274
  strategy tools and techniques use
      70, 71, 88
open book agreement   236
operations and production tools and
    techniques   21, 159, 191–2
  barriers to implementation   214–8
  companies surveyed in the 1998–2004
      research project for   317–9
  objectives of   204, *205–6*
    functional   207–10
    operational effectiveness   204, 207
    strategic   207
  performance of   204, 210–4, 221–3
  use of   192–6, 218–21
    by business activity   196–200
    by function   *288–9*
    by industry sector and grouping
        200–3
    by level of risk   221–2, 300
optimised production technology (OPT)
    180
organisation (*seiri*)   42

outsourcing procedure   5, 49, 236
  usage rate   64, 255

Parasuraman, Zeithaml, Berry (PZB)
      Model   116
Pareto analysis
  for operations and production
      management   181, 187
  for procurement and supply
      management   237, 255
  for strategic management   27, 49–50,
      51
Pareto, Vilfredo   49
partnership sourcing   182, 237
payback analysis   51
penetration pricing   110
perceived-value pricing   110–1
perceptual mapping   106–7
performance management
  use of marketing and sales tools and
      techniques for   129, 291, 292,
      293
  use of strategy tools and techniques
      for   65
performance measurement
  use of operations and production
      tools and techniques for   194,
      196
Peters, Tom   10
pipeline mapping   237
planning, design and work organization
  use of management tools and
      techniques for   293
  use of operations and production
      tools and techniques for   192,
      194, 196
plan-o-grams   104, 106
Platts Gregory procedure   182
Platts, Ken   182
political, economic, social, and
      technological (PEST) analysis
      51–2, 104
  usage rate   64
Porter, Michael   22, 54, 59
Porter's five forces model   54, *55*, 106,
      150
  usage rate   64, 87, 128
portfolio analysis   106
  usage rate   128
portfolio planning   39–40
positioning   106–7